HIGHEST AWARDS IN THE WORLD

RODS, REELS, FLIES & TACKLE FOR ALL PARTS OF THE WORLD

TRADE MARK.   TRADE MARK.

FIRST CLASS AND GOLD MEDALS AWARDED.

INVENTORS, MANUFACTURERS AND PATENTEES OF FISHING RODS, TACKLE, GUNS, ETC.

Hardy's Book of Fishing

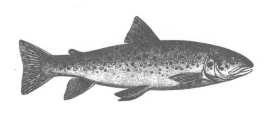

HARDY'S BOOK OF FISHING

compiled by

PATRICK ANNESLEY

HEINEMANN : LONDON

William Heinemann Ltd
15 Queen St, Mayfair, London W1X 8BE
LONDON MELBOURNE TORONTO
JOHANNESBURG AUCKLAND

First published 1971

434 02220 9

Photoset and printed in Great Britain by
BAS Printers Limited, Wallop, Hampshire

CONTENTS

Foreword

For 100 years the name of Hardy has stood for the highest quality fishing tackle. To own a Hardy rod has been the ambition of generations of fishermen not only in Britain but throughout the world; for it was for rods—split-cane rods especially—that Hardy Brothers became famous. Experiments in splitting and glueing cane had been undertaken by Higginbotham's, a London fishing tackle firm, early in the 19th century and a few rods of this sort continued to be produced and sold through the ensuing years (see "Rods of Rent Cane", p. 10); however, the first real advances in the use of this material were made on the other side of the Atlantic, when Samuel Phillippe of Pennsylvania began to produce rod sections using strips of the hard outer shell of the bamboo only. The technique was taken up by Charles Orvis of Vermont, who built a factory for the manufacture of split-cane rods in 1856, and by the most famous American rodmaker of all, Hiram Leonard, in the same decade. The English sporting press of the 1870s and early 1880s contains many suitably conservative queries—and not a few complaints—about the "new-fangled" American cane rods; it contains too a mounting volume of testimony that Hardy Brothers were now outstripping all other manufacturers, English and American, in sheer technical excellence. There emerged an enduring rivalry between Hardy and Leonard as to who produced the finest split-cane rods in the world. Many Americans favoured Hardy, though it is ironic that in 1902, while Hardy continued to collect their transatlantic testimonials, G. E. M.

Skues, already on his way to becoming one of the famous trout fishermen of all time, began a life-long love affair with Leonard rods.

Hardy Brothers did more than manufacture rods and sell these and every other kind of fishing tackle. Over the years they filled their catalogues with information and advice, with notes on the far-away places an angler might visit, and with the testimonials and anecdotes of their patrons. This catalogue material forms the basis for this book. I have selected those pieces which seem to me best to illustrate the fishing of the time—to be most informative, nostalgic or simply entertaining—and added extracts from other writers which seem to me complementary.

These pieces are all of them, I hope, worth reading in their own right. Taken together they provide a picture of the practice and development of angling over the past hundred or more years. Some innovations have been notable: the marriage of split-cane rod and dressed silk line boosted the developments of the dry fly; the replacement of silkworm gut by nylon rendered obsolete one of the most characteristic of anglers' rituals—the use of dampers and cast box. Yet it is notable too how often "development" means something less than real change. Nineteenth-century fly minnows are, in profile, identical to today's Polystickles. Scrope in 1843 was advising his readers, as Wood of Cairnton was to advise his disciples 90 years later, to delay the strike when fly fishing for salmon in low water; and while Scrope knew nothing of greasing his line it is likely that his small summer fly, fished on a light horsehair line, behaved not very differently from the Blue Charm of the modern greased line fisherman. Stewart, writing of the upstream wet fly more than 100 years ago, recommended drawing the fly across in front of the known lie of a trout, thus anticipating the modern "induced take" style of nymph fishing. Hardy's "Filip" line, introduced in 1911, looks forward to today's distance casting with forward tapers and shooting heads. And the "modern" demand for ultra-light rods followed on quickly from the split cane revolution. "Light rods have come to stay," acknowledge Hardy Brothers in 1907, introducing their Fairy and Featherweight rods. American demands went further than British: while Hardy were offering their home customers nothing lighter than 4 ounces, they were already shipping "abnormally light and supple rods of 3 ounces" across the Atlantic.

Within the different sections of this book, the broad pattern of arrangement is firstly by subject matter and then by date. Thus the section on "Salmon" begins with a number of pieces on fly fishing grouped together roughly chronologically and this is followed by pieces on other techniques, similarly grouped. But this book does not pretend to be a strict chronology: with some pieces their relative dates are unimportant, and these are grouped in whatever way enables them to complement one another. Similarly, while most of the pieces come from within the period covered by the catalogues, there are a few which are earlier and which are included because they set the scene for, or counterpoint, some part of the main area covered. There are pieces too which bear no intimate relationship to the material from the Hardy catalogues: in particular this is true of many pieces dealing with people.

Since this book recalls so many of the places where people have fished and still fish, it seemed right that it should include something about the sort of people who fish and have fished. The pleasure of angling includes not only the catching of fish and the use of good tackle but also fellow-anglers. This book will, I hope, recapture all those pleasures.

Patrick Annesley

Acknowledgements

The idea for this book first took shape in the course of a conversation between Toby Eady and myself one rainy day while we were failing to catch trout on a stream in Ireland. I am most grateful to him for much of the effort involved in translating the idea into reality, and for his research and suggestions on items for inclusion.

In preparing the book, the first essential was of course the consent and co-operation of Hardy Brothers Limited. In particular, I thank Mr. William Hardy for approving the project in principle and for giving me access to the catalogues and documents from which much of the material in the book is taken.

I am most grateful to Mr. David Colquhoun, Editor of the *Journal of the Flyfishers' Club* for permission to reprint from the Journal the articles which appear on pages 30, 49, 57, 87, 126, 128, 158, 231, 269, 275 and 298 of this book. I am grateful also to the following publishers who have given me permission to use extracts from books in which they control the copyright:

Ernest Benn Ltd. (H. Plunket Greene, *Where the Bright Waters Meet*); A. & C. Black Ltd. (G. E. M. Skues, *Minor Tactics of the Chalk Stream* and *Nymph Fishing for Chalk Stream Trout*); Eyre & Spottiswoode Ltd. (H. T. Sheringham, *Trout Fishing Memories and Morals*); Faber & Faber Ltd. (G. D. Luard, *Fishing Fortunes and Misfortunes* and *Fishing, Fact or Fantasy?*, and Henry Williamson, *Salar the Salmon*); The Hamlyn Publishing Group Ltd. (Negley Farson, *Going Fishing*); The Bodley Head (Charles Ritz, *A Fly Fisher's Life*); Lady Tweedsmuir and the Houghton Mifflin

Co. (John Buchan, *John McNab*); The Bodley Head (O. S. Hintz, (*Trout at Taupo*); John Murray (Publishers) Ltd. (A. H. Chaytor, *Letters to a Salmon Fisher's Son*); Oxford University Press (S. Aksakov, *Years of Childhood*, translated by J. D. Duff).

The quotations which appear on the part-title pages for *The Equipment, Fish and Fishing* and *The Angler at Large* and at the head of the sections on *Salmon, Trout* and *Coarse Fish* are, in the order of their appearance, from the following sources:

The Equipment, from Hardy Brothers' 1886 catalogue and from a letter printed in the 1887 catalogue; *Fish and Fishing*, from Robert Venables, *The Experienc'd Angler* (1662); *Salmon*, from *The Treatyse of Fysshynge with an Angle* (1496), attributed to Dame Juliana Berners; *Trout*, from William Lauson's notes to his 1630 edition of John Dennys, *The Secrets of Angling*; *Coarse Fish*, from *The Arte of Angling* (1577), by an unknown author; and *The Angler at Large*, from Izaak Walton, *The Compleat Angler*, Part I (1653).

The majority of the illustrations in this book are taken from Hardy Brothers' catalogues, and the date of the catalogue is given below each such illustration, either as a simple number or, in the case of captioned illustrations, as part of the caption. A small number of illustrations have been taken from other printed sources and from picture libraries: the provenance of every such illustration is given in its caption. Decorative woodcuts, notably those on angling themes by Thomas Bewick (1753–1828), also appear throughout the book. In selecting these I am grateful to Dover Press for permission to reproduce from their publication *1800 Woodcuts by Thomas Bewick and his School*. And I am grateful to W. D. & H. O. Wills for the use of four cigarette cards in the jacket design.

The Equipment

A good rod is, without doubt, the Angler's chief requisite.

Hardy Brothers Catalogue, 1886

Dear Sirs,

My take this year has been 506. I credit the rod with 1,226 deaths since it has been in my possession. *Yours truly,* M.B.

Letter to Hardy Brothers, 1887.

A FAMOUS NORTHUMBERLAND MANUFACTORY

Few of the implements which man has made in order to facilitate an indulgence in sport afford more pleasure to those who are expert in its use than a fishing rod. Yet how few of the disciples of Izaak Walton have any conception of the numerous and delicate processes through which the materials must pass before the perfect rod is revealed; how few have any idea of the careful and judicious selection of material required, and the severe tests by which its quality is proved, or the mathematical accuracy with which the numberless parts must be fashioned and fitted together in order that a strong, reliable, and useful rod may be placed in their hands. A visit to a manufactory would astound most followers of the gentle craft, and would inspire them with a respect for their instruments in other senses as well as that of a means to the enjoyment of a gentlemanly, exciting, and healthy recreation. "It takes ten men to make a pin," so the school books of 20 and 30 years ago informed us, and that was the marvel of the juvenile minds of a generation ago. To make a complete fishing rod of the best type ready for use it requires as many men, and they must be skilful and able to work to the most minute precision.

We have experienced nothing so interesting for a long time as a visit paid to the new manufactory of Messrs. Hardy Brothers, rod, reel, and tackle makers, Alnwick, who in the course of a comparatively short career have established a reputation and a connection which is world-wide, and made the name of the little Northumbrian

"Alnwick, where the best men buy their fishing tackle." The Times, *8th September, 1925*

town in which they are located familiar to all who whip the waters in pursuit of their finny denizens. Scarcely 20 years ago Messrs. Hardy opened a factory for making guns, fishing rods, reels, and gear in Paikes Street, Alnwick, thus introducing to that neighbourhood an entirely new industry. They had an uphill task at the outset to establish themselves, but north-country determination, a prolific inventive faculty, and sound workmanship carried them through, and in time enabled them to force themselves to the front. As business increased they were obliged to seek larger premises, and they, therefore, entered new workshops in Fenkle Street in the same town. These in turn were subsequently found too cramped for a constantly increasing demand upon their resources, and recently they erected entirely new and extensive premises in Bondgate Without, where now a large staff of workmen are actively engaged in turning out fishing materials to meet orders from far and near.

Messrs. Hardy Brothers served their time as engineers, and afterwards learned the business of gun makers. An inherent love of sport, and all connected with it, impelled them to enter upon the manufacture of the instruments required for shooting and fishing, the former of which, although a good, sound, local trade, supplying most of the gentry and sportsmen in North Northumberland, takes a very second-rate place to their fishing rod and tackle business, in which they have displayed an aptitude which has done more to advance the trade and promote the interests of rod fishermen everywhere than any other firm in the world. In their earlier career they made the ordinary wood rods, but subsequently, struck with the superiority of cane, took up the cane-built work, and we believe we are correct in stating that they are now the largest manufacturers of cane-built rods in the world, and have transactions with all parts. The excellence of their workmanship, as well as the improvements they have invented and patented, have constituted a lever by which their work first forced itself into notice, and then into great demand. Among the customers of the firm may be numbered Royal personages, including Prince Albert Victor, the King of Belgium, the Emperor of Germany, and others, also Mr. C. Pennell, Major Turle, Mrs. G. Selwyn Marriott, Mr. H. S. Hall, Mr. W. Senior (*Field*), Mr. R. B. Marston (*Fishing Gazette*), Mr. G. M. Kelson, Mr. F. M. Halford, "Hi Regan", and many other distinguished anglers at home, and also in France, Germany, Austria, Switzerland, India, New Zealand, Spain, America, and elsewhere.

The new premises, which are built in the Jacobean style, are situated in close proximity to the railway station, and form a striking contrast to some of the buildings in the neighbourhood that have long contributed their quota to the quaintness which is one of the charms of the old ducal town. All that modern progress could suggest towards rendering them suitable to the business for which they are intended, promoting the comfort of the workpeople, and securing the convenience of those who trade with the firm, has been worked into the plan of the building, and the result is eminently satisfactory. Attention is first drawn to the handsome frontage, which is wide and striking, and the varied display of sporting implements in the windows of that part of the premises which does duty as a sale shop; roomy and well-stocked without being overcrowded, the shop gives one a favourable impression of the place from the beginning of the visit. Access may be had to the factory from the rear of the front or sale shop, or by a wide archway opening from the footpath. We will conduct our readers there by the former way. Behind the sale shop is the packing room, where the various consignments are made up and packed, and in due time sent out for delivery. Leading from this room is a spacious staircase, affording means of approach to the ground floor of the main part of the building, which is, of course, the factory, and which stands higher than the front premises, as the whole block is built on the side of a hill.

On the ground floor of the manufactory is the office, which is so situated as to command through the glass panels of the partition almost the entire floor. In front of the office is an 8-horse-power cycle engine of the newest type, which works all the machinery of the establishment. It is on this floor that the wood rods are made. To facilitate this branch of the business there is a useful little machine, a sort of variety worker, which does sawing, planning, grooving, and a number of other operations with the utmost celerity. One man is occupied the whole of his time at this machine selecting and cutting material. Another man spends his time in putting handles on rods. Throughout the place there is an endeavour to keep one man, or one set of men, always to the same operations. Messrs. Hardy have found, as others have, that work is done quicker and better when men are kept to one thing than when they are required to turn their hands to anything and everything. Especially is this the case in some of the finer work connected with the building of fishing rods. After the material of the wood rod is cut, as stated, it is then rounded and taken to a lathe which describes about 2,700 revolutions. Then it is passed to another man who finishes and balances it.

The next step is to send it upstairs, where the silk tyings and rings are put on and affixed, and where it is varnished. Lastly it goes back to the finisher to be finally finished off and made ready for use. An ordinary wood rod goes through about seven different hands before it arrives at the complete state. The rod itself is made of greatheart and the handle of cedar. So far we have only referred to the wood portion of the instrument, but Messrs. Hardy make the whole implement right from the ground, and on the first floor is found all the essential equipment for brass work, brazing, making of reels, and packing boxes, &c. Here it is that notice is first attracted to the fact that no fires are used. Fires are dirty and dangerous, and the work can be done equally well, if not better, with the aid of gas. The heating of the shops for the comfort of the workpeople is effected by pipes put in by Messrs. Dinning and Cooke, Newcastle, through the entire building.

Another flight of stairs conducts one to the first floor, where cane-built work is done. Here it is that one is most struck with the commanding strides that have been made in the manufacture of fishing rods during the past 20 years. Two decades ago the making of fishing rods used to be a rough and ready art. Now things are quite different. The rods which satisfied the last generation would be regarded with a feeling of contempt by the present. Great mental activity and manual skill have been brought to bear upon this branch of industry, and now we have angling appliances that it would seem difficult to further improve upon. In this progress Messrs. Hardy Brothers have taken a large share, and indeed their fame has grown with the progress which has been made in the trade, and this would seem to be conclusive evidence that the latter has received no small portion of its impulse from their endeavours to get established and afterwards to maintain a front place in the market. The medals they have gained fully corroborate this idea, and show how much the angler is indebted to this firm for many of the improvements which have been effected in fishing appliances.

India supplies the best bamboo for the cane-built rods, and the number of bamboos imported by this firm is simply astounding. On the occasion of our visit to Messrs. Hardy's factory we saw no less than 10,000 bamboo canes waiting for the processes of manufacture on the second floor, which, as well as the first floor, is devoted to cane-built work. Of these, we were informed, probably only 30 per cent would be fit for use. At the other end the agents satisfy themselves that the bamboos look serviceable, but it is impossible from the outward appearance to judge with anything like accuracy. A consequence of this is that a considerable number are received which are of no use. When a cane is being selected a portion is cut off the thick end, and then it can be seen whether there is sufficient fibre to warrant its being further dealt with. One out of ten, on an average, are found ultimately to justify the hope that they may come unscathed out of the test to which they are subjected. But a portion of the cane is available, as for a considerable distance from the top the material is unsuitable, and only part of the remainder actually goes into the rod. The portion of the selected canes which are fit for the purpose is rent into strips, and then it has to withstand the severest test or it is cast aside as useless. About twenty-five canes that have stood the test are needed to furnish the material for one 18-foot salmon rod. In the case of the double-built cane rod, which this firm introduced, forty-eight different strips of cane are required. Each section of the rod is composed of six strips forming the outer portion, and six other strips forming the inner portion, so that there are really two rods, one within the other. The accuracy with which these strips are cut and fixed together is really wonderful. Right to the minute end of the tapering rod the double set of strips are continued and fixed with the same exactitude as if they had grown that way. The more expensive cane rods have steel centres. Within the inner rod of cane a steel rod is introduced, which adds greatly to the power.

It is in the second or top storey from which, over the roofs of adjacent buildings, a fine view of the surrounding country is obtained, that the bamboos are stored, and they are selected and tested, rent

He examined my rod, asked me to let him have a few casts with it, then came back, took his own rod, chucked it on the ground. "I'm off home, I'll sell my rod to someone and get a 'Hardy' rod like yours."

Letter quoted in Hardy Brothers Catalogue, *1912.*

into strips, cut to the proper size, straightened, and have the knots removed. The rod has to be thoroughly balanced before the parts are fitted together, as to interfere with the hard enamel of the cane would greatly impair the serviceability of the instrument. The strips are fitted together and secured by cement. Ordinary glue would be valueless for this work; something more adhesive and less susceptible to wet is required, and Messrs. Hardy have invented a cement which has never failed to give satisfaction. Next the rods are finished and bound and tied down in order that they may dry straight. Afterwards they are sent downstairs to have the handles put on, and then on to the joint maker who makes the joints to fit. Next they go to the tying shop and the varnishing shop, and finally back to the finisher, who completes them ready for sending out.

I am sending you for repairs the VERY FIRST *rod you sold at the Exhibition of 1883, and though* PRO-GRESS *no doubt despises the* PAST, *you have not a better in your establishment, and it may interest you to examine it.*

Letter quoted in Hardy Brothers Catalogue, *1907.*

Hardy's patent lock-fast joint is one of the specialties of the firm, and one that has given the greatest satisfaction all round. Its advantages are simplicity, quickness, strength, and the impossibility of putting the joints together without being locked. When the old clumsy and ineffectual devices are remembered, fishers will readily admit the importance of this invention. The point of contact between the cane or wood and the metal which forms the joint is the weakest part of a rod, as the unyielding nature of the metal throws the whole strain on the cane or wood. To obviate this Messrs. Hardy have extended and split the end of the ferrule and tapered it down so that there is no sudden arrest of the vibration and less susceptibility to

1888

strain at that particular point. Since adopting this plan they have never heard of a rod breaking at the joint. But this is only one of the inventions of Messrs. Hardy. They began to win medals in 1881. At the Fisheries Exhibition, London, 1883, they won the gold medal for the best trout rod, and were awarded £10 for the best collection of trout rods against fifty-two competitors. This signal success they have followed up by winning thirty-one medals since for improvements in rods and reels. Besides manufacturing these, they also make artificial flies, and this is a very pretty work, and also a delicate work, as the variety of types, of colours, and shades of colour needed in order to suit the requirements or whims of fishers are legion. Gut cast-lines and almost every kind of tackle are also made in this department, including artificial baits, &c., too numerous to mention.

Newcastle Daily Journal,
Thursday, 29th May, 1890.

YOUR ROD
FOR FLY FISHING

For the length of your Rod, you are always to be govern'd by the breadth of the River you shall chuse to angle at; and for a Trout River, one of 5 or 6 yards long is commonly enough, and longer (though never so neatly and artificially made) it ought not to be, if you intend to Fish at ease, and if otherwise, where lies the sport?

Of these, the best that ever I saw are made in *York-shire*, which are all of one piece; that is to say, of several, six, eight, ten or twelve pieces, so neatly piec't, and ty'd together with fine thred below, and Silk above, as to make it taper, like a switch, and to ply with a true bent to your hand; and these are too light, being made of Fir wood, for two or three lengths, nearest to the hand, and of other wood nearer to the top, that a Man might very easily manage the longest of them that ever I saw, with one hand; and these when you have given over Angling for a season, being taken to pieces, and laid up

"SALMON ROD FOR THE GERMAN EMPEROR.—*His Imperial Majesty the German Emperor intends to resume the sport of angling next season, and has commissioned Messrs. Hardy, of Alnwick, to build him one of their best 17-foot split-cane salmon rods. This English rod is superior to the best American I have ever seen, and at its best, there is no better in the world. The Emperor used a borrowed one in Norway last year, and was so delighted with it that he has determined to have a special one for himself.*"

The Field *quoted in* Hardy Brothers Catalogue, *1907*.

in some dry place, may afterwards be set together again in their former postures, and will be as strait, sound, and good as the first hour they were made, and being laid in Oyl and colour according to your Master *Waltons* direction, will last many years.

The length of your line, to a Man that knows how to handle his Rod, and to cast it, is no manner of encumbrance, excepting in woody places, and in landing of a Fish, which every one that can afford to Angle for pleasure, has some body to do for him, and the length of line is a mighty advantage to the fishing at distance; and to fish *fine, and far off* is the first and principal Rule for Trout Angling.

Charles Cotton,
The Compleat Angler, Part II, 1676.

RODS OF RENT CANE

The beautiful rent and glued-up bamboo-cane fly rods, which I turn out to the greatest perfection, are very valuable, as they are both light and powerful, and throw the line with great facility. The cane for these rods must be of the very best description, or they will not last any time. They will last for years if properly made, and of course the fisher must take care of them; they are best when made into pocket rods, in eight joints, with all the knots cut out, and the good pieces between each knot rent and glued up; these may be had in my shop of as good a balance as a three-joint rod, most superbly made of the lightest brazings. They make capital perch and roach rods with a bait top added to the extra fly top, with bored butt to hold all. These rods can be made to suit a lady's hand for either boat or fly fishing.

The salmon rod should be made in four pieces or joints. The butt of the best long grained solid ash, the wood of which is not so heavy as hickory, and is not liable to break at the ferrule, that is, if the ferrule is put on "flush", without letting it into the wood by scoring it; the piece above the butt, and the joint next the top, should be of

Twenty-foot Built-Cane Rod has arrived all right. I am very much pleased with it. The balance of it is perfect. The lock-fast joints and winch fittings are a great improvement.
Letter quoted in Hardy Brothers Catalogue, *1886.*

the very best well-seasoned hickory, without crack or flaw; the tops to be made of the best yellow bamboo cane, either rent and glued up in three pieces, or spliced in short lengths with the knots cut away; the first joint to be nearly as stout as the substance of the wood above the ferrule at the end of the butt for $1\frac{1}{2}$ feet, to prevent the rod being limber in the middle; the next joint that holds the top should be very smart, and come up at a touch when bent with the hand, and the extreme lightness of the cane top prevents all appearance of its being top-heavy, which cannot be prevented with lance-wood, unless it is made very fine indeed, and then it becomes useless. The length of the rod should not exceed 17 or 18 feet long, and for light rivers, 16 feet is quite long enough.

William Blacker,
Art of Fly Making, 1844.

CAPRICE AND CUSTOM

Caprice and custom regulate largely the fancy of individuals in respect to this implement; one holds stiffness as a requisite, another pliancy; one prefers the single-handed, another the double-handed rod; some use a butt piece of hickory, some of ash and others of fir wood: this angler, again, in the matter of the top piece esteems lance,

I am greatly pleased with the 16-foot Steel-Centred Salmon Rod. Compared with the American and English rod in my possession, I give your rod the preference, equal in power to a 19-foot hickory for a long cast.
Letter from France quoted in Hardy Brothers Catalogue, *1886.*

The 17½-foot Greenheart Salmon Rod you made to my order in September last has turned out in every way satisfactory. It is beautifully made and balanced, and casts with great ease. The rod has been made of grand stuff, and the spring has been put in the right place. One can tell this from the clean way in which it lifts and throws. With such a rod, it is a great pleasure to fish, as there is little or no fatigue necessary, the rod doing the work itself.

Letter quoted in Hardy Brothers Catalogue, *1907.*

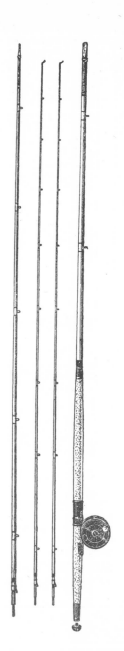

that bamboo; and, as to the ferrule, I meet with one who commends the plain joint and socket, another who countenances the Scottish screw, and a third who disclaims the use of brass joinings altogether and stands up on behalf of the tie system. In short, there is no termination to the variety of tastes and prejudices on the subject of fishing rods. The rings, the colouring, the varnish, the lower fittings all fall as matters of dispute, within the contentious circle; nor, indeed, does the observation of many years, and the most ample and un-prejudiced testing of rods of every description, stiff and pliant, light and heavy, single and double-handed, enable me so decisively to pronounce an opinion upon one and all of those matters, or even to approach an adjustment of differences in respect to them.

Thomas Tod Stoddart,
The Angler's Companion, 1847.

THE VIRTUES
OF SPLIT CANE

I bought my first split-cane rod, a powerful two-piece 10½-foot rod, of Messrs. HARDY in 1884. The butt and joint of that rod are still as sound as ever, after landing many fish of all weights up to 10 pounds, and though I have worn out one or two tops, not one has ever broken suddenly in the act of fishing, and they have stood faithfully against the most fearful shocks caused by weeds or bushes in the act of casting. It is this toughness of split-cane which, in my opinion, settles the question decisively in its favour, and though, after several seasons' hard work in all sorts of weather and in contending against down-stream winds, a split-cane top may weaken, mine have always given

The Alnwick greenheart rods were made by Hardy Brothers in lengths ranging from 9 feet to 20 feet and cost (in 1888) from 30s. to £5 7s. 6d.

I have had a fair trial of one of your 16-foot Cane-Built Steel-Centre Salmon Rods, and have great pleasure in testifying to its superiority to all the other rods of various kinds I ever tried or possessed. The rod responds so nicely to all the movements of the fish that he can scarcely even free himself, and at the same time there is a powerful pressure upon him. Whilst a friend of mine, who was fishing in the same water with me, lost four out of six fish with a spliced greenheart rod, I landed my first six fish, and I attribute my success entirely to my rod, as my friend is a practical fisherman. The casting of the rod is excellent, either against wind or otherwise, and there is no difficulty in throwing 26 yards of line in a calm and more with the wind from behind. The rod is very light to work with, and instead of being knocked up, as I have been with a greenheart rod, I never feel tired now, and in short, nothing would induce me to return to the old rods, so soon would I think of taking "Brown Bess" with me into the turnips.

Letter quoted in Hardy Brothers Catalogue, *1886.*

The Redspinner Rod.—Is of built cane, and fitted with all the latest improvements, which are applied by this firm to their justly celebrated rods. But it has two specialities. The first is a telescopic arrangement, by which the rod can be lengthened from 9½ feet to 10½ feet. The difference does not appear to be great, but every angler knows how much more work can at critical times be got out of an extra foot of casting power. The butt has one of those cork handles of about 18 inches long, which have of late years been applied to the built-cane rods, and it is in this that the extra length is made to slide. At the point where the handle ceases, and the comparatively slender continuation of the piece commences, there is a nozzle which screws tightly down to a chunk in three detached sections, and these, when the screw is worked, close round the telescopic length and neatly. Three turns of the screw release the extra foot length, which may be drawn out, or not, as required, and screwed up with ease.

The Field, *July, 1887.*

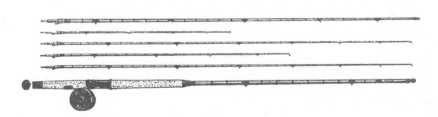

H. Cholmondeley-Pennell's General Rod.
This rod is 14 feet in three pieces, all Cane-built, with Steel Centre and four Tops, fitted with Lock-joints, "Universal" Winch-fitting and Rubber Button. Made by us to the order of H. Cholmondeley-Pennell, Esq., and approved by him as the best rod made for general work.

It is suitable for all kinds of fishing. Has two full length fly tops, which make it either a double-handed, trout, or light salmon rod; and for boat work, is one of the best of salmon rods (as 28 yards of line can be got out with it). It is very powerful and quite light. It has also a spinning top, two-thirds the length of fly tops, and with it makes an excellent spinning rod for salmon, sea trout, trout, pike &c. It is also suitable for all kinds of float-fishing. For heavy trolling it has another shorter top, and is altogether one of the most useful rods any angling tourist can carry, as it is (says Mr. Cholmondeley-Pennell) "three rods contained in one".

Hardy Brothers Catalogue, *1888.*

The Perfect Test: an 11-foot two-piece dry-fly rod of built cane in the Perfection range. Cost (in 1888), £5. Perfection rods are still made today

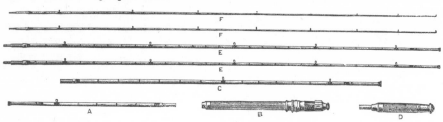

Hardy "Quadruple" Rod in built cane for trout and sea trout anglers (Hardy Brothers Catalogue, 1907). F F, two tops; E E, two middles; C, long butt piece; A, short butt piece, B, handle, into which fit C and A; D is a short handle which is fitted to B when the rod is used double-handed. F E A and B make a rod of 11 feet; F E A B and D 11½ feet; F E C and B 12½ feet; F E C B and D 13 feet.

The N.B. Perfection Rod

Is a complete outfit as regards rod and landing net. It is a similar rod to our ordinary "Perfection", but with detachable handle, C, which with A A forms the rod. D is our folding Y net head, which screws into landing handle, B, at E. The handle, B, is hollow, and carries A A when not in use, completely protecting them. The net head and handle are carried in the bag with B, or carried in a leather protector hung on the waist belt, leaving B to be used as an Alpine stock. The arrangement of detachable handle allows the total length to be reduced, an advantage in travelling. The 10 feet 6 inches, when packed, measures 5 feet 2 inches, made in lengths 9 feet, 9½ feet, 10 feet, 10½ feet, and 11 feet.

The handle may be either cork, cedar, or pigskin. Lockjoint to handle and parts A A; all best quality.

This is a splendid rod, up to any amount of hard work, and the compactness of the arrangement may be left to commend itself. Price, complete, £4 15s.; with steel centre, £5 15s.

NOTE.—*In using this rod where the landing handle is much in the water, it is advisable, on reaching home, to take out the rod and leave off the cap until it is dry.*

Hardy Brothers Catalogue, *1906.*

me ample warning; never in trout fishing, since I have used split-cane, have I lost a minute's fishing by the breaking of any part of my rod. Split-cane is the most staunch of all materials; like an old and faithful servant, it is incapable of treachery or sudden change, and when it fails it does so gradually. My own original split-cane rod has become a trusted companion, used to all winds, and weathers, to burns, chalk streams and rivers of many kinds; to trout, sea trout and grilse; doing all that is asked of it, having more than once risen to the occasion of playing a salmon, and remained straight erect and fit after landing it.

Sir Edward Gray, *Fly Fishing* (1899),
quoted in *Hardy Brothers Catalogue,* 1906.

IN BAMBOO PROTECTOR, Price, Five Guineas.

"THE IDEAL"

TROUT ROD,

No. 564 I.

All anglers are well aware that the fewer the joints in a rod the better, and for this reason many had so great an affection for the old spliced rod, which, however, since the introduction of short hard ferrules, carefully gauged in their thickness to spring in unison with the parts of the rod has become quite a thing of the past as any of our rods fitted with our patent ferrules, with splint-ends, are better and much more convenient than a splice. Still, it cannot be said that theoretically, any jointed rod is so perfect as a rod in one piece; and, therefore, we have, after much trouble, succeeded in producing a cane-built rod from 9 to 11 feet long, in one perfect piece. This is a very perfect article, and, where rods can be kept full length, a very beautiful tool to work with. Fitted with Cork Handle, Patent "Universal" Winch Fittings, and Bridge Rings, Five Guineas. If with Steel Centre, Six Guineas.

Hardy Brothers Catalogue, *1898.*

LONG OR SHORT?

The old rods would, of course, do *some* work, but not the kind of work one wants of a rod in many circumstances now. You cannot use a heavy line with a rod which does not play well down. The strain on the top part is much too severe. The lines such rods were accustomed to were light, made of horsehair, or horsehair and silk, and propelling them was no great strain. Presumably their owners never attempted to fish against a strong wind, and if they wanted to make longer casts they used longer rods. That must be the explanation of the 22-foot salmon-rods of which heroic tales are told. No one would fish with a 22-foot rod out of sheer gaiety of heart, though possibly the actual labour of using it with a light line would be no greater than the labour of using a modern 18-foot rod with a heavy

If prime cost is not an object, a really good built up cane rod, made by a first-rate hand, of thoroughly seasoned cane, with the bark untouched, each section properly worked and set straight before glueing up, the glue itself of the right description, and the entire rod coated with varnish which will stand, although costing something like £6 or £7, will in the end prove an economy, and will, beyond doubt, if properly handled, cast into the wind with far less exertion than any sort yet known to anglers.

The Field, *October, 1885.*

line. The common use of trout-rods measuring 13 or 14 feet was probably due to a similar need which exists no longer. Now that a 10-foot rod will cast 20 yards with ease and comfort, there is no reason to be bothered with a weapon which requires two hands. . . .

I think the evolution of this kind of rod is one of the chief triumphs of tackle-making, and we certainly owe a debt of gratitude to America for stimulating our first interest in it. The slender split-cane rod weighing little more than $\frac{1}{2}$ ounce to the foot, with a resiliency like steel and with what seemed almost miraculous power of casting,

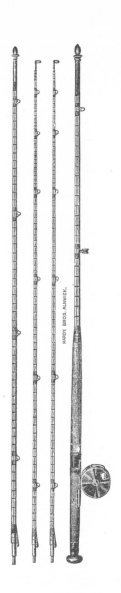

Some extraordinary fly-casting was witnessed yesterday morning at the Tir aux Pigeons in the Bois de Boulogne, Paris. Mr. John James Hardy, British champion salmon and trout fly caster, gave an exhibition of fly-casting for which he used what is probably the lightest fishing rod in the world. *It is made of "Palakona" bamboo, 7 feet in length, and weighs only $2\frac{3}{4}$ ounces. With this rod Mr. Hardy cast 25 yards, which is much further than the average cast of an expert fisherman using a rod three times this weight.*

Fishing Gazette, *quoted in* Hardy Brothers Catalogue, *1937.*

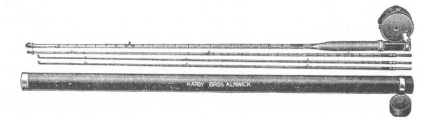

The Fairy rod was being made in lengths of $8\frac{1}{2}$ to 10 feet and weights of $4\frac{1}{2}$ to 6 ounces in 1907, while even lighter rods were being produced for export to America

The Connemara salmon rod (1908): lightness with power —a 16-foot steel-centred rod which weighed $28\frac{1}{2}$ ounces whereas the standard weight for such rods was over 2 pounds. A 14-foot cane rod without steel centre introduced the previous year weighed only 19 ounces

was a revelation to some of us at one time. But it has proved that there is no miracle about it, and our own makers now turn out light rods which answer every requirement of the angler's ideal. For all that we owe the impulse to America. So long ago as 1873, when W. C. Prime wrote *I Go A-Fishing*, our cousins were using 7-ounce rods. Twelve years later Francis Francis, in *A Book on Angling* (sixth edition), was weighing the merits of four of his rods, which varied in length from 11 feet 7 inches to 12 feet 8 inches, and in weight from 13 ounces 4 drams to 14 ounces 6 drams. Not, of course, that light rods were unknown here till the American type was discovered. I have a little greenheart of 9 feet 6 inches which is essentially a light rod and is perhaps 40 years old. But it is not split cane.

H. T. Sheringham,
Trout Fishing, Memories and Morals, 1920.

I used the Hardy "De Luxe" rod almost exclusively during my entire vacation. I had with me fishing rods made by the best fishing rod manufacturers in the United States and used these for a few days, but I wish to say for the "Hardy" rod that it was far superior in action to anything else I had in my rod case.

Letter from Kansas quoted in Hardy Brothers Catalogue, *1925.*

RODS FOR LIGHT LINE FISHING

The new principle in light line and threadline fly-fishing in rivers is that the line, instead of being in or on the water is in the air. This is achieved by the use of a small device called a controller or caster. Although it is small it has three functions. It enables the thin, light line to be cast easily up to distances of 40 yards, it informs the angler where his fly is, and it keeps the line out of the water. The latter is achieved by opposing pressures. The current presses on the controller; the angler keeps the point of his rod approximately at the perpendicular. The line is straightened between the two.

The effects of this provision are important. The fly does not drag but is fishing from the moment it falls in or on the water. The strength of the line is not diminished by saturation. Disturbance of the water and therefore of the fish is reduced and very often eliminated.

These practical considerations are reinforced by lightness of the equipment used. This adds greatly to the angler's comfort and pleasure. Even in the largest rivers in salmon fishing it is not necessary to use a rod longer than 12 feet 6 inches, weighing approximately 16 ounces. With such a rod heavy or light lines can be used;

he "Casting Club de France", led in 1911 as "the lightest actical fishing rod in the orld". As early as 1887 ardy were producing an -foot Gem fly rod weighing ly 6 ounces

heavy means lines with a breaking strength of from 12 pounds to 15 pounds, light means of from 6 pounds to 10 pounds. Flies and casts correspond with the thickness of the line.

In trout fishing the b.s. [breaking strain] of the line varies from 2 pounds to 4 pounds to suit conditions. Superfine casts can be used. Thus in low water 6x gut can be safely employed but, of course, calls for high skill in its manipulation. Normally 4x gut suffices.

The little Gem Featherweight has killed sea trout up to 3½ pounds and has played two fish over 5 pounds, but as I usually fish fine and carry no landing net, I failed to land either. The rod to date has killed under all sorts of conditions about 2,500 fish from 3 ounces up to 3½ pounds.
Letter quoted in Hardy Brothers Catalogue, *1924.*

This 25-year-old rod brings back many happy recollections, for it is a copy of the one you built for the late Princess Victoria, with whom at that time I had several chats about fishing matters.
Letter quoted in Hardy Brothers Catalogue, *1937.*

An interesting feature of both salmon and trout fishing is that when the flies are fished near the surface the fish makes a small splash. In salmon fishing the angler may strike at once or delay his strike as suits his temperament. In trout fishing the angler strikes at the splash. The reason the fish splash is of course that the flies are so close to the surface that they cannot be taken without the surface being broken. Normally, for the greater part of the season the flies are fished high but they can be fished at any depth the angler requires.

This is especially useful in loch fishing where the flies, the angler using a small, invisible sinking controller, can be fished virtually on the bottom, close to the surface, or at any preselected intermediate depth. Further, in loch fishing, if there is a good fishing breeze, the line and part of the cast are suspended in the air while the flies are bobbed, dapped, or otherwise manipulated. This method is especially useful for dapping with natural flies, such as Daddy-longlegs or May. If there is no wind these natural flies can still be cast without injury and fished floating; a most exciting variation. Fixed spool fishing greatly extends the technique of loch fishing whether from boat or bank. The bank fisher has much greater command of the water.

That is an important feature of fly fishing with fixed spool reels whatever kind of fish is being angled for. In river fishing it means that the angler can fish fly in situations impossible with the heavy line. The reason for this is that in casting only the cast is suspended from the rod. Normally it is from 10 feet to 12 feet in length; that is the distance between fly or end fly and controller. In salmon fishing

It may interest you to hear that I have landed a tarpon weighing 118 pounds on the Cholmondeley Pennell Rod I purchased from you some time ago.

Letter quoted in Hardy Brothers Catalogue, *1907.*

an ingenious use of a slip knot enables the angler to fish with a cast considerably longer than his rod if he desires to do so.

In casting the controller is drawn into the end ring of the rod. Thus, by keeping the line taut when the controller is cast, weakening of the end of the line from the stress of casting is virtually eliminated. This is important when such fine lines are being used. Tight line casting is, however, rarely necessary in brown trout fishing in river or loch as the stress of casting is not then severe. In loch fishing "stripping" the flies, perhaps the deadliest tactic for brown trout and sea trout, is done to perfection when using a No. 1 or No. 2 Altex. And the angler can fish successfully with artificial flies for trout rising in calms.

Hardy Brothers Catalogue, 1952.

USING THE THREADLINE

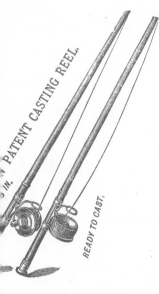

...re-runner of the fixed spool ...l: a Malloch-type casting ...l (1888)

The growth of the popularity of fixed spool reel angling, especially for trout and salmon, has been the greatest phenomenon of angling history which changes slowly down the ages. It was in 1930 that the first book devoted solely to the art of spinning—*The Science of Spinning for Salmon and Trout*—was published; the position has now been reached when no fisherman can consider himself properly equipped unless he has mastered the use of the fixed spool as well as the easier revolving drum reel.

This generalization applies to angling in river, lake and reservoir whether for trout, sea trout or salmon. It applies to fly fishing as well as spinning and other forms of bait fishing; for fly may now be successfully and fascinatingly used in conjunction with the fixed spool reel in running or still water, often in situations where because of obstructions the heavy line cannot be cast a sufficient distance.

DIAGRAM

Shewing Positions in Casting a Prawn or Spinner from Hardy's
Patent " Silex " Reel

THIS illustration shews the correct positions in casting a prawn or spinner with our new patent "Silex" reel, direction of stream indicated by the arrows.

Position (1) Angler's face to river, with rod as at F in fishing, feet at A.A. Position (2) Angler's face from river, holding rod as at C, preparatory to making a cast, feet as at B.B.

Stand on position A.A., reel up your line until not more than $1\frac{1}{2}$ yards projects from rod point; make a right wheel until your feet are on positions B.B., rod at C. Swing bait gently to and fro a few times, press your finger on the little projection on reel, then with a steady, sweeping, upward motion, cast your bait towards G, at same time turning to the left into position A.A. again. In doing this, when you come to D try to carry the rod to E as nearly as possible at right angles to the river, by drawing the elbows in as you approach E. This will cause your bait to go straight. The stroke or cast must be stopped at or before reaching E. If this has been done correctly, and the bait dropped at G, commence to reel up, holding rod as in position F, as fast as the nature of the stream or pool may require.

From Hardy Brothers
Catalogue, *1898.*

Mr. Emery, who used a No. 2 "Silex", commenced to cast, and at his third attempt he made an enormous CAST of 309 feet 6 inches. This constitutes a world's record, a truly remarkable cast.

Fishing Gazette, *July, 1911.*

1924

Fixed spool fly fishing embodies the new and revolutionary principle that the line instead of being in or on the water remains in the air. This eliminates involuntary drag and, as ordinary spinning lines are used, longer casting and greater command of the water is assured.

Fixed spool angling is now practised in many parts of the world. It is widely practised in Europe, especially in France; in Britain its increasing popularity has created problems which should eventually lead to the more intelligent management and therefore the improvement of our fisheries.

As invariably happens in periods of rapid change new ideas are adopted by numerous individuals before they appreciate their value; use precedes understanding. The result is the mis-use as well as the use of the fixed spool method. This rights itself in time as the individual learns from experience and gains confidence but a lot of time would be saved if at the beginning care is taken to understand the principles of fixed spool angling and the various devices embodied in the reels to put them into practice. There are no dark mysteries to be solved; everything is straightforward and logical. The basis of success can be simply stated: the equipment must be suited to the conditions and the size of the fish which the angler wishes to catch.

To reduce it to a single axiom: it is folly to use trout gear to catch salmon, or salmon tackle to land trout. . . .

Until I used your "Silex" I was a perfect duffer, always getting overruns and tangled up, a ruffled temper that made me say things that I should not.

Letter quoted in Hardy Brothers Catalogue, *1925.*

1924

The mistake of using too fine lines in salmon angling is so important that it is highly desirable that the angler, attracted by the apparent ease of the method when practised by experts, should grasp thoroughly the principles of what has universally come to be known as threadline fishing. Even at this late day, nearly 20 years after the term was "invented", it seems to be necessary to explain its meaning. It has less to do with the reel than with the line. The correct analogy is the ordinary domestic thread used in sewing. The thickest thread so used corresponds in diameter and strength to the fishing line with a breaking strength of 6 pounds. A line of that kind is strong enough to land the largest class of fish. The heaviest fish taken on a 6-pound line weighed 54 pounds and was caught on a river in Norway. Other authenticated fish of 35 pounds and upwards have been taken in this country on the same line. It is because of the efficiency of the 6-pound line properly used that it was fixed as the highest limit of b.s. to which the term threadline can be applied.

But before attempting to use such a line for large fish the angler must be sure of two essentials. He must have freedom of movement, especially down-river, so that if necessary he can lead or follow a large exhausted fish falling back in the current until he has worked it into a suitable place for gaffing. The other essential is that the river bed is reasonably clear of obstructions; since guile takes the place of force in this kind of angling.

Here are the line standards of threadline fishing:

For brown trout the line should have a breaking strength of from 1 pound to 4 pounds; for sea trout, from 3 pounds to 4 pounds; for salmon, 6 pounds.

If the angler uses a 5-pound or 6-pound line for brown trout or small sea trout he is not threadline fishing; nor is he if he uses an 8-pound line for salmon. The weights of line used with fixed spool reels for salmon can be conveniently classified as follows: threadline 6-pound, light line 8-pound to 10-pound, heavy line 12-pound to 15-pound. The correct reel to use in conjunction with these lines is as follows: 6-pound to 10-pound No. 2 Altex; 12 pound to 15-pound No. 3 Altex. For trout and sea trout up to a few pounds in weight, the No. 1 Altex. And the correct rods are: for trout and sea trout, single-handed 7-foot Hardy-Wanless 2-pound or 4-pound test curve; for sea trout, same series 4-pound and 6-pound test curve; for salmon, 6-pound line, 6-pound test curve, light lines, 6-pound, 8-pound and 10-pound test curve (latter may be double-handed); heavy lines, 12-pound to 15-pound; double-handed 10-foot, 10-pound test curve.

Observance of these standards will put the beginner on the right road and save him weary ploddings.

There is another important matter to which, especially when the finer lines are used in salmon or pike fishing, the angler should give serious thought. That is the prevention of loss of strength in the line from stress of casting and saturation and also from the tying of knots in nylon lines. This applies whether the angler is spinning, roving a prawn or bunch of worms or fly fishing. . . .

As to the weight of the lure or controller in relation to the line; if the weight at the end of the line is too light for the weight of the line long casting is impossible. If, on the other hand it is too heavy over-casting is the result and that is a bad fault. Moreover the heavy bait

The Perfect reel (1890). A fly reel with ball-bearings, regulating check, and ventilated drum

The Field reel (1892). A fly reel with exposed rim for fingertip braking. The partial replacement of brass by aluminium alloy gave birth to a new generation of lightweight fly reels in the 1890s

is sure to foul the bottom. This applies in all forms of bait fishing.

For the proper use of equipment rough guidance may be given. For clear-water worm fishing for trout, lines from 1 to 2 pounds are used, with, if necessary, a single split shot. For spinning with natural minnows $1\frac{1}{2}$ inches long with appropriate tackle the line can be of 2- or 3-pound b.s. An ordinary artificial minnow 1 inch long needs a 4-pound line, and the Hardy Heavyweight, used in salmon fishing, will need a line of 6 or even 8 pounds.

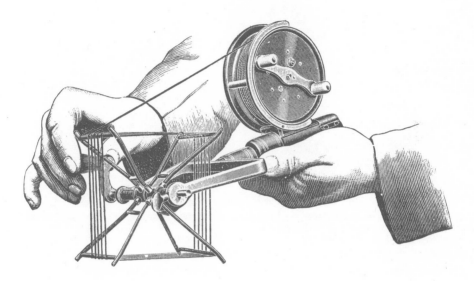

The Bethune line drier (1898)

Finally the device which makes the fixed spool reel so efficient when fine lines are used to catch heavy fish, the slipping clutch, must be used and not misused if success is to be achieved. This device is operated automatically through the tension of the line. The principle is simple. The tension is so adjusted when a fish is being played that at no time does the pull of the fish on the line exceed the b.s. of the latter. . . .

The amount of pleasure the fixed spool, properly used, can give the intelligent angler cannot be measured in words.

Alexander Wanless,
in Hardy Brothers Catalogue, 1952.

A RARE LIST OF
Irish Salmon Flies.

Most of these Irish patterns, both salmon, sea trout, and trout, were collected by one of our partners in 1901, who for the purpose made an extended fishing tour in Ireland.

In the selection of the sea trout (see page 78) and salmon flies (see page 90) for Recess lakes he had the valuable assistance of General Beresford and W. Wickham, Esq., to whom we are much indebted.

	Sizes—	4/0	3/0	2/0	1/0	1½	1	2	3	4	5	6	7	8
* 1	Claret Grey (PRICES)	2/-	2/-	..	1/9	..	..	..	1/3	1/2	1/-	1/-		
* 2	Lemon Grey (x)	?.	..	..	..	1/6	..	..	1/3	1/2	..	..	..	10d
3	Orange Grey (x)	..	..	..	..	..	..	..	1/3	..	..	1/-	..	10d
* 4	Black and Orange	2/-	2/-	..	1/9	..	..	..	1/3	1/2	1/1	1/-	10d.	
5	Black Jay	..	..	..	..	..	..	..	..	1/2	1/1	1/-	10d.	
* 6	Olive Jay	..	..	..	..	..	..	..	1/3	1/2	1/1	1/-	10d	
* 7	Orange Blue	2/-	2/-	1/9	1/9	..	1/6	..	1/3	1/2	1/1	1/-		
8	Lee Blue	..	..	..	..	..	..	..	..	1/2	1/1	1/-		
* 9	Black Goldfinch	..	..	1/9	..	..	..	..	..	1/2	1/1	1/-	10d.	
10	Yellow, Black & Orange	..	..	..	..	..	..	..	1/3	1/2	1/1	1/-	10d.	
11	Claret Palmer	..	..	..	..	..	..	..	..	1/2	1/1	1/-		
12	Blue Palmer	..	..	..	..	..	..	..	1/3	..	1/1	..	10d.	
*13	Nondescript No. 1 (x)	..	..	..	..	..	..	1/6	1/3	1/2	1/1	1/-	10d.	
*14	Nondescript No. 2 (x)	..	..	..	..	..	..	1/6	1/3	1/2	1/1	1/-	10d.	
15	Silver Jock Scott	..	2/3	..	..	..	..	1/9	1/6	1/3	1/2	1/1		
16	Durham Ranger (Irish)	2/6	2/3	2/-	..	..	..	..	..	..	..			
17	Orange Jock Scott (x)	..	2/3	..	..	..	..	..	1/6	1/4	1/3	1/2		
18	Spring Blue (x)	..	2/-	1/9	1/9	..	..	..	..	..	..			
19	Moray Doune	2/6	2/3	2/-	..	..	..	..	..	..	..			
20	Orange and Green (x)	..	..	..	1/9	1/6	1/6	1/6	1/3	1/2	1/-	1/-		
21	Claret and Orange (x)	..	..	..	1/9	1/6	1/6	1/6	1/3	1/2	1/-	1/-		
22	Black and Claret (x)	..	..	..	1/9	1/6	1/6	1/6	1/3	1/2	1/-	1/-		

NOTES.

Summer and Autumn Patterns.—Group 1. Embraces all dressed on hooks Nos. 3 to 7.

Spring Patterns.—Group 2. Nos. 15 to 19 are entirely Spring patterns, suitable for the Suir and other large rivers in early Spring. Dressed on sizes 4/0 to 1/0. To these should be added the Dusty Miller.

Corrib and Mask.—Group 3. Nos. 20, 21, 22. These three are selected as being specially good on these lochs.

Those marked (X) are the choice of the lot, and may be used all the season dressed in different sizes. (*) Nos. 1 and 2 "Nondescript" dressed and used successfully by one of our partners.

We have only given the prices under the size of hooks the flies are generally dressed on, and this will serve as a guide to the seasons for which they are intended, the small of course signifying Summer, and the larger Spring.

From Hardy Brothers
Catalogue, *1907*.

1924

The Trout Flies tied by this firm on eyed hooks, with semi-transparent india-rubber bodies are the most natural artificial lure we have seen. Placed on the hand, and held up to the light, they are so like the real thing that the trout must be wary indeed who can detect the imposture.

Land and Water, *1883.*

ODD TROUT FLIES.

No. 740.

Almost every angler has some pet flies which on occasions have stood him in good stead, and in a long experience (about thirty years) of fly fishing, we have, like others, found some curious patterns, of these we select a few which we think will be useful.

1. "The Defiance." Wings, woodcock; body, bright scarlet; with one turn of gold; tail, two red whisks; red legs. This fly kills well, especially when the March browns are thick on the water, and although the trout are feeding well they will not take your imitation, and all you can get is a few small fish. This is the time for the "Defiance," and large trout take it well.

2. "Kingsley's Cock-tail Spinner." Blea Wing; tail end of body olive quill, other half bright green quill; hackle and tail, honey dun. We are indebted to that good angler the Rev. W. Kingsley for this excellent pattern. He found it good on every stream and lake he fished. We find it especially good in cold showery weather. It kills well when any of the duns are on the water.

3. "The Ghost." Jungle cock wings; black body, hackle and tail; ribbed silver. This fly is most deadly in the twilight. At the head of streams, large trout take it well.

4. "Never Fail." Blea wing; dark green body ribbed with fine gold; red hackle and legs. One of the best all-the-season-round flies which can be used. The pattern is little known, but we confidently recommend a trial.

5. "Scarlet-ribbed Hare's-ear." Blea wing; scarlet and gold body; with hare's-ear picked out for legs. This is a most deadly fly in a full water. It is one of our inventions many years ago, and may always be tried when at a loss.

6. "Yellow Hammer." Blea wings; dull primrose yellow body; with yellow legs, and two white tails. A useful fly at almost any time, and the only one which will kill when the fish are feeding on these pale watery duns which defy the fly-tyers' skill.

7. "Little Favourite." Blea wing; dark olive green silk body; with blue legs and tail. A small clear water fly, and a grand killer.

8. "The Mystery" (No 1). In dead low clear water with this fly we have killed good baskets when it might have been said fly fishing was impossible.

9. "The Mystery" (No. 2). To be used as a dropper to No. 1, only two flies being on the cast. For dead low water these have no equals.

The first six are on ordinary best sneck-bend hooks. The three last are on very fine wires, and in using them care should be taken when striking or landing a good fish. Price 2s. per dozen, not less than half-dozen of any one kind.

From Hardy Brothers Catalogue, *1907.*

THE 'FILIP'

This is an attempt to help the Angler—to make casting easier and more accurate. These are desirable objects, and we are glad to say that with the kind co-operation of the late Philip F. Ch. Trench, Esq., of Dublin, we evolved (after many experiments), *this* the latest thing in fly lines.

Roughly, the idea is, that a longer foreline can be thrown when shooting, owing to the special form of back taper, and the fact that, the principal weight of the line is nearer the fly. Thus a longer line can be shot, with a comparatively short casting line; a consideration when in difficult places, with bushes, &c., behind. Possibly there is also something of advantage in the forward weight of the line, working the fly deeper in salmon fishing.

The same idea has been carried out in trout *dry-fly* lines. Here accurate casting is absolutely necessary. In this they are a great help, as they shoot most perfectly, and make continuous casting much less tiring.

Last season's experience (both by clients and ourselves) showed these lines to be quite a success; they cast with greater ease and shoot fully twice as far as the ordinary fly line.

Hardy Brothers Catalogue, 1911.

TROUT FLIES WITH WINGS OF NATURAL INSECTS

Mr. J. Richardson begs respectfully to inform Anglers and Fishing Tackle Trade generally, that he has brought his Invention of Preserving, Strengthening and Waterproofing the Wings of Insects to perfection, for the purpose of utilizing same in the manufacture of Artificial Flies.

1886

Hardy's "Midgets."

75 M—Hardy's Midgets, on Special Hooks. Black Midge, Black Gnat, Sky Blue, Pale Green, Jenny Spinner, Golden Dun, Brown Midge, Red Midge. Dressed on finest gut on 000, 00, 0 hooks with short shanks, specially designed by us for Midges, price 2/- per dozen. NOTE.—The flies are really less than the illustrations

From Hardy Brothers
Catalogue, *1902.*

By this patented process the Wings are Strengthened to such an extent, that they will be found to be stronger than feathers. This fact should be well borne in mind, as many are deterred from giving these flies a trial, owing to the natural Wings of Insects hardly allowing their being touched without falling to pieces, which is obviated by my patented process. These flies are guaranteed to stand more usage than any Artificial Fly ever made.

This marvellous strength is obtained without perceptibly deviating from their natural and original appearance.

The following are some of the advantages claimed by those using these life-like Artificial Flies:—the Wings have a more natural cock; they dry more quickly, being waterproof; will not kink the line; thoroughly flexible; considerably more life-like than any other Flies made.

The Wings are put on in such a manner as to prevent their drawing out.

The wings being transparent throw a light over the whole of the Fly—manifestly a considerable advantage.

The Moth will not attack them.

Richardson's brochure, 1890.

I have bought a large quantity of tackle from you this year, and I must say the result has been very successful, and in every respect most satisfactory. As for your idea of India-rubber bodied flies, they are marvels, and I have advised all my friends on the Test, if they have not tried them to do so for next season. The worm tackle with eyed hooks is to my mind quite the best I have ever used. I should like also to say that at the beginning of last season I bought one of your split-cane trout rods with a steel bar up the centre; I have used it regularly for the whole season, having killed 2,000 trout with it, both with fly worm, and minnow, and now the rod is as straight as it was when it left your works.
Letter quoted in Hardy Brothers Catalogue, *1907.*

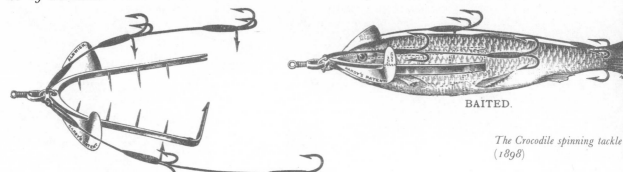

OPEN READY TO RECEIVE BAIT.

BAITED.

The Crocodile spinning tackle
(1898)

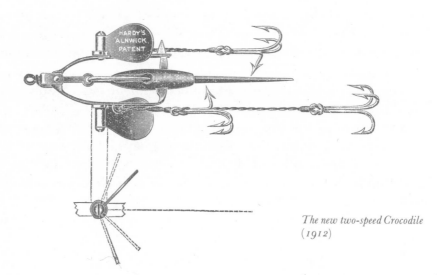

The new two-speed Crocodile
(1912)

ZULULAND.—*Of all the Spinners I have had the "Crocodile" beats everything else.*
Letter quoted in Hardy Brothers Catalogue, *1907.*

OF GARMENTS

And let your garments Russet be or gray,
   Of colour darke, and hardest to discrye;
That with the Raine or weather wil away,
   And least offend the fearful Fishes eye;
For neither Skarlet nor rich cloth of ray,

Nor colours dipt in fresh Assyrian dye,
   Nor tender silkes of Purple, Paule, or golde,
   Will serve so well to keep off wet or colde.

John Dennys,
The Secrets of Angling, 1613.

What the well-dressed angler was wearing (1888)

A COMMON BEAVER HAT

A common *beaver hat* is the best thing to *hook*, and *keep* flies on; and, if you have not two rods by the river side, always keep a gut length and flies ready to put on, round your hat, in order to avoid the waste of time and torment which you would have, if you had much entangled your line.

Peter Hawker,
Instructions to Young Sportsmen, 1814.

A 'WILD WEST' FELT

. . . No angler should look grotesque (if he can help it), and there are two things which he should always studiously avoid, and they are a white straw hat and patent leather boots, as these frighten the fish.

   Some angling advertisements lay it down as a rule that anglers should wear "all wool", and nothing but wool, and that by so doing they will be able to avoid rheumatism and such like ailments; but in my case I got the woollen clothing and rheumatism as well, so this statement is not to be relied upon.

   Apart from advertisements, a soft "Wild West" felt, a loose Norfolk jacket, grey flannel trousers, and a coloured pocket handkerchief seem to me a nice romantic "rig" for a dry-fly fisherman, especially if he is one of those who like to have a copy of Izaak Walton, or one of the classics, in their pocket (to read when anyone is passing by) as does,

Yours faithfully,

G.F.E.

Journal of the Flyfishers Club, 1918.

BY ROYAL APPOINTMENT

A most excellent compound of essential oils, which we have proved effective on many a midge-infested riverside. It is a clean, healthy preparation, not unpleasant in odour, and has no deleterious effect on the skin. Some form of midge preventative is a necessity for anglers, and this compound does all that is required in most parts. The bottle is of a convenient form to fit the waistcoat pocket, and has a sprinkler stopper. Price 1/6 each.

Hardy Brothers Catalogue, 1925.

BY ROYAL WARRANT OF APPOINTMENT MANUFACTURERS TO

HIS MAJESTY KING GEORGE V.,
His Majesty the King of Spain,
AND
His Majesty the King of Italy.

Patronized by Her Majesty the Queen, and H.R.H. Princess Victoria.

𝕿estimonials.

WHITE LODGE, RICHMOND PARK, SURREY.

I am desired by H.R.H. the Duchess of Teck to thank you for your kind present of a fishing rod to H.S.H. Princess Victoria of Teck, and to say Her Serene Highness has much pleasure in accepting it.   MARY THESIGER.

MARLBOROUGH HOUSE, PALL MALL, S.W.

Captain GREVILLE is desired by PRINCE ALBERT VICTOR to express his complete satisfaction with the Steel-Centre Cane-built Rod which was recently supplied to him by Messrs. HARDY BROTHERS.

PALAZZO REALE, QUIRINAL, ROME.

The new rod, etc., arrived safely, and Her Majesty the Queen of Italy desires me to thank you and say she is pleased with it.   S. DICKINS.

AMBASSADE DE RUSSIE, LONDRES.

The Secretary of the Imperial Russian Embassy is instructed to transmit you the thanks of His Imperial Majesty.

From Hardy Brothers
Catalogue, *1907*.

The only complaint that I have to make is that I have never been able to find out a single fault.
Letter quoted in Hardy Brothers Catalogue, *1907*.

The anglers (from The Compleat Angler, *third edition*).

Fish & Fishing

Many have supposed angling void of delight, never having tried it, yet have afterwards experimented it so full of content, that they have quitted all other recreations.

Robert Venables

SALMON

The Salmon is the most stately fish that any man may angle to in fresh water.
                                                                    Juliana Berners

1888

SALMON FISHING WITH THE FLY

For the salmon, tackle must be employed of a description much stronger than that used for trout. In principle, however, it is nearly similar, and a salmon rod with its line may be compared, in all respects, to a trout rod magnified with a slight power of the microscope.

The fly is worked very differently to the trout fly, which is generally on the top; whereas the salmon fly should always be sufficiently under the water to avoid making any ripple, as it is drawn towards the thrower, and yet not so deep as to be wholly out of sight; the cast should be made at an angle 25 degrees across the stream and the fly worked round to the side.

In the beginning of the season the fly may be worked near the surface, but late in the autumn it will be found most killing when thrown across the stream, at right angles to the angler, and allowed to float down with the current, working it round to the extreme edge before recasting, as fish often follow a fly, and will take it just at the edge.

A salmon fly with gut loop (1888)

Avoid disturbing the fish; it is better to get quickly over the pool, when, if they will not take, give them a rest and a change of fly.

STRIKING.—When anything is felt to obstruct the line such as a pull from a fish, the rod point should be thrown gently upward, when, if the fish is fairly felt, the hook should be well driven home, by a firm stroke, excepting in a rough stream, where the fish will hook himself. We have seen as many as six salmon lost in a single day after being half played by an angler who may fairly be considered good, but who did not sufficiently attend to this all-important matter.

It is much the fashion now to use double hooks, and it is really very difficult to say which is best; although we are inclined to favour the double, yet we had a very curious bit of practice this last season. After hooking and losing four fish in succession on a No. 4 double hook, we changed to a No. 5 single, and killed seven fish without a miss, losing the eighth from a mistake on the part of the gaffer. On the whole, if a fish fairly take a double wire its holding power over the single cannot be doubted, and late in the season, for kippers with their large open jaws, they will often hook a fish where a single would miss. Yet we generally find that fish take the single more freely than the double, especially in thin water.

PLAYING A FISH.—Immediately after striking you may prepare for a little desperate play. If your fish rushes off any great distance from you, get near him again as quick as possible, and never allow a foot more line than is necessary. Keep your rod well up, and a good firm strain on your fish at all times. Lower your rod point quickly if he leaps out of the water to avoid his striking the line, and tighten the instant he falls. Always keep your fish moving. Never allow him to settle, and fight him up-stream, keeping below him if possible. As soon as his wild rushes are over, press him as hard as you safely can (this according to the strength of your tackle), and work him towards the gaffer. He will generally make off again; in which case let him go a safe distance, then turn his head toward shore, and firmly and quietly draw him over the gaff. He will generally come fairly well the third time, but of course according to his power you and your tackle must deal with him. If your fish sulks, it is a good plan if you can get below him, to drop the point of your rod so as the weight of the stream puts the greatest vibration on the line. They cannot stand this, and will generally move. If this should not succeed try a firm pull on the line with your hand. These manœuvres may seem somewhat rough, but they are what we find most useful, and who would ever think of being laid up for the best part of the day with a fish, when you might kill half a dozen. Should your fish go fast down-stream where you cannot follow, and is likely to run your line out, and break you, hold him a little with your right hand, while with the left throw off some 5 yards of line from the reel. At the same time your rod should be well up, and when you have your slack ready, throw your rod forward as if switching. This we have some-times done successfully when no other means would have saved us from a break. The fish either turns on feeling the slack line before him, or more probably on being freed from the pressure of the line fancies he is free, and turns his head up-stream again, when our angler must wind up his slack as quickly as possible.

GAFFING.—There are many ways of gaffing a fish, but the following we find the most certain, and, besides, it does not destroy the fish as when struck through the shoulder:—The attendant should stoop down to be out of sight as much as possible (where the angler intends to bring his fish) with the gaff extended in the water upside down, and in this position he should remain perfectly still until the fish is fairly over the gaff, when he should strike, and draw the fish quietly out. On no account is he to strike until perfectly sure of his stroke.

Hardy Brothers Catalogue, 1886.

FLY FISHING FOR SALMON

Fishing with the fly is, undoubtedly, the form *par excellence* of angling for this game fish. *Salmo Salar* is far and away the best of all fish for sport. Possessed of great strength and vigour, he affords when hooked a vast amount of play and excitement to the angler. Small wonder is it then that the army of salmon anglers is ever on the increase. "Once a salmon angler—always a salmon angler" is a true saying, and he who has not tasted the pleasure it affords, may regret that one of the many charms of existence has been denied him.

No branch of the art of making rods and tackle has received more careful attention and study than that of making suitable gear for this form of sport. Nor has any department made such rapid strides. The introduction of so light a material as bamboo, with its great tough-

Messrs. HARDY, *of Alnwick, have made up a steel-centred split-bamboo salmon rod for my use. Having generally used greenheart rods (Castle Connell) pattern, this* "HARDY" *rod seemed a little too stiff near the hand for me, but though I am now an invalid, and not able to use a double-handed rod with my customary power, I believe that I can cast further with it than with any other rod I ever grasped. Of one thing I am quite certain, i.e. that it recovers better from the water, and brings back a longer line than any rod I ever saw. To try its actual strength, I tied a heavy shooting boot to the line, and swung the boot from side to side. I then put some shot in the boot, and raised the rod suddenly, but no break ensued. I added more shot till I filled the boot, but the rod lifted it from the dry ground easily. On release, the rod resumed its straightness at once, and* without a quiver. *On the whole, I think this is the best salmon rod I ever saw. The compliment Messrs. Hardy pay me in applying my* nom de plume *to such a magnificent rod confers on it a sort of immortality quite beyond my deserts as an angler or subscriber.*
        Letter from "Hi Regan" *quoted in* Hardy Brothers Catalogue, *1900.*

ness and strength, the system of doubling the enamel, and the introduction of a centre of highly tempered steel, has enabled us to produce lighter rods of greater power so that one can now fish comfortably and without undue fatigue. . . .

The length of rods generally used for fly-fishing for salmon vary from 14 feet to 18 feet. The more general length "nowadays" appears to be 16 feet to 17 feet 9 inches. The 15 feet to 16 feet is perfectly suitable for small rivers or larger when a boat is used. As all-round rods, 16-foot and 17-foot are the most popular. Personally we prefer a somewhat longer rod, and in the "Champion" we have 17 feet 9 inches only weighing about 39 ounces. (A 17-foot of this class has been added, weighing about 36 ounces.) We have tried this rod in every conceivable way, and find it sufficiently strong and powerful for any kind of fishing, while its lightness when mounted with a suitable "Perfect" reel and line make it, in our opinion, as an all-round rod, the best of its kind. We have fished a good many Scotch, English, and Irish, and some very heavy Norwegian rivers with one of these rods, during the last few years, and although there are certain rivers where one might, with advantage, use a heavier rod, we have found it perfect.

Suppose, then, that the ghillie has put into the hand of our young angler such an equipment as above, and directed him where the fish lie, and what part of the pool to fish; he should begin by casting his fly across the stream at an angle of about 45 degrees, working it across (as it sweeps round with the stream) to his own side. A very good measure for covering the water effectively, is to take a yard and a half between casts. Do not dwell at any particular place unless you have seen a fish, or know of one lying there, but get over the water at a regular and moderate pace. Then, if you are not going on to a fresh pool, rest the one you have already fished, put up another fly and try it over again. In this, as indeed in most other things,

The "Hi Regan", a powerful 16-foot salmon fly rod introduced in 1897 which remained one of the most popular salmon rods for some 50 years

remember that perseverance brings success. Therefore keep pegging away, and sooner or later you will be rewarded with a pull which sets every fibre of your being in motion; you need not be told to strike, instinctively you will do this, but avoid doing it too rashly, and yet it should be firmly done. It is seldom that on hooking a salmon he goes off with a rush, more generally he seems puzzled and undetermined what course to take, and this gives you a moment to breath. See that your line is clear, but at all times carefully look to this, as you never know when you may hook a fish, and to have the line caught round the handle or under the reel means disaster, for which you will hardly forgive yourself, as it may be the one chance of your day has been lost, and you go home "clean" to tell people stories they never believe. Having hooked your fish, stand ready for action, keep a steady pressure on him and the line clear; don't touch it with your fingers, the friction on the rings and resistance of the reel check will be sufficient pressure. It is probable your fish will rush across and up- or down-stream; do not be too hard on him, keep your rod well up and, if possible, get opposite him. Now you must have patience, for you cannot expect to kill him much under 1 minute to the pound. Carefully watch him, be quick and prompt to act, either in following or taking in line the moment you can. If he leaps, drop the point of the rod at once to avoid his striking the line, and tighten again as quickly as possible. Keep a steady pressure on and keep your fish moving. If you think he is going for a dangerous place, such as may place a large rock between you, where he may lie up or cut your gut line, use such discretion and means as occur to you at the moment to prevent him, but do not be afraid to ply the butt. As soon as he seems exhausted, try to work him in to the side, so that the ghillie may gaff or net him. It is not likely he will be brought within reach the first time, for as he catches sight of the gaff he will be off again into the middle, or possibly quite across the pool; try him again until he is exhausted, when your ghillie will get a chance. Personally, we always prefer to clip a fish through the belly; this does not destroy it so much as when done in the shoulder, and we are inclined to think it safer. Let the ghillie get down on his knee and place the gaff stretched out under water, then work your fish over it, when he cannot fail to clip him.

The reel and line should be carefully selected to match the rod in order to give the best results in casting, and your gut trace partly twisted or plaited, and partly single, should be regulated by the state of the water and the probable size of the fish. It is a mistake to use very thick gut, unless the water is heavy. In choosing a fly, always select one on the small side. Flies up to 3/0 irons may be either single or double; larger sizes are generally single.

As to the method of working the fly, it is curious to observe the different methods employed, almost every man works differently; one will cast his fly across the stream and allow it to sail round without moving his rod. Another will sink it deep and with long slow draws work it round. While another will work his rod top quite vigorously.

In the very early spring and late autumn we like to sink the fly deep and give it a moderate movement. When the season advances, say into May, and one uses comparatively small flies, they should be fished nearer the surface and a little quicker. Fishing rivers like the Moy in Ireland (which is deep and clear), in the summer and using the customary point fly and dropper on about a No. 7 "Oval" wire hook, the usual method of casting and fishing general in England and Scotland is useless. To be successful, the flies must be worked quickly on the top as in fishing for trout. We do not say one cannot kill fish in these rivers with slow fishing, but six fish will be killed fishing quick for every one fishing slow and deep in this particular river and its locality. As to why it should be better to fish one river or even one pool quicker or slower than another, we cannot here enter. It is sufficient to say that in fishing a strange river, it is best to experiment a little, and having found the best method, stick to that.

In wading swift rocky rivers, or one to which you are a stranger, it is wise to be provided with a wading staff of some kind. . . . It is handy, saves many a tumble, and gives confidence, as, should the water be discoloured, you can feel before you and so prove the depth. Besides, on hooking a fish, you can get out of the water more quickly, as it practically serves the purpose of a third leg.

Hardy Brothers Catalogue, 1911.

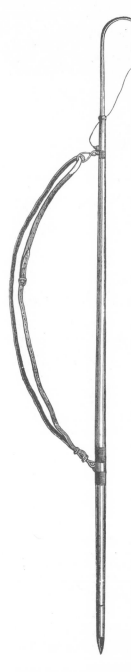

Combined gaff and wading staff (1896)

1924

SALMON FLY FISHING IN SLOW RUNNING WATER

The writer, who fishes a good deal of slow running water 3 to 5 feet deep, has for some 3 years adopted a style which gives good results, and may be interesting to other anglers. The method is to cast the fly across the water, and bring it round, gathering the line in with the left hand by a series of "jumps". The motion is given as stated, with the left hand, therefore the whole weight of the rod, after making a cast, comes on the right forearm, so that an ordinary man cannot comfortably use a rod longer than 15 feet.

Hardy Brothers Catalogue, 1931.

HARRY OTTER LEARNS WHAT IS A FISH

The rod was hastily put together; a beautiful new azure line passed through the rings; a casting line, made like the waist of Prior's Emma, appended, with two trout flies attached to it of the manufacture even of me, Harry Otter. An eager throw to begin with: round came the flies intact. Three, four, five, six throws—a dozen: no better result. The fish were stern and contemptuous. At length some favourable change took place in the clouds, or atmosphere, and I caught sundry small trout; and finally, in the cheek of a boiler, I fairly hauled out a 2-pounder. A jewel of a fish he was—quite a treasure all over. After I had performed the satisfactory office of bagging him, I came to a part of the river which, being contracted, rushed forward in a heap, rolling with great impetuosity. Here, after a little flogging, I hooked a lusty fellow, strong as an elephant, and swift as a thunderbolt. How I was agitated say ye who best can tell, ye fellow tyros! Every moment did I expect my trout tackle, for such it was, to part company. At length, after various runs of dubious result, the caitiff began to yield; and at the expiration of about half an hour, I wooed him to the shore. What a sight then struck my optics! A fair 5-pounder at the least; not fisherman's weight, mark me, but such as would pass muster with the most conscientious lord mayor of London during the high price of bread. Long did I gaze on him, not without self-applause. All too large he was for my basket; I therefore laid the darling at full length on the ground, under a birch tree, and covered over the precious deposit with some wet bracken, that it might not suffer from the sunbeam.

I had not long completed this immortal achievement ere I saw a native approaching, armed with a prodigious fishing-rod of simple construction guiltless of colour or varnish. He had a belt round his waist, to which was fastened a large wooden reel or pirn, and the line passed from it through the rings of his rod: a sort of Wat Tinlinn he was to look at. The whole affair seemed so primitive; there was such an absolute indigence of ornament, and poverty of conception, that I felt somewhat fastidious about it. I could not, however, let a brother of the craft pass unnoticed, albeit somewhat rude in his attire; so, "What sport," said I, "my good friend?"

"I canna say that I hae had muckle deversion; for she is quite fallen in, and there wull be no good fishing till there comes a spate."

Now, after this remark, I waxed more proud of my success; but I did not come down upon him at once with it, but said somewhat slyly, and with mock modesty:

"Then you think there is not much chance for any one, and least of all for a stranger like myself?"

"I dinna think the like o' ye can do muckle; though I will no say but ye may light on a wee bit trout, or may be on a happening fish. That's a bonny little wand you've got; and she shimmers so with varnish, that I'm thinking that when she is in the eye o' the sun the fish will come aneath her, as they do to the blaze in the water."

Sandy was evidently lampooning my Higginbotham. I therefore replied, that she certainly had more shining qualities than were often met with on the northern side of the Tweed. At this personality, my pleasant friend took out a large mull from his pocket, and, applying a copious quantity of its contents to his nose, very politely responded:

"Ye needna fash yoursel' to observe aboot the like o' her; she is no worth this pinch o' snuff.''

He then very courteously handed his mull to me.

"Well," said I, still modestly. "she will do well enough for a bungler like me." I was trolling for a compliment.

"Ay, that will she," said he.

Though a little mortified, I was not sorry to get him to this point; for I knew I could overwhelm him with facts, and the more diffidently I conducted myself the more complete would be my triumph. So laying down my pet rod on the channel, I very deliberately took out my 2-pounder, as a feeler. He looked particularly well; for I had tied up his mouth, that he might keep his shape, and moistened him, as I before said, with soaked fern to preserve his colour. I fear I looked a little elate on the occasion; assuredly I felt so.

"There's a fine fish now,—a perfect beauty!"

"Hoot toot! that's no a fish ava."

"No fish, man! What the deuce is it, then? Is it a rabbit, or a wild duck, or a water-rat?"

"Ye are joost gin daft. Do ye no ken a troot when ye see it?"

I could make nothing of this answer, for I thought a trout was a fish; but it seems I was mistaken. However, I saw the envy of the man; so I determined to inflict him with a settler at once. For this purpose I inveigled him to where my 5-pounder was deposited; then kneeling down and proudly removing the bracken I had placed over him, there lay the monster most manifest, extended in all his glory. The light—the eye of the landscape—before whose brilliant sides Runjeet Singh's diamond, called "the mountain of light", would sink into the deep obscure;—dazzled with the magnificent sight, I chuckled in the plenitude of victory. This was unbecoming in me, I own, for I should have borne my faculties meekly, but I was young and sanguine; so (*horresco referens*) I gave a smart turn of my body, and, placing an arm akimbo, said, in an exulting tone, and with a scrutinizing look, "There, what do you think of that?" I did not see the astonishment in Sawny's face that I had anticipated, neither did he seem to regard me with the least degree of veneration; but, giving my pet a shove with his nasty iron-shod shoes, he simply said:

"Hoot! that's a wee bit gilse."

This was laconic. I could hold no longer, for I hate a detractor; so I roundly told him that I did not think he had ever caught so large a fish in all his life.

"Did you now?—own."

The Tweed near Kelso (from
The Angler's Companion, *1847*).

"I suppose I have."

"Suppose! But don't you know?"

"I suppose I have."

"Speak decidedly, yes or no. That is no answer."

"Well, then, I suppose I have."

And this was the sum-total of what I could extract from this *nil admirari* fellow.

A third person now joined us, whom I afterwards discovered to be the renter of that part of the river. He had a rod and tackle of the selfsame fashion with the apathetic man. He touched his bonnet to me; and if he did not eye me with approval, at least he did not look envious or sarcastic.

"Well, Sandy," said he to his piscatorial friend, my new acquaintance, "what luck the morn?"

"I canna speecify that I hae had muckle; for they hae bin at the sheep-washing up bye, and she is foul, ye ken. But I hae ta'en twa saumon,—ane wi' Nancy, and the ither wi a Toppy,—baith in Faldonside Burn fut."

And twisting round a coarse linen bag which was slung at his back, and which I had supposed to contain some common lumber, he drew forth by the tail a never-ending monster of a salmon, dazzling and lusty to the view; and then a second, fit consort to the first. Could you believe it? One proved to be 15 pounds, and the other 12! At the sudden appearance of these whales I was shivered to atoms: dumbfoundered I was, like the Laird of Cockpen when Mrs. Jean refused the honour of his hand. I felt as small as Flimnap the treasurer in the presence of Gulliver. Little did I say; but that little, I hope, was becoming a youth in my situation.

I was now fairly vaccinated.

William Scrope,
Days and Nights of Salmon-Fishing, 1843.

HOW TO FISH

When you have learnt to cast a fly tolerably, you then begin to tackle the real craft. That is, how to fish; how best to make use of your power of casting so that salmon may be induced to take the fly you throw for them.

There are few subjects in sport upon which more theories are held, or about which more nonsense is talked. These theories are held almost as articles of faith and are stated with angry conviction. Gillies and fishing-keepers are proverbial for their ignorant omniscience. Nearly all of them believe that there is only one way— and that, of course, is their way—to do everything, and the moment that they see a newcomer fish otherwise, they regard him as little better than a fool, and if he does not speedily conform to their ways, he will receive neither information nor help from them—and you want their information as to where the fish lie and where they take. The truth is that there are many ways to fish well, and no one way is the best in all cases. You may fish either deep or on the surface, with flies large or small, plain or gaudy, working the fly or bringing the rod round perfectly steady, and in general you may do well with each method.

The fact that different styles of fishing do hold their ground amongst good fishers suggests—as I believe is the case—that no one style should be adhered to slavishly, and that to fish with the greatest effect one should vary the methods of fishing with the varying waters fished. And not only do salmon pools differ greatly in character, but the same pool often requires fishing in a totally different place and manner according as the river is high or low. Personally I was taught to hold the rod almost level over the water and to fish a long line, letting the fly sink deep, and fishing without the least lifting motion of the rod point. A fine fisher, then always fishing near me, used the opposite method. With rod held high, as in trouting, and with a rather short line, cast lightly upon the water, he kept a much larger fly always skimming near the surface with a constant lifting motion intended to give the fly a lifelike play. Over our first 5 years of fishing together he maintained a slight but distinct lead in the number of salmon caught, but in every single year the fish taken in the same water by the deeper fishing of a small fly averaged from 1 to 3 pounds heavier than those taken by the larger fly played near the surface. Other results we noticed. One method succeeded constantly in places where the other fisher used to fail, and in a big dark water the surface method was greatly inferior to the other. So we came to vary the style of fishing to suit, as we judged, the different pools and waters. The result is that now in the rough stream of a medium-sized river, or in deep, strong waters, we fish with a long line cast well down-stream, and allowed to come round as deep in the water as possible without any playing of the rod, which is held with the tip only 2 or 3 feet above the water. But in low water, and in quiet streams or grassy swirling pools, unless very strong indeed, the fly is cast much more across the stream and worked round by a series of short lifts until the rod is almost upright, and often line is drawn in by hand before making the next cast.

Fly reels (1886)

The clearer the water, and the more shy the fish, the more I find myself fishing on the surface and playing the fly quickly. There are many tricks and variations. Across a glassy swirl one constantly casts at right angles to the central stream or even somewhat up-stream. After almost every deeply fished cast one allows a slight hang to the fly and then slowly draws it up with a series of short lifts. In fishing from the inner side of a curving stream a quite exaggerated hang, after the fly *appears* to have swung below you, and then a slow, jerky lifting, with rod stretched out far over the stream, has constantly produced fine fish just as the fly was about to be taken from the water. They seem either to follow it, or—as I have seen them do— to rush at it out of the part already fished, as they see the fly being drawn past them up the edge of the stream. Often the heaviest fish

will thus take the fly, and take it so late that the only way to strike
the hook home—as you must do with the line just about to leave the
water and the rod nearly upright—is to jerk the top violently backward so that the weight of the line may jerk the hook hard into the
fish. Often when a pool has been fished down blank in the ordinary
style you may get a fish or two at once by fishing it over again, either
by starting to fish from the bottom and backing upwards, or by
fishing from the top downwards, and in either case casting straight
across the stream and keeping the rod top well up-stream as the fly
comes round. I have even seen a fish that in a dead low water had
been pricked, and would not rise again, taken by the fisher standing
at the head of the shrunken stream, holding out his rod over the
current and letting down the same fly to his fish.

One more caution to you. Be most careful not to bring round the
rod point faster than the line is being brought round by the current.
This is a very common fault, especially when one is impatient or
pressed for time, but it is a bad fault, for it keeps the line slack
instead of taut to the fly. Rather do the opposite and keep the point
of your rod out over the stream, particularly if the fly has to swing
close in below you. When fishing from the inside of a curving stream
you should be most careful to do this.

I would not have any one think that any of these methods are
stated as being necessarily the best, still less as the only good ways
of fishing. The more you can vary your fishing with the water the
better you will fish, but some idea of the ways that others find to
succeed may help you when no mentor is at hand and the fish utterly
decline your offers.

In quick, narrow rushes, when the river is dead low, a way that
often succeeds is this: with a sea trout fly or a big March brown on
a light line and thin gut, make your cast straight across the rush, then
with outstretched rod let the fly sink as deep as possible into the
centre of the current, then with a short, jerky motion begin towing
it up-stream as it approaches the side on which you stand. Constantly
the fish will grab the fly just after the jerks begin.

On one, as I thought, quite hopeless afternoon in September, 1904,
hot, hazy, and windless, with a glaring sun, in a dead low water, in
one short stream, I took in this way, with a double-handed trout rod
and a small green-bodied, heckam-peckam fly, three fish of 13, 12,
and 5 pounds, and lost a fourth. Many and many a time the odd fish
that has saved a blank day in August or September has come by

this method when the ordinary salmon fly and its manœuvres were quite useless. Again on 2 days in the season of 1907, in the dead low September waters of that year, I took four salmon each day with the same trout rod and tiny fly. For this kind of fishing I use a thin sea trout cast ended off with 3 feet of ordinary trout worming gut, but gut always new and sound, and watched most carefully to detect the least sign of weakening. Such gut costs only a couple of shillings or so for 100 strands, and one must simply throw away the cast so soon as it becomes frayed or weakened and make up a new one in its place. It sounds alarming to hook large salmon upon such thin gut, but if sound and new, such gut is very strong indeed, and with a light rod you need have no fear of a break unless the fish can get round some rock or snag. These things, of course, are generally more dangerous than ever in low waters, and of them you must take your chance, and must, when broken on them—as I constantly have been broken in low summer waters—reflect that you might easily have fared no better with the strongest gut, and that with it you would probably never have hooked the fish at all, nor had the fun of his fight and loss.

But for very low, clear water a very light line is almost as important as thin gut. Not only is the splash of its fall much less, but the feebler current can float a light line and give the fly a lively motion when the ordinary salmon line is almost useless except in the rush of the streams. However, when in despair you have taken to your small flies and trout tackle, it is worth while occasionally to try a big salmon fly in the streams. Occasionally a fish that has not seen a big fly for some time will seize one in the very smallest water. When you have risen a fish and failed to hook him, you may be in doubt as to what is the best thing to do. If he has been pricked he may come again, but he is not likely to do so. But the mere fact that you have had a hard pull is nothing against the fish taking the fly again. I have taken a fish at the fourth offer which had taken my fly hard three times within as many minutes. Sometimes they will again take the fly cast to them instantly, and some people advise a long wait, but personally I almost always remain where I am, pull in 3 or 4 yards of line at the reel, and from the same stand fish down to the fish by letting out at each cast about a yard of the line drawn in. If that fails and I do not want to fish on, I go out of the stream and begin 20 yards higher up and fish down to him again.

A. H. Chaytor,

Letters to a Salmon Fisher's Sons, 1910.

WHEN THE WEATHER CHANGES

Salmon never take well when the weather is about to change; it is therefore useless to go out when the mercury remains at this point. When it first sets in for a continuance of dry weather the fish will rise about your hook, and only break the surface of the water; but before a flood they will spring clean out of it, for the purpose, perhaps, of filling their air-bladder before travelling.

> William Scrope,
> *Days and Nights of Salmon-Fishing*, 1843.

HOW TO TELL A SALMON POOL

One is sometimes asked, and sometimes asks oneself if one can tell a Salmon Pool, and for my part I answer, rightly or wrongly, in the affirmative. Before laying down any precepts on the subject it is necessary to have an idea as to what sorts of places the salmon like to lie in, and I would say, firstly, that they like fairly swift water. If the water is very cold they want it deeper and less swift, and if that is not available they may content themselves with water which is slack and almost still, but deep; but they will move up into the swifter and shallower waters as it gets warmer. Conversely they will, if the water is very hot in summer, frequent the deep waters by day and move up into the swift and shallower water at night. When I say shallow water I do not mean really shallow water and the depth must vary on different rivers, but I would lay down not less than 6 feet in ordinary cold weather and not less than 5 feet in warm weather, but much deeper than 6 feet in cold weather if possible. Next they favour some shelter from the incessant flow of the stream; some rock behind which to lie or some promontory or projection from the bank which causes a backwater, on the edge of which they like to lie, but not actually in a swirly backwater with the stream coming all ways. I have, nevertheless, known salmon to lie with their heads facing down the river in a backwater with a steady flow up-river, and have, in particular, watched one so situate steadily taking March Browns like a trout. If there are trees on the bank they will go near them, other conditions being favourable, and for this reason it is always a little risky recklessly to cut down bushes and trees in order to get at the water, as, with the trees gone, the fish are apt to forsake their old lies. Writing of old lies (not unsuitable, I believe, in an angler), it is remarkable how, year after year, salmon will lie in precisely the same spot, provided no floods alter the bed of the river.

Bearing these observations in mind when one goes to a strange salmon river, assuming that the water is reasonably clear, one looks first for those deep, dark, forbidding, quick-running waters and knows that either just inside the backwater made by some projection from the bank or anywhere in the dark deep stream proper, fish may lie and take anywhere from the top to the bottom of the deep run. If the water has an apparently even flow right across, but is deep with a good stream, then one looks for certain swirls which appear from time to time from below, and which denote that a little up-stream of them there is a rock behind which a salmon should be. There may be many salmon elsewhere too, but, if there are no such swirls, one cannot be guided as to where the fish actually will lie, only probably in the deepest part of the stream and more especially near bushes over the deep water. Supposing that the water is quite slack, what may be termed pike water, then I do not think that a stranger will be able to make up his mind as to where the fish lie— it may be anywhere. I do not say that in the swift waters he will be infallible, but that without local aid he should be able to select the best waters. And here I would lay stress on the importance of fishing the best water and not wasting time on indifferent places, even if one knows the river. Another method of diagnosis which I hope many of my readers who have not gleaned anything from the above suggestions, and those who have too, may be able to employ is to see the salmon rise and to mark the spot. Apropos of this, as I think I have already recorded in the *Journal*, a large stone or stick or even a human body, thrown into the water in the neighbourhood of where salmon lie, but not too near them, or beating the grass bank smartly and repeatedly with a walking stick, will usually make the salmon show and enable the angler to locate them. This will not prevent the fish from taking, but rather will rouse them and make them take the more readily.

Journal of the Flyfishers' Club, 1925.

HOOKED THROUGH THE BACK FIN

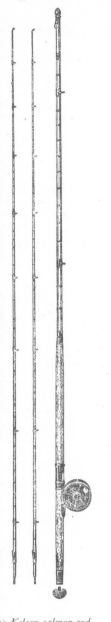

he Kelson salmon rod 888). An 18-foot cane-built d weighing 46 ounces

It was a perfect day for salmon fishing. The sky was overcast, the air light, with just enough wind. The river was in perfect order. Oh, that Conway, that sad and sullen river! You can flog it day after day without reward. A bag of two fish a week is something wonderful, and three or four are enough to make a fisherman happy for the rest of his life. I had been flogging persistently for 5 or 6 days, but had touched very few, and caught none. But the way in which they were rising on this eventful morning was enough to make the nerves tingle. There were salmon running from 10, 20, 30, and even 40 pounds weight. A friend, who had been with me for 2 or 3 weeks, had only a few days left, was very anxious to see me get hold of one of these monsters. I had fished the Tyn-y-cae Pool, which was in perfect order. All the morning I had flogged the tempting water, but without success, and as I had to meet a friend down the river, I left the pool in sheer disgust. The fish would not take. I went down to the Crooked Pool, with the same result. We turned again to Tyn-y-cae just about lunch time, and I was setting my rod against the old toll bar, preparatory to going in to lunch, when my friend H. said, "Just try another cast over the tail of this pool, it is perfect." Just to please him I did so, and fished very closely for about 10 yards, when my man said, "There, did you see that?" On enquiring what he had seen, he said a fish had made a boil at my fly. At that instant a fine salmon jumped right over the cast. I struck with all my might, hoping to get the fly in some part of him, but I missed. I tried three or four more casts, but he would not come again. David was sent to ask Mr. Hall to come and have lunch at the toll bar. After my man had gone I thought I would try just once more, and put a silver-bodied fly on. I commenced fishing a little above where the fish had risen, and had only made a few casts when I saw a boil. On tightening, I felt that I had him. The salmon was just at the tail of the pool, and, being afraid lest he should make a dash down the river, I brought him up quietly until he got opposite the little island, and then, with a rush, he bolted to the other side. With about 60 yards of line out, he jumped clean out, showing well. With the rocks at the bottom, I knew the danger of having so much line out, and slowly but surely got him to my side. My friend H., who was looking down into the water, announced that the line had got round the fish. This did not make me feel very comfortable, but in less than a minute I felt I had him unwound and secure. Then he made up the pool and my man declared I had hooked him through the back fin; he could see the jungle cock feather. I was fishing with one of Hardy's cane-built, steel-centred rods, 18 feet long, made specially to my order. It was stiffer than most men like, but when once used anglers were compelled to say of it "What a beauty!"

The fish all along meant fight, so did I. For the next 10 minutes my work was well cut out. Up the pool, down the pool, across the pool went the fish. Still I held on, allowing between 5 and 6 pounds pressure, which, from the length of the rod, was equal to 90 pounds on my arm. Flesh and muscle could not endure this long, and I said to my friend H., who had persuaded me to try for the fish, and was in some way responsible, "It's not a question of my killing the fish, but rather a question of the fish killing me. My arms are almost paralyzed. Just put your hand under that rod and hold it up." He did so, easing me a little, but only a little. In another 5 minutes the fish made up his mind to go out of that pool if he could. As I made up my mind that he was going to do nothing of the kind, when he got at what I considered a fair angle from the point of the rod, I dropped on one knee, keeping the rod perpendicular, throwing the butt into the hollow of my right foot, pressed my hand rapidly up, and held on. Now it was a question of what was going to give. "You will smash," said my man. "Smash away," I replied. But it was no smash. Slowly but surely I felt the fish coming to the top, nearer and nearer, and at last the salmon lay athwart the stream, fully one third out of the water. But he sailed up the river once more, and putting on a good bit of pressure I brought him in; he went under the bushes. I was as far back as I could get on account of the trees behind me, and, holding my rod nearly perpendicular, tried the risky game of pulling the line through the rings to bring the fish up to David's gaff. The fish objected, and I was determined. So, one pull, a second pull, and still a third pull, and then I saw David reach over the bushes, the steel of the gaff flashing through the air. The pressure was taken off the top of my rod, and a 25-pound salmon lay gasping on the bank, truly hooked through the back fin. My arms were so stiff that I could hardly raise or drop them. The time of landing the fish from the moment I hooked him was just 30 minutes. Fortunately, before starting out in the morning, I put a small box of Homocea in my pocket. I went into the toll bar, and before a nice warm fire I rubbed it in for the space of 10 minutes, and was just as fresh as if I had never had this hard battle.

Hardy Brothers Catalogue, 1894.

MY BEST FISH

My best fish—so far, may I say without touching wood—was no great monster. Four-and-twenty pounds it was for a long time, and then for some years a fish of 28 pounds held the field. In 1904 it became 32 pounds, and now—this last week "as ever was"—his place has been taken by a fish of 34 pounds. But he is nothing to feel very proud of, because he was taken on the minnow, with a trace of steel wire, and so his last gallant battle was but brief and brutal.

The 24-pounder was the best sportsman of the lot. He was a beautiful spring fish, his back blue-grey and his sides of burnished silver, and with that peach-coloured or rose-pink iridescence over the glistening under sides that you never see upon a late autumn fish. Yet he was taken on the 28th of October. A big flood had lasted for a week, and the river had begun to run clear, though it was still very high. On the 27th I had touched a fish on the fly, but had done nothing else. It was a perfect day for a minnow, but I used no minnow in those days. I began on the 28th at the same spot, and immediately got a heavy pull from this fish, but the hook got no hold, and he could not be induced to come again. All day I fished blank, and about 5 o'clock I returned to give my friend another trial. When I reached him I felt the faintest draw on the line, yet it was a quite slow draw such as only a good fish can give. I made the same cast again, and this time with a snatch he made sure of his fly. The current ran strong, and the very butt seemed to creak as the top of the rod was dragged down to the water. Like so many strong fish that are well hooked, he didn't show himself at first, but kept deep down in the water, and after a few moments of heavy "jagging" he began steadily to bore his way up the stream. In 25 minutes he showed himself but once, and then it was only one sudden leaping somersault about 10 minutes after he had been hooked. At last his strength began to fail and I tried to strand him on the gravel bed, but every time that he touched the stones he turned and splashed out into deep water, and stubbornly refused to be coaxed to shore again. The rod was a most powerful steel-centred cane rod, and I knew that the tackle was strong, so I did not spare him in the least, and I can remember to this day how my left arm ached with the cramped strain of holding the rod so hard against him. However, at last, after 35 minutes of the severest treatment that I ever remember, he was safely stranded and lifted out by the tail. I had, of course, seen for some time that his whole colouring was very unusual, and each time that he had stranded upon the shallows I had noticed that his wet back showed as a sort of warm yellowish grey—like the wet back of a great trout, and entirely unlike the colour of the autumn fish, which, even at their brightest, show a dark and rather dull-looking back as they are drawn on to the shallows. But until I saw this fish out of the water I had never thought of the chance of taking a clean spring fish at that time of year, and I could hardly believe my eyes when I saw him shining before me with that unmistakable rosy pink bloom, and his fins and tail standing out in contrast almost as black as ink. Well, he was a cock fish, and, as I have told you, he weighed 24 pounds. He had taken a fly that I had made the night before— a silver body with a pale blue hackle and a plain dark mallard wing —and he was sent off to a very young lady who is now your mother; and I believe that she thought then that I caught fish just like that every day.

For a good many years 24 pounds was my best. I caught fish of

1907

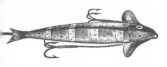

*The famous phantom"
1886)*

22 pounds and 23 pounds often, I caught even several of 24 pounds, but I could go no higher. At length in the course of one season I rose to $25\frac{1}{2}$, then to $26\frac{1}{2}$, and then to 28 pounds. The 25-pounder I caught as a small flood was rising. A week later, when it had fallen again, and the water had become dead low, so low that for days we had caught no salmon, I was fishing one evening with a very light double-handed sea trout rod, a trout cast, and a small green heckampeckam fly, about the size of a large March brown, when I saw the flicker of a big tail in the shallow rushing water right at the throat of a pool. I got into the river well above the place and fished down to it almost inch by inch, for I knew that the fish must be lying just where the water deepened, and that the fly would almost touch his nose. Whatever it did he took it. There is little to be said about the next hour and 5 minutes. There never—or very rarely—is hard or quick fighting with a heavy salmon on a light rod in a big pool where the fish has plenty of sea-room. I was as gentle as possible, merely doing my best whenever he grew quiet to urge him to keep up his struggles. At the end of that time I floated him, dead beat and lying on his side, on to a sand-bank a quarter of a mile below the place where he was hooked, and there lifted him out. He was a cock fish and weighed $26\frac{1}{2}$ pounds, and the hook of the little green fly had opened out a good deal, but I keep it as a pattern; many salmon have since died upon copies of it. The 28-pounder was caught in September and upon the rising water of a flood. He had been fished for in vain for many days, but had been hooked and lost that same morning. Fortune must have been smiling that day, for the line was badly "knuckled" above the cast, and though it was strained almost to breaking-point in turning the fish away from some logs, yet it held then, although it snapped like rotten thread when tested—as you must always do—after the big fish was landed.

It was several years before I got to 30 pounds. Then one day in a heavy, muddy flood, on a river on which we were guests, two of us had been fishing with fly and minnow all day on the only pool quiet enough to offer us any chance of a fish. At 5 o'clock we decided to give it one last turn with the phantom, and in that turn my big fish boiled up at the minnow on the shallow tail of the pool. He missed the minnow, but turned and rushed after it along the top of the water and seized it a few yards farther on. I was wading waist-deep, and as soon as I had got back on to the shallows the fish flung himself out of the water. None of your wild somersaults, but a stately dive, head first out and in again, like that which one sees done by each one of a school of porpoises as they dive into the air out of the side of a wave and pop in again in the trough. I saw, and said on the spot, that he must weigh 30 pounds, and, as you may suppose, I was very careful with him. But care does not mean easing the strain and playing gently; it means watching every move of the fish to be sure that if he gives a sudden dash or leap the rod and reel are ready to respond to it. Well, he made a fine fight; twice more he leaped clean out and repeatedly dropped down to the edge of the rapids and there lashed about on the surface. In one long run up the farther side of the river he caught the line upon a great round boulder, and it seemed as if he must break it, but after a few moments of horrible grating I felt a twang, and the line was released from the boulder and sprang into the air again taut upon the fish, some 10 yards higher up the stream, but carrying fast upon it a lump of moss about the size of a cricket ball torn from the side of the boulder. The last effort of the fish was to bolt down the rapids into the pool below, where, after a stubborn fight, he was brought to the gravel and taken out, 35 minutes after he was hooked. Thirty-two pounds he weighed, and proud as Punch I was of him in those days, making an outline model of his tubby figure in strong drawing-paper and touching it up with ink, to fill in the eyes, fins, and other details, and the spots and shading of the back.

This remained the best fish until September, 1908, when on the 18th I took six fish weighing as they came 15, 5, 15, 14, 18, and 34 pounds. The big one was caught upon a minnow in a quiet slow-running pool where I had never dreamed of taking a very big fish.

But that pool must have been well suited for big fish, for 7 days later—and since I wrote what you have just been reading—I was lucky enough to hook there and land a fish of $40\frac{1}{2}$ pounds, my heaviest salmon up to the present, and one that I am not very likely to beat. During the morning three fish had touched my fly, two, weighing 14 and 16 pounds, had been landed and the other lost; but after midday not a rise could be got, so as a last chance before going home I went to try this pool. Whilst I took one turn over it with the fly I got Tom to put up the spinning rod, and then I mounted a small phantom minnow and at the second cast hooked the big fish. He fought and walloped and plunged on the surface for a long time, taking a great deal out of himself and also showing me that I had a very big fish to deal with. It was growing dark and the bank was fringed with willows, but luckily the fish kept to the open water and put up a very active plunging fight, so that in about 15 minutes I was able, at a gap in the willows, to bring him near enough to use the gaff. Up to then I believed that he was a big fish, about 30 pounds perhaps, but until, as I dragged him ashore, I saw his great length and his thick back, I had no idea that I was in for the long-coveted 40-pounder. But when I saw him come out of the water I hoped for even more than 40 pounds, and I am certain that if he had not been bitten, as he was, he must have weighed from 45 to 50 pounds. For he measured just over 48 inches from the snout to the centre of the tail, and these big fish usually weigh about a pound to the inch, or if in really fine condition, a little more than a pound to the inch. But my victim had lately received a frightful double wound from the teeth of some predatory beast—some seal or porpoise most probably—and although he showed no sign of autumn redness, in spite of a large "gib" and a hooked jaw, yet he was not as deep as he ought to have been, and he must have lost many pounds in condition from this injury.

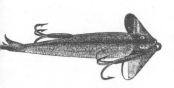

A soleskin phantom (1888)

His would-be captor had quite obviously seized his salmon from underneath, for there were two great gashes on each side of his belly, and the scrapes of his captor's teeth backwards and downwards to the anal fin were quite plainly to be seen. What a meal he would have made for almost anything!

A. H. Chaytor,
Letters to a Salmon Fisher's Sons, 1910.

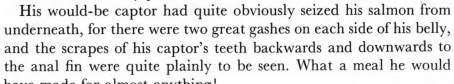

SALMON FISHING—OR THE SPORT OF CHANCE

I suggest that, given some slight knowledge of fishing ways, the catching of salmon is not a matter of skill but of luck. Here is my proof. Three fishermen find themselves in possession for the month of May, of the best stretch of water, about 5 miles both banks, on one of the most charming and famous of Scottish rivers—over twenty pools, fairly easy wading, and a fly can in most places be put upon the opposite bank.

The water is divided into three beats, fished alternately by an Expert who has fished the water for 10 years and known every stone and his gillie, equally expert, each with a rod, likewise an Expert of less mature experience and his gillie, each with a rod, and lastly the Novice and his gillie with one rod between them.

The Novice is easily tired and being fond of his afternoon tea is generally home by 4 p.m. The others, hardier and with fewer years of angling behind them, usually return just before dinner and so gain 2 or 3 hours more fishing in a day. All start at the same time, 10 a.m.

At the end of the first day the Novice brings home two fish, the others one. The second day the Novice brings three fish, the others nil. This day seems proof of the title to these notes. Of these three fish, two were seen to rise in a pool where a fish had not been taken for some considerable time, it being looked upon as just a temporary stopping place. The Novice took one, had his lunch and then grassed the other. That evening the Novice, partly in a spirit of humility, and partly of belief, expressed the view that salmon fishing was a chancy sport demanding nothing like the skill required for dry-fly trout fishing. He was duly and amply censured by the Experts, who, although not saying it, wore a look of "And what did you take them on?"

Another day when the water was getting very fine the Novice had the top beat, and, after fishing without result the first two pools with a small fly on a fine grilse cast, passed the rod to his gillie, an excellent fisherman and fellow, who changed the fly and fished them again without success. Whilst watching the gillie and meditating over a pipe the Novice was inspired with the idea that the flies were too small and asked for his fly-box, which by the way was a small cardboard box holding a dozen loose flies, the Novice being somewhat indifferent to appearances. Selecting one, without any knowledge of its species, upon a hook twice as large as the size previously fished, he asked his gillie to tie it on. The gillie seemed surprised and somewhat amused, but being by this time accustomed to the Novice's eccentricities, complied. Thus armed, the Novice fished again the two pools already fished over twice and after a few casts took a fish from the top pool and likewise one from the lower pool. The gillie, looking first at the fly and then at the fish, exclaimed, "That's going against nature."

One further incident in proof that salmon fishing is a sport of chance. There had been several more or less blank days for all rods when the morning of the last day arrived and the Novice prayed for one more fish. This day his beat held one of the largest pools on the water, always full of fish often sporting and leaping. Although the pool had been systematically fished every day and at some time or other with every legal lure by each fisher in turn throughout the month, only one fish had been taken from it. The water by now had got very low and clear and was running but slowly through the pool and the Novice discussed with his gillie the wisdom of trying the dry-fly (so-called) which he had read of but never tried; the gillie, being of the opinion that conditions permitted opportunity for any experiments the Novice desired to make, proceeded to grease the line and cast up to within an inch of the fly (this time a small one). The hour was about 10.30 a.m. By 11.15 a.m. a fish had been risen and missed and two really nice fish lay on the grass. The other four rods had a blank day.

To sum up, a month's fishing on first-class water, five rods (four experts, one novice), forty-nine fish, of which nineteen were taken by the Novice's rod (nine the Novice, 10 his gillie), all nineteen being clean fresh run fish.

After dinner on this the last evening the Novice confidently asserted that salmon fishing was a chancy sport and that reduced to an arithmetical basis he would apportion the credit for results: as to 10 per cent, the tackle; 15 per cent, the fisherman; and 75 per cent, the fish.

The Experts were silent.

Journal of the Flyfishers' Club, 1930.

TIMING THE STRIKE

In a low clear water you must be somewhat dilatory in striking: you often see the heave of the water and a break before the fish has actually seized your fly. Give him time to turn his head in his way back to his seat, to which a salmon always returns after rising at the fly. Tom Purdie gave me an account of a fish that had perplexed him greatly by his non-observance of this rule, as nearly as possible in the following words. He might have used fewer certainly, but Tom was not laconic.

"I had," said he, "risen a sawmon 3 successive days at the throat of Caddon-water fut, and on the 4th day I was determined to bring him to book; and when he rose as usual, I went up to Caddon Wa's namely, the pool opposite the ruins of Caddon Lee, where there had been a terrace garden facing the south; and on returning I tried my old friend, when he rose again, without touching the heuck: but I got a glimpse o' him, and saw he was a sawmon o' the biggest sort. I then went down the river to a lower pool, and in half an hour came up again and changed my heuck. I began to suspect that having *raised* the fish so often, I had become too anxious, and given him too little law—or jerked the heuck away before he had closed his mouth upon it. And as I had a heavy rod and good line, and the castin' line, which I had gotten thrae the *Sherra*, had three fadom o' pleit gut at the end of it, and the *flee* was buskit on a three plies o' sawmon gut, sae I was na feard for my tackle. I had putten a cockle-stane at the side o' the water fornent the place where he raise; forbye I kend fu' weel where he was lyin': it was at the side o' a muckle blue clint that made a clour i' the rough throat, e'en when the Queed was in a brown flood, as she had been for twa days afore. Aweel, I thought I wad try a plan o' auld *Juniperbank's* when he had raised a sawmon mair nor ance. I keepit my eyne hard closed when the heuck was commin owre the *place*. Peace be here! I fand as gif I had catched the branch o' an aik tree swingin' and sabbin' in a storm o' wind. Ye needna doobt I opened my eyne! An' what think ye was the sawmon aboot?—turnin' and rowin' doon the tap o' the water owre him and owre him (as ye hae seen a hempie o' a callant row down a green brae side) at great speed, makin' a fearfu' jumblin' and splashin', and shakin' the tap o' the wand at sic a rate, that deil hae me but I thocht he wad hae shaken my arms aff at the shouther joints, tho' I said to mysel' they were guy firm putten on. I never saw a fish do the like but ane i' the Auld Brig pool in the Darnwick-water. I jalouse they want to unspin the line; for a fish has far mair cunnin' and wiles aboot him that mony ane wad think. At ony rate it was a fashious plan this I fell on; for or he war to the fut o' the pool I was tired o' him and his wark, and sae was he, Ise warrant ye. For when he fand the water turnin' shallow, he wheeled aboot, and I ran up the pool as fast as I could follow him, gien him a' the line I could at the same time; and when it was just about a' off the pirn, and he was commin into the throat, he wheeled again in a jiffy, and cam straight for my feet as if he had been shot out o' a cannon! I thocht it was a' owre atween us, for I fand naething at the wand as the line was soommin' i' the pool a' the way doon. I was deed sure I had lost him after a' my quirks; for whan they cast a cantrip o' that kind, it's done to slacken the line to let them draw the heuck out o' their mouths wi' their teethy toung—an' they are amaist sure to do sae. But he was owre weel heuckit, this ane, to work his purpose in that gyse, as ye sal hear; for when by dint o' runnin' back thrae the water as fast as I could, and windin' up the line I had brought a bow on the tap o' the rod, I fand the fish had riestit in the deepest part o' the pool, trying a' that teeth an' toung could do to get haud o' the heuck; and there did he lie for nearly an hour, for I had plenty o' time to look at my watch, and now and then to tak' mony a snuff too. But I was certain by this time that he was fast heuckit, and I raised him again by cloddin stanes afore him as near as I durst for hittin' the line. But when I got him up at last there was mickle mair to do that I thocht of; for he ran up the pool and doon the pool I dar' say fifty times, till my feet wur dour sair wi' gangin sae lang on the channel: then he gaed owre the stream a'thegither. I was glad to let him change his gait ony way; and he gaed down to *Glenbenna*, that was in Whitebank's water, and I wrocht him lang there. To mak' a lang tale short, before I could get at him wi' the gaff, I was baith hungry an' tyrt; an' after a' he was firm heuckit, in the teughest part o' the body, at the outside o' the edge o' the wick bane. He was a clean sawmon an' 23 meal pounds."

William Scrope,
Days and Nights of Salmon-Fishing, 1843.

THE NEW PHASE OF SALMON ANGLING

For many years we have made stout single-handed rods for salmon fishing in Great Britain and America. These rods have been much used by anglers who delight in giving the fish a fair sporting chance, and at the same time taking as much enjoyment out of their sport as possible.

Mr. E. R. Hewitt has lately written an instructive book, called *Secrets of the Salmon*. This work we have pleasure in recommending to clients. The special feature in Mr. Hewitt's book is that he largely favours the "dry fly". This strongly appeals to us, as we feel sure it must make the sport more enjoyable. To kill a salmon on a light rod of 6 to 7 ounces with a dry fly is the highest art.

So far as the practice of fishing with single-handed rods is concerned, much credit is due to Mr. A. H. E. Wood, of Cairnton, as he has piloted the development of this on the Dee for many years. We are fortunate by favour of Mr. Wood, to lay before our readers a letter from him containing a full and interesting description of his methods:

I was most interested in Mr. Hewitt's book, although I do not use a "dry fly" specially made for that purpose. I have caught a lot of my fish on a dry fly; that is on my Silver Blues, Blue Charms and March Browns made to float. As you know our water does not always suit the "dry-fly" fishing, but many a time some of the pools or bits of the pools work nicely, and I have caught quite a number fishing exactly as Mr. Hewitt describes. Some of my friends have asked me to show them how the fish come to the dry fly. I have often succeeded in getting a fish to come up that we could see lying in the water close to us. When we can see them close, no doubt they can see us, and I have noticed on these occasions that the fish generally allow the fly to come straight over them, and when about a yard below, they will suddenly turn down-stream and snatch it; otherwise, when fishing with fly floating they take it quietly like an old trout. When the water is suitable, I find it the most deadly; but the fishing I enjoy and love most is when the water is in the right condition, and the stream not too rapid, where I can fish with a wet fly just under the surface. I do this by greasing everything except the last few feet of the cast. My aim and object is to keep the fly about ½-inch under the surface, not more, and to keep my line slack on the surface of the water. The fly moves very slowly across and down-stream, and is some way round before the line straightens, and the fly begins to travel faster into the bank. In making this cast I invariably throw about 25 degrees up-stream, as I find the fish so often take it, in the first few yards when it must be travelling almost directly down-stream.

1898

When the water is suitable, this is what I find so deadly.

It was in 1904 that I first fished for salmon in Ireland during the summer months, and I then started "light" fishing as the water was so clear. From then, until 1913, I did not have a rod in my hand. When I came up here in 1913, the water being clear, I worked out these methods, as I found they paid best; I did not know there was anything novel in them, and I have never considered them so.

As you know, I have not used such a light rod as Mr. Hewitt. I think my lightest one, 12 feet, which you made for me 2 years ago, was a little over 11 ounces. This I find a beautiful rod, and gives me full control of the line and the fish. I generally land my fish quicker than those using a big rod. I think one feels the fish better, and although one has not the power to control him when he makes a run, one has far more chance to worry him between the runs. . . .

There is one point I should like to differ with Mr. Hewitt, and that is, the temperature of the water. I find on the Dee, it is worth starting fishing with small fly, that is, No. 1 hook, as soon as the temperature of the water is 38 degrees to 40 degrees, and from 40 degrees to 45 degrees one can drop to a No. 6 or 8 hook. Above 45 degrees anything down to No. 12. I notice he wants a far higher temperature.

Yours sincerely,

A. H. E. WOOD.

While we think this new style of fishing most delightful in rivers of moderate depth, where one may wade and stalk the fish during the late spring and summer fishing, for general work we must retain our 14 to 17-foot rods, as necessary for spring, autumn and general use. While there are rivers on which one may practice this comparatively new art, there are also rivers in which these small rods and fine tackle may be worse than useless.

Hardy Brothers Catalogue, *1924.*

I killed with the 9-foot trout rod six salmon, largest 7½ pounds, smallest 5 pounds, in 2 hours' fishing. Four were killed in the first hour exactly.

Letter quoted in Hardy Brothers Catalogue, *1925.*

I now use the Fairy for all my low-water Salmon fishing, and it has landed twenty-seven weighing 227 pounds including two of 18 pounds and 16½ pounds respectively. This year, on 1st October, it lost what might have been an even bigger one—a lovely autumn fish the hold giving way when the played-out fish was being steered ashore for landing after not more than 15 or 20 minutes.

I have not a complete record of the rod's trout captures, but can vouch for 1,335 weighing 603½ pounds.

Letter quoted in Hardy Brothers Catalogue, *1954.*

SPINNING AND PRAWNING FOR SALMON

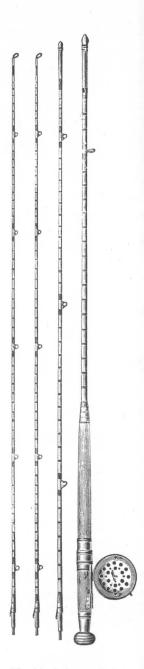

It is absolutely necessary in order to enjoy this form of angling for salmon, that the appointments should be perfectly suitable. The haphazard way in which some men will occasionally put up a prawn or a phantom on their fly rod, and have a cast with it, does the style an injustice; nor can they by such modes appreciate what an amount of artistic skill is required, and enjoyment derived from casting and spinning with suitable tools in a proper manner. We feel sure one of the chief reasons why until recently, spinning and prawning was so little practised, lies in the fact that really suitable rods and reels were not procurable.

Last month when I was fishing in the Isle of Lewis with a Trout Perfection Rod and Small Double Short point flies I killed thirteen salmon in 1 day, weight from 5½ pounds to over 9 pounds.
Letter quoted in Hardy Brothers Catalogue, *1937.*

The difficulty in casting from an ordinary "Nottingham" reel is indeed great, and not a few will remember when for the first time they tried the experiment; how the bait would insist on going on all sorts of expeditions of its own, and generally where it had no business. How the reel itself would insist on over-running, and getting the line into such a hopeless tangle, that a quarter of an hour between casts was generally necessary to unravel it. Nor was this all, for the heavy rods heretofore generally used, were by no means conducive to easy and graceful sport. This is the more evident when we remember that in addition to guiding the line on to the reel, the left hand and arm have all the weight of the rod to bear; while the position of the left hand (just over the reel) naturally gives one at any time very little power, so that with a stout rod of say 14 feet of heavy greenheart, the work was more than trying.

Like others we struggled on with these things in the past, and have tried not a few experiments in our efforts to improve which, however, we are glad to say have been so successful that we can now work with efficiency, ease, and comfort. A short, light, but powerful

The Murdoch, a typical 11½-foot spinning and prawning rod, which cost £5 in 1898

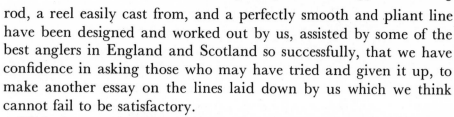

rod, a reel easily cast from, and a perfectly smooth and pliant line have been designed and worked out by us, assisted by some of the best anglers in England and Scotland so successfully, that we have confidence in asking those who may have tried and given it up, to make another essay on the lines laid down by us which we think cannot fail to be satisfactory.

With the question as to whether it is right or wrong to use either a prawn or minnow for salmon, we have nothing to do. We have of course our own opinion on the point, and prefer the fly whenever possible or productive; but, to go home fishless after a long day is not one of our desires. Besides, almost every angler nowadays carries a spinning rod as well as one for fly, and, as manufacturers, it is our business to provide up-to-date gear.

It may interest you to know that the prawns you sent a short time ago were the best I ever had—hard and stony—I killed a fish with nearly every one of them.

Letter quoted in Hardy Brothers Catalogue, *1934.*

One may prawn or spin with anything in the shape of a rod and reel, and we as well as others have often done it with an 18-foot fly rod, reel, and line, but such a method as we have before said is unsatisfactory, clumsy, and tiring. *The Rod* we use and now introduce is the "Murdoch", 11½-foot, fitted with a 4-inch reel, and 100 to 120 yards of line. This rig is light, handy, and strong enough for anything. The rod is of a nice easy balance, with great power, which enables even a very moderate fisherman to swing out a bait and lead 30 to 40 yards with ease. The reel is on the "Nottingham" centre pin principle, but so constructed that it is under the control of the operator by the aid of our patent regulating brake, which is simplicity itself, and prevents over-running and entanglement.

There are many methods of using a prawn or spinning bait, but the pleasantest and most sporting, to our mind, is to cast at an angle almost across, but rather down-stream, and as soon as the bait falls, to drop the point of the rod a little and reel up just sufficiently fast to keep your bait off the stones, while it is working round and across the stream or pool. It should then be wound up to the end of the trace, which should not be more than 1½ yards long. The motion of casting must be an easy swing, never jerk or try to make an extra long cast by any spasmodic effort, as it is sure to be fatal. . . .

*e Sandeman prawn tackle
98)*

Of course the leads must be varied to the strength and depth of water. In shallow, rocky pools the bait should not be allowed to sink more than say 2 feet, while in deep water fairly free from rocks it

may be more heavily leaded, and allowed to sink deeper. The method
we have tried to describe applies equally to the phantom, natural,
or other artificial baits, only the winding up should be a little
quicker.

When a heavy bait and lead is used, and a short cast of say only
20 yards is required, it will not be necessary to press the regulator of
the reel, as in its normal position it will allow the heavy bait to draw
off sufficient line to enable the cast to be made.

Hardy Brothers Catalogue, 1894.

PRAWNING FOR SALMON

There is probably no sport that varies so much as salmon fishing—
varies, that is, in the sport itself, the methods of pursuing it, and in
the sportsmen who make it their hobby. Yet there is a very general
opinion that a fish killed on the fly is somehow better than a fish
killed on any other lure.

The method of using the small prawn on the single hook has its
headquarters in Galway, where it is safe to say that over 1,000 fish
annually have often been killed on it.

I can say this for it, that in English, Scotch, Irish and Welsh waters
it has given me many a good fish when fly-fishing and even spinning
had proved a weary failure. Furthermore, I can say this for it, that
it is a pleasant change after long hours of casting. Amongst your
casts you have laid a trace and amongst your flies half-a-dozen hooks
to gut. Not eyed hooks, and on no account any triangles. Now for the
only extra. In an empty 2-ounce tin of baccy you have placed about
a dozen or more prawns, received from Galway that morning. Of
course ordinary small prawns will do, or even large shrimps, but
you will see the difference if you get them from the fountain head.
They lie amongst plenty of salt; it keeps them fresh but it makes them
brittle, and you take out a couple to soak in a little pool, which takes
the brittleness out of them and makes them easy to mount. By the
time you have your trace and hook ready they will be soaked enough,
and you can begin right away.

Can you though? What about mounting them? True. Certainly

there is a knack about that. But an easily avoidable knack. Take your hook "to gut" (Ah! now you see the use of that), off your trace, and with a baiting-needle run gut and hook up through the soaked prawn from throat to tail, replace baited hook on trace and there you are. Moreover, this only till you have acquired the knack. Attach a foot of finest copper-wire to your hook previous to putting on the shrimp, which, wound round it, will serve to keep it on.

One word more. The prawns used in this method are small ones, about as big as we should call fine shrimps in England. Galway shrimps are often very scarce even in Galway, where they have a knack of cooking them to such a consistency that they will readily slide on and stay on the hook and to such colour that the salmon simply cannot resist them.

One more small item, a few coils of lead wire, readily bendable. But if you bury this in your prawn because you think a fish will be alarmed if he sees it on your cast, then I have nothing further to say to you. Our acquaintanceship, so promisingly begun, is closed; I should not care to introduce you to a clever, shy, timid little fish like a salmon, for even he, stout-hearted fellow as he is, would have nothing to say to such a weighted bait, lying inert like a mere dead thing on the bottom. You *will* be given that advice, as sure as a gun. Don't listen to it. Roll the wire round the trace, at least a foot from the hook; one coil say round the end of the trace, and if another is necessary put it a foot higher up, and so on. As to how much, you will understand in a minute, that if you never touch the bottom with a light skimming touch you are not deep enough to meet the fish, and if you keep on getting caught up in weeds and rocks it is because you have a coil too much on.

Now cast in your prawn with a gentle, underhand, lob-bowler's action, and let it come round, throwing it higher or lower according to the pace of the stream and the depth of the water, remembering above all to let it come well round to your own bank nearly to your feet. I once saw a curling back straighten as its owner grabbed my bait within 4 feet of me one evening on the Lyon, and such a back I never did see before or since. He left me half-an-hour later. I can scarcely bear to refer to it. He was an immense fish.

Remember if you rise a fish on fly and it will not come again or to another fly, it almost certainly will to a shrimp. And remember too that you may shrimp a pool in this manner and revert to fly without any fear of your pool being disturbed. The shrimp will wake the lazy dozer, and he'll take it or your fly with a rush.

For the most part I have fished as a guest, and in many beautiful waters where no other bait than fly was permitted, so, there was no chance to give a trial to my favourite method. But in Avon (Hampshire) and Coquet in England; in Add, Lyon, Dee, and Orchy in Scotland; in Corrib, Clare, Galway, Slaney, Boyne, Shannon, and Blackwater in Ireland; and Towy and Dee in Wales, I have had splendid sport, owing to this way of shrimping.

But the most wonderful pool I personally have ever fished is a hole 35 feet deep. You stand on a flat rock in 6 inches of water, fishing in 30 feet, and all the time noble, fresh-run, flexible silver bars are flashing and splashing around you. Owing to your single hook you do not catch in the waving weeds along the rocky shelves; your bait just swims through them so great is the pull of water at those depths. You do not fish full deep all the time; you attempt rather to induce Mr. Prawn to swim along and roundabout the smooth, worn rocks, and where a ledge or projecting corner shelters some fish straight out of the sea while in this apparently mad soda-water he studies your fairy shrimp, just as pretty, just as artistic, just as coy, as any Jock Scott or Silver Doctor and smelling ever so much nicer, comes swimming round the corner and—Oh! Oн! OH! is in a second seized by ruthless jaws and borne off, right, left, up, down, in, out, all over the place. So steep, overhung and slippery are the rocks you stand on, that only the most expert of Spey-casters could fish it with a fly, while spinning might entail spinning oneself into the whirlpool; but for the gentle swing of the shrimp well-adapted.

Hardy Brothers Catalogue, 1934.

PRAWNING FOR SALMON
IN LOW WATER

A low and clear water, with every stone visible, a windless day with brilliant sunshine—not ideal conditions for salmon fishing as generally understood, but quite a favourable day for using a small prawn or shrimp in this most artistic and deadly method.

As may be anticipated, the tackle must be the neatest and finest that can be used with safety. Salmon do not always rush wildly at a prawn; some do, but the majority do not. Their usual way is to follow it round in the stream, leave it, come back again, maybe two or three times for further inspection, and then when satisfied, take hold.

As the bait has to bear frequent inspection without raising the slightest suspicion, the utmost care must be taken when mounting.

The outfit may be a short, light spinning rod with "Super Silex" reel, and the cast made direct from the reel; or a 12 foot 6 inches stout fly rod, such as the "Wye", and the cast made from a coil of line held in the hand. The line is important, and should be waterproof dressed,

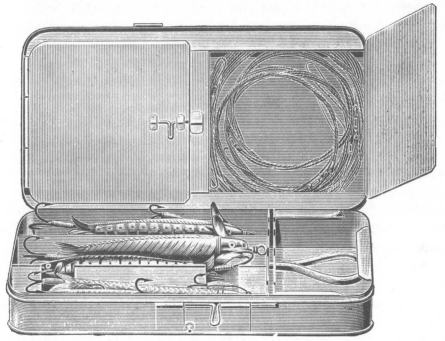

Spinning bait and trace box (1907).

particularly when used in casting from the coil in the hand. The trace is 4 foot of 5/5 single gut, with a swivel at one end to attach reel line, and at the other, for easy attachment and detachment when rebaiting, a special steel link. The tackle is a light, single wide bend hook bound to a length of 5/5 gut. It is better not to loop the gut, as when a loop is drawn through a small prawn it is sure to tear it.

To mount, use a fine ordinary wire needle, pass the end of the hook gut through the eye and bend it back about $\frac{1}{8}$ in. or less; this holds quite well when threading. Insert the point of the needle between the eye and the "spear", run it through the body as low as possible, and out under the tail. Remove needle, take hold of the gut and pull the hook (point uppermost) into the bait until it cuts a little into the head shell; this will keep the hook from turning when casting. As the point of the hook is uppermost and over the back, it covers the neck of the prawn, where usually attacked. Complete the mount by binding down the tail with two or three turns of white waxed silk which is practically invisible when wet. Attach the baited hook to the link on trace by the figure of eight knot, for easy undoing when rebaiting. A "Jardine" lead or lead wire, $\frac{1}{8}$, $\frac{1}{4}$, or $\frac{1}{2}$ oz. as may be required, is fixed to the trace, about two feet above the bait. The amount of lead is important; it should be sufficient to keep the bait well down in the water, yet not too heavy to catch the bottom when the prawn is allowed to drop downstream as it swings round across the current.

In fishing, it is quite unnecessary to cast long distances, 10 to 15 yards is sufficient. Cast across and a little upstream, and as the prawn is coming "square" to you, draw in a yard or two of line. Work it in the "sink and draw" method, letting out this yard or two of line, a little at each "sink"; the bait must not be held up to the stream as a fly. Fish the cast out, then gently and gradually gather in the line. After the cast has straightened out under your bank, raise the bait to the top of the water, then let it fall slowly back. Shake your rod up and down and pull in line at the same time, so as to make it "shudder". A fish will often follow and rush at the last moment, taking the prawn quite close to the bank. Should you see a fish, keep on casting to him, a dozen times if necessary. Try from both banks if possible. Hang the bait over him, working it in all sorts of little jumps.

If you can get above the fish, drop in the prawn and pay out line down to him, swinging the bait about a little as it goes down. Do not hold it up, as he will take it best when dropping down. Should it pass him, bring it back quite slowly when he may take hold. As a fish frequently takes the bait when dropping, a good plan is to keep rod, line and prawn in a dead straight line, so as to feel the slightest touch.

Strike only when you feel the fish really tighten; they often hold or nip the prawn without getting the hook in their mouth. Keep the hook *very sharp*, then if he does get it into his mouth you are more sure of a hold. By striking at every touch you may frighten fish. Have a loop of loose line between your hand and reel, holding it with the finger and thumb. When the hook has penetrated, let this line free to enable you to get the point of your rod up and avoid breakage.

The foregoing method of fishing a small prawn or shrimp is especially suitable where there is a reasonable current. There are, however, many stretches of water in which fish lie, and where there is little or no current. To fish such places, so as to get the prawn over fish, a float is necessary. The tackle previously described, but with a lead bullet instead of the "Jardine", is used. The float is adjusted so that the bait is just clear of the bottom. The cast is made as before, across and slightly upstream. Hold up the float to allow the bait to swing slowly round with the current. Try to arrange that the prawn will go straight to the fish, or just cross close in front of him.

An alternative method to either of the above is spinning the prawn. In low and clear water, special tackle is necessary, the usual mount with spinning fans attached is often too clumsy for this work. The correct tackle is that with the spinning fans fixed into the trace about 18 inches in front of the bait. The flight may be either a single hook or small treble with fastener to hold the bait. The prawn is fixed on the needle and the hook or hooks fastened in. The method of using is as in ordinary spinning, working the bait as slowly as possible. The usual Antikink lead should be used.

Hardy Brothers Catalogue, 1927

FINE SPINNING FOR SALMON

At the beginning of this article there are two things I want to make quite clear. First, by Fine Spinning I do *not* mean Thread Lining in the accepted sense of the word with lines of about 4 lb. breaking strain. Salmon can, of course, be killed with this tackle on easy rivers, and when everything goes well, but the percentage of losses on fast rocky streams is far too high to be borne. There are few things I dislike more than losing a salmon I have hooked, possibly because I have to work pretty hard for every one I do induce to take my fly or bait. If the parting comes as the result of a break then, in my eyes, it is an almost criminal offence, and I feel that hanging is the only fit punishment for the criminal!

Second, my remarks apply chiefly to the streams of the moors and mountains, such as one finds in the North-west and South-west of

England, Wales and the Highlands, small for the most part, and almost always shallow, rocky and rapid. The technique of salmon fishing in such waters is entirely different from that required on great rivers like Wye or Tweed or Tay. Personally, I am a confirmed "small river" fan. One may not, almost certainly will not, kill as many salmon, but the fishing is so much more interesting, and in my, possibly prejudiced, view needs a higher standard of skill.

For this specialized form of spinning one needs a specialized outfit if the best results are to be obtained. It may be of two kinds. The first based on a fixed-spool reel like the "Altex" with a rod designed for its use, and the rod for work with a fixed-spool reel should have quite a different action from the one to be employed with a multiplier. To the best of my belief Hardy's is the only firm which has realized this and carried their ideas into practice. I used various fixed-spool reels for some ten years, but when, just before I went to Ireland in July 1939, an advance model of the "Elarex" was sent me to try, my love for the fixed-spool began to wane, and for the last five seasons I have used nothing but the multiplier, which, to my mind, is an incomparably superior type for lines of 8 lb. breaking strain and upwards which do not need the safeguard of a slipping clutch.

My rod is a "West Country Light Spinning", the first of which Hardy's designed to my ideas in 1944. It is 7 feet long, weighs about 6 oz. and is the most accurate rod I have ever used, a point of primary importance for Accuracy with a capital A is an essential requisite for Fine Spinning in the kind of rivers I have mentioned. The line is an 8-9 lb. braided nylon which is infinitely stronger and more reliable than monofil nylon of the same diameter.

Fine Spinning is best practised in the same conditions which suit the greased-line fly, and when rivers begin to fall, and salmon lose that first fine, free abandon which characterizes them when they enter the river, these methods make up two-thirds of the whole art of salmon fishing, the remaining third being represented by natural baits such as the prawn, shrimp and worm. The great advantage of combining Fine Spinning with greased-lining is that each is superior in a particular type of water, and between them they enable one to fish every part of the river, except the deep dead pools which are only really useful in floods, to the best advantage. Everyone knows the ideal sort of pool for the greased-line, and it is least effective, and most difficult to fish, where the river is broken by rocks into different channels each running at a different pace, and in very fast broken water generally. The latter are the ideal places for Fine Spinning.

As I have already emphasized an essential for success in Fine Spinning is accuracy. One must be able to place the bait exactly at, and not somewhere near, the required place, for when salmon are lying in narrow streams, or tight up against rocks, the bait is only fishing for a few feet, and so much pitch in just the right place to show properly as it comes into the salmon's "window". Fine Spinning indeed demands just as high a standard of accuracy as does dry-fly fishing for trout. In another way the two have much in common for often one is fishing over individual salmon, or at any rate individual lies, and not just casting "into the brown" as is so often the case on large rivers. Well done, it will kill salmon in the lowest water as long as they are not so "potted" that they will look at nothing.

One of the great charms of the method is that one is rarely snagged on the bottom. As in greased-lining the aim is to keep the bait high in the water. I like mine to be more than a few inches deep. One cannot, of course, always ensure this as eddies and down currents will allow it to drop vertically at times, but experience gives one a sort of sixth sense which, generally speaking, affords a pretty good indication of the under-water lay-out.

There is no standard method of casting. One throws up, down or across in whatever direction seems right to cover the particular lie, and if that brings no response another angle is pursued, always being careful to avoid the cardinal sin of "plastering" the fish for too long. In trying a stream without visible boulders, or boils which indicate underwater rocks, I normally cast straight across, or slightly up, and then point the rod downstream and lead the bait over broadside on as one likes to do in greased-line fly fishing. A strong up- or down-stream wind which will belly the light line in the air is fine because it gives the fish plenty of time to get the bait well into its mouth before feeling any resistance, and prevents the angler tightening too soon.

There is another method I often employ when trying deep, narrow guts. Here fish often lie under rocky shelves, and for them to see the bait it must get well down. I make a short cast and then let out line slowly until I think I am near the bottom. All this time the light bait is fluttering in the stream like a live thing, and sometimes when I begin to recover line I find there is a fish on. This must have taken the devon as it was going down, but salmon do not quickly eject even a hard, bulky thing like a spinning bait, and such fish are almost always very well hooked, often far back in the throat. In hot weather try very carefully the white-water below falls. Because it is highly aerated salmon and seatrout like to lie here in such conditions, and will often snap at a bait allowed to play for a few minutes in the froth and foam.

Because one is for the most part fishing fast, broken water very fine traces are quite unnecessary. I never go lighter than one yard of 9/5 gut; I don't like wire, as a light bait needs a flexible trace to allow it to play freely in the stream, and monofil nylon in fine sizes is, in my experience, quite unreliable for salmon. Owing to the need for extreme accuracy the main weight for casting *must* be in the bait, the only lead being a tiny pierced bullet for anti-kink purposes. Better still, use a Hardy ball-bearing swivel at the top of the trace, and you can dispense with a lead in low water.

Most of my spinning is with devons, although a quill minnow is excellent. Weights are light $\frac{1}{8}$-$\frac{1}{4}$ oz., seldom heavier, and sizes small, 1-2 inches, depending on the speed and roughness of the water. Shape is very important, and I like a bait with a fat bulbous body, or one that is flattened slightly on back and belly. In all cases fins should be big. Such baits are bouyant, sink slowly and spin freely. One can throw at an angle up-stream and let the lure come tumbling down in the rough water on a loose line without getting hung up on the bottom. A wooden devon with celluloid fins, and a brass tube through the middle to give it enough weight for casting, without seriously impairing its buoyancy, makes a first-class bait.

Kenneth Dawson,
Hardy Brothers Catalogue, 1952

A NEW TECHNIQUE IN THE ART OF CASTING AND SPINNING FOR SALMON

I use the term "up-stream casting" as in this style of spinning the cast is made up-stream. The actual spinning is very much down-stream, the bait moving at great speed.

Before attempting to describe the new style of casting, it may be well to give a brief history of recent developments in spinning generally.

It has long been known that in certain conditions, especially those of low clear water, very small baits such as 1¼-inch Devons and smaller are much more attractive to salmon and sea trout than the more usual baits of 2 to 3 inches in length. But when using the old style single action rotating drum reels with their comparatively heavy lines, not only was it very difficult to make long casts with small baits, but almost impossible to recover line down-stream at speeds which would prevent the bait from sinking and getting snagged up on rocks, or other hazards.

With the advent of fixed spool and such multiplying reels as the

Hardy's 'Special' Traces
Made in Single & Treble Salmon Gut, also Punjab Twisted Wire,
for Salmon, Mahseer, Pike, Etc.

From Hardy Brothers
Catalogue, *1912*

"Altex" and "Elarex", both of which have a gear ratio of about 4 to 1, up-stream casting and rapid down-stream spinning became a practical proposition. Even with these reels there were difficulties to be overcome. When using the so-called threadline and stationary drum reels, light weight baits of the smallest size could be cast great distances, but the light lines required for such small baits were not strong enough to play a heavy lively fish; consequently far too many salmon broke away with the bait and several yards of line attached. Finally this light line fishing was generally and rightly condemned as unsportsmanlike, and heavier stronger lines were recommended. But here again, with the use of the stronger lines of greater diameter, except when helped by a brisk following wind, the resistance of the spool-lip, the rod rings and the air was so great that baits of the required small size could not be cast far enough.

To overcome this trouble, I made a series of experiments with small Devons made of various alloys of metal and finally succeeded in producing the now well-known Hardy "Heavyweight" Devon which, to a great extent, overcame the trouble. Then came the new series of braided nylon lines which, with the heavyweight Devons opened up further possibilities in the shape of longer and more accurate casts combined with the correct size of bait and lines of adequate strength to hold the heaviest fish without the former constant fear of a smash.

Now I have always found that greater accuracy of direction can be obtained by using a directly overhead cast, that is a cast in which the rod makes a vertical arc, than is possible with the side swing cast so much in vogue. When using the ordinary overhead cast, however, much of the energy expended is absorbed by the bait flying at too great a height, so that the problem boiled down to one of simple ballistics. Given sufficient "muzzle velocity", all that one required was a "flat trajectory" so that the energy, instead of being lost in climbing into the air, may be properly used in obtaining distance. For if the bait rises high in the air the lost distance is pro rata to the height, also the long line in its upward flight is exposed to the resistance of the air and wind all along its length. Whereas, if the bait flies low with the line following in a more or less horizontal direction, the air resistance is greatly reduced.

With the foregoing facts in mind, I set to work on the development of a special rod, which I have recently succeeded in perfecting. By the use of this rod very long and accurate casts can easily be made, and it should be remembered that during low clear water conditions, when fish are lethargic, the bait must be cast well above the "lie" and retrieved in such a manner that the fish has only to travel a few feet to the side in order to seize it, and at such speed that he has no time to examine it. No doubt many fish follow the bait and grab hold, seeing only a lively escaping object. Also it is important in low clear water conditions that the angler should keep far enough below the fish to be out of sight, especially as salmon occasionally move or cruise about. As this style of fishing is often practised in streamy or fast running water, very rapid recovery of the bait is obviously necessary.

The new rod, "The Marksman Precision", is a very light two-handed one of 8 feet 3 inches in length, having an action making a continuous curve right from the button to the tip. The rod is built for use with the No. 2 or No. 3 "Altex" or "Elarex" Reel, which is seated 16 inches from the button. The long cork grip is on the thin side in order that the butt action shall not be impeded. The curve of the rod in action is of the parabolic order, giving when casting, great power and speed to the tip. The location of the reel on the rod butt and the thin handle combine to make a very comfortable position for winding in or recovering the line and bait. The rod butt is tucked under the right or left armpit which avoids a bent and tired back.

Mount the heavyweight Devon on a trace of about 3 feet in length. A ball bearing swivel to be attached between the trace and the line. As an additional safeguard, a celluloid anti-kinker may be used. Ordinary plain swivels are useless for this high speed spinning, as they quickly jam and cause the trace and running line to snarl and twist up after a few casts.

Take up your position as directly below the "lie" of the fish as possible and fixing your eyes on a point well above the "lie", swing the rod back in line behind your right shoulder. As you make the forward cast raise the right hand and, as the rod tip passes the apex of the forward arc, release the running line which is held by the index finger. It may seem that this apex point of release would be wrong, but unless the release is made exactly at the apex, or very slightly forward of it, you will not be able to cast the full distance, as the bait will fly too high. As the right hand and arm are driven forward, the left hand holding the button of the rod is pulled down and in smartly towards the body. The timing of the release is of great importance. Your right hand is now the fulcrum, and that part

'The Angel or Devon' (*1888*)

of the rod between your hands becomes a powerful lever which causes the full length of the rod, from button to tip, to bend like an archer's bow, thereby imparting to the bait a tremendously powerful forward impulse.

When properly cast the bait will fly in a long flat curve, with a speed and accuracy comparable to the flight of an arrow, straight to the mark. Indeed, this cast differs from archery only in the fact that the "arrow" (the bait) is shot from the point of the "bow" (the rod) instead of from its centre, and that the fulcrum is below instead of at the centre, the impulse being given directly by the hands instead of through the string. . . .

When using a stationary drum reel, it should be remembered that apart from the tendency to twist given by the rapidly-spinning bait, there is another source of twist. When casting and recovering line the twists put into the cast by the corkscrew action of the line as it leaves the spool are corrected when the line is replaced on the spool by the pick-up and flyer. But when actually running a fish the line is pulled off over the pick-up bollard and the spool rotates. The reel during this process is converted into a rotating drum reel, and the line being drawn off will have no twists in it; but when you wind to recover as the fish gives line, twists will result and these twists are trapped on the line as the fish pulls it off again, so that during a 15 or 20 minutes' fight the line will be considerably twisted. The function of the ball-bearing swivel and anti-kinker is to allow the line to relieve itself of these twists during the fight, and during the first few casts when resuming fishing afterwards.

SPEED OF RECOVERY

When fishing streamy or really fast running water great speed of recovery is necessary if the Devon is to be kept clear of underwater snags, etc., which means very rapid winding even with multiplying reels such as the "Altex" or "Elarex". In short, the Devon must travel faster than the stream. Some anglers may at first find this quick winding difficult, but if the reel handle is held lightly and the wrist used loosely, a little practice will enable this to be mastered.

CASTING AND FISHING

Take up your position directly below the "lie", or as nearly so as possible, and far enough down-stream to be sure you are out of sight of the fish.

Cast as far as you can, or as is desirable, directly, or at a slight angle, up-stream. Recover as fast as possible. Keep on casting for a long period, even up to half-an-hour, over a good "lie", and sooner or later in very many cases a fish will take your Devon.

L. R. Hardy,
Hardy Brothers Catalogue, 1952.

SALMON FISHING
WITH THE WORM

In worm-fishing for salmon there is this peculiarity, that it cannot be indulged in as a common or every-day sport, but is dependant more closely upon circumstances than any other branch of the gentle art I am acquainted with. Thus, to insure success, one must have the water at a certain reduced state to act upon; he requires to be favoured in general with a clear sky, none the worse of there being a disposition in the air towards frost. The streams, also, to which he has access must possess that degree of depth and rapidity which are necessary both to conceal the fish and assist the play of the bait; moreover, it is essential that, notwithstanding one and all of them may have been angled over repeatedly with the salmon fly, they shall not previously, during the decrease of the river, have been disturbed with the worm itself; if so, should the angler impatiently have resorted to it before they were in order, every fish then descrying it would, at its re-appearance on a favourable occasion, hold it in distrust.

The most approved of tackle for this description of angling consists of a large hook of the round-bend shape, Nos. from 14 to 16 of Adlington's. It requires to be tied upon picked salmon-gut, fresh and round; the shank-end of the wire in tying ought to be left bare to the extent of nearly a quarter of an inch.

The single gut or foot line, from the hook upwards, should extend at least 6 feet, and terminate with a loop, so as to allow of its being readily annexed to the higher casting line. It should also be furnished with a box-swivel fixed below the uppermost length.

With regard to the leads or plummets, these ought to be placed at a distance of 18 inches from the hook, and should consist of at least five or six pellets of large shot, Nos. 2 and 3. In all cases, the tackle in question requires to be heavily shotted, but in regulating the quantity of weight, it is quite necessary that attention be paid to the power, depth, and swerve of the cast or stream fished in.

As to the worms best adapted for salmon fishing, I require to say little. The lob or large dew-worm is esteemed the favourite. This is easily obtained in the desired quantity from almost any piece of garden ground. It is met with, stretched at length on the earth during mild nights, and especially after a shower when the surface of the soil is damp. Besides the lob-worm, the large button-worm is sometimes used, and possesses this advantage, that it is easily scoured and becomes tougher and redder than the other. It is not, however, found in such great abundance or in all localities, and with respect to size is decidedly inferior to the lob-worm.

In baiting the hook, two, sometimes three worms are made use of. These are attached in the following way: Holding one of them betwixt the thumb and forefinger of the left hand, insert the point of your hook a short way below the head of the worm, which, I shall suppose, measures in length 8 or 9 inches; run the bend of the wire carefully along through the bait, to the full extent of an inch, in the direction of the tail; bring the point out again, and passing over an equal portion of the worm, re-enter it further on, drawing up, as you do so, what has already been transfixed, along the shank of the hook, then, as before, bring out the point an inch lower down. Repeat this proceeding a third time, and at its completion pull the worm up quite free from the hook to the gut above. Select a second worm, and insert, as formerly, the barbed wire below the head; run it along underneath, until the shank, bend, and point are completely concealed. Then, with your finger and thumb, press down the first bait close against the shank, so as to hang over in small loops or folds.

In the event of a third worm being thought necessary, string on the one preceding it in the manner I have already described, and use the worm in question to cover the hook.... The performer requires to use a long, stiffish rod, 18 feet and upwards, such as is employed for pike trolling. The rings should be large, allowing the line to pass through them without the smallest restraint, and the reel itself ought to be facile in the extreme, having neither catch nor multiplicator. With regard to the quantity of line employed in casting, it should not greatly exceed the length of the rod itself. Considering the manner in which it is weighted, and the mode of using it I am about to point out, it is difficult to manage more.

Having baited his hook, let the angler take his place at the head of the cast or salmon-stream he intends fishing. Immediately on commencing operations, there is a matter of observance to which he must pay particular attention. It forms, in fact, to some extent the secret of the successful worm-fisher, and is embodied in this simple piece of instruction, viz.: Let him draw out with his hand, over and above what he uses in casting, a yard or so of line from off the reel, allowing the same to hang loosely down towards the butt-end of his rod. The intention of this is, that he may afford instant and unresisting compliance with the movements of the fish, on first seizing the bait. Should the least check occur in the running off of the line, the salmon will, in most cases, quit before gorging. . . . I have placed the angler at the head of a cast or salmon-stream. Let him heave his bait across, and, in some measure, with the current, which I take to be so heavy or rapid as to bring round the weighted line, at a deliberate rate, until it attains its full stretch or tension. It is necessary, during this circuit, that the worm travel deep, in contact almost with the channel of the river, otherwise it will not prove attractive to the fish. On completing its range, the angler should allow it to hang, as it were, for a few seconds in subjection to the current, and when recovering, in order to renew the cast, should do so with extreme caution and deliberation.

When a check occurs, no matter from what cause it may, on the instant, be imagined to proceed, he ought at once to give line, not merely exhausting what he has in preparation, but dealing out ungrudgingly a further supply from his reel, and this by means of the hand, so that it may run off easily, and, as it were, humour the movements of a supposed fish. The check itself may very possibly be occasioned by collision of the plummets with some stone or jut of rock, or it may proceed from the interference of a trout or eel, but this being quite uncertain, the angler has himself to blame, should he, by dealing with it as such and uncircumspectedly, give opportunity for a good fish to escape. In general, however, I may remark, a mere check or stoppage is not the usual indication of a fish having

Coming to the gaff (from H. Cholmondeley-Pennell, Fishing, 1885).

seized the worm. What takes place has more the nature of an attack, quick and vigorous as is that of the pike on a running bait. The progress of the hook downwards is disturbed by a violent jerk or pull, sometimes in the direction of the current, but as frequently to the side, towards the lair or retreat of the salmon. Should this attack on the bait be met with unresistingly by the angler, and sufficient line allowed on the occasion, it will generally, after a short pause, become repeated, with less violence indeed, but with more earnestness and effect. In the interval between the charges, however, care must be taken to sustain and give an animated appearance to the worms. If allowed to drop to the bottom, the salmon will no longer assail them. Accordingly, recover line with the hand, and be a little more chary than at first of yielding it when the fish renews the attack. At this point it is, that a slight measure of resistance will act as a provocative; previously its effect was to alarm and beget suspicion.

The salmon will now, after two or three successive assaults, bolt the bait; and his doing so may be inferred from a peculiar strain upon the line, more fixed and continued in character than any it had yet been subject to, during the attack. The resolute and quick elevation of the rod will suffice to fix the hook deep among the entrails of the fish, and nothing further is left to be done but to fatigue and land him.

Thomas Tod Stoddart,
The Angler's Companion, 1847.

WITHOUT A REEL-HANDLE

Perhaps the most exciting encounter with a large, strong fish, I ever engaged in, took place on the 21st of November, 1864, on Teviot. I had not taken above three or four throws, when the nut or screw by which the handle of the reel was fastened on, becoming detached, the handle itself, by the force of my throw across the pool, was precipitated forwards and lodged among some large stones lying at a depth of nearly five feet, and at a corresponding distance from the spot which I occupied when making the cast. It was some time before I could detect where it lay, and nearly an hour passed before I succeeded, by means of a large hook fastened to a stick, in recovering it. Although I had regained possession of the handle, I was unable, from want of the nut, to make active use of it in the way of recovering line. I could still manage, however, to apply it in the manner of a watch-key, so as to accomplish a few revolutions at a time, when it would invariably become detached and require replacement. Under this drawback I recommenced fishing, using as a fly the silver-doctor. Before long, the gleam of a large salmon in the act of seizing my hook discovered itself below the surface. Raising my rod, I felt that I had him fast, not by the mouth, however, but, as it turned out, by the tough skin which lies under the pectoral fin on one side.

After the pause of a second or two, off he set at a tremendous pace up the pool, exhausting, at the first rush, nearly my whole supply of line, about seventy yards, and concluding the heat with a vigorous somersault. He then, after another short pause, doubled in upon me in such a way as completely to slacken the reins, and compel me, in order to retain the master-hand, to use speed in an opposite direction; nor was it until a minute or two of high excitement had passed, that I became satisfied as to the fact that we were still in firm conjunction. The only resource left me was to make use, as I was best able, of the loose reel-handle, and recover line as quickly as possible. This, to a certain extent, I had succeeded in doing, when the fish again set off at steam-speed on a cruise down the river. To humour this movement, I was compelled not only to follow as fast as the nature of the bank permitted, but to pay out the larger portion of my recovered line, in doing which the handle of the reel was again thrown off and fell, lost to view among the rank grass. Taken up, as I was, with my fish and his vagaries, I had no time to search for it, but, marking the where-abouts of its fall, hurried, or rather was dragged, forwards in rear of the chase, the respectful distance of seventy yards being kept up betwixt us. Still the salmon pressed on, but at a more leisurely rate, and, to keep pace with him in his way towards the foot of the pool, I had to pass my rod across the stems of several trees and bushes; also to hold it low, and in a direction nearly parallel to the water, in order to avoid coming into contact with the branchwork overhead. On reaching the shallows which divide the Nine-wells from the Turnpool stream, the fish once more doubled rapidly in upon me, skimming the surface, as he did so, and making the water fly on all sides of him. In order to keep a *taut* line, I had again, with all possible speed, to retrace my steps upwards, and managed at length, in spite of a good deal of manœuvring on his part, to arrive at the place where my reel-handle had been jerked off. Fortunately, I stumbled on the object of my search, and notwithstanding that I could only derive slow and imperfect assistance from it in the way of winding-up, it was to its recovery alone that I owed, after a protracted and exhausting contest, my good fortune in securing what turned out to be a fine newly-run male salmon of twenty pounds' weight. The casting-line, I may mention, was of single gut, and the hook of size No. 8 in Philips' arrangement.

Thomas Tod Stoddart,
An Angler's Rambles, 1866.

1898

CONCERNING WADING

Wading in the water is not only an agreeable thing in itself, but absolutely necessary in some rivers in the North that are destitute of boats; and that you may do this in the best possible style, procure half a dozen pair of shoes, with large knobnails at some distance asunder; if they are too close, they will bring your foot to an even surface, and it will glide off a stone or rock, which in deep water may be inconvenient. Cut some holes in the upper-leathers of your shoes, to give the water a free passage out of them when you are on dry land; not because the fluid is annoying, for we should wrong you to say so, but to prevent the pumping noise you would other-wise make at every step. If you are not much of a triton, you may use fishermen's boots, and keep yourself dry: it is all a matter of taste. When you are wading through the rapids, step on quickly and boldly, and do not gaze down on the stream after the fashion of Narcissus: for running waves will not reflect your beauty, but only make your head giddy. If you stop for a moment, place your legs abreast of each other: should you fancy a straddle, with one of them in advance, the action of the water will operate upon both, trip you up, and carry you out to sea.

Avoid standing upon rocking stones, for obvious reasons; and never go into the water deeper than the fifth button of your waistcoat; even this does not always agree with tender constitutions in frosty weather. As you are likely not to take a just estimate of the cold in the excitement of the sport, should you be of a delicate temperament, and be wading in the month of February, when it may chance to freeze very hard, pull down your stockings, and examine your legs. Should they be black, or even purple, it might, perhaps, be as well to get on dry land; but if they are only rubicund, you may continue to enjoy the water, if it so pleases you.

*　　*　　*

For the less hardy wader: rubberized canvas wading trousers (1886)

It is really refreshing, and does one's heart good, to see how some that are green in the sport will, in the language of stag-hunting, "take to soil". I heard of a very fat man from the precincts of Cheapside, who was encountered in the river Shiel, in Inverness-shire, by two gentlemen—merrier ones than whom "I never passed an hour's talk withal". The corpulent man looked at the water for some time like a child that is going into a cold bath, and does not half like it; he then broke forth in the following guise:—"I am convinced, gentlemen, that your waders catch most fish. I say, gentlemen, that those who wade are the most successful." His opinion being greatly encouraged, he put forth one foot in the pool; and not finding the sensation very alarming, for the weather was warm, he walked soberly forward, saying at every step, "Ay, ay—your waders catch the most fish." Now the rock is shelving down near the bank, in progressing he was soon up to the hips—

Waders are useless on the Waikato rivers, if not dangerous. I found it much safer and more comfortable to wade in knickers, and if the fisherman has a tendency to rheumatics, he can keep it down, and even charm it away, by indulging every evening in one of the beautiful natural hot baths of the district.
　　　　　Letter from New Zealand quoted in Hardy Brothers Catalogue, *1907.*

Tendebatque manus ripæ ulterioris amore; but he could not reach the desired spot even then. In this dilemma he looked wistfully at the shore for advice. "How deep should I go?" said the enterprising man. One said to the fifth button of your waistcoat, and the other to your shirt-collar. He preferred the fifth button; and soon treading on a faithless stone, fairly toppled head foremost into the pool. His hand relaxed its grasp, and away went the fishing-rod down the stream. He himself was soon placed out of danger by the gentlemen, an attention that, considering all things, he was fairly entitled to; but his rod lay across the river, the butt end opposed in its passage by one rock in the middle of it, and the top by another; so the weight of the stream bore upon the centre, and snapped it in twain. The corpulent gentleman took all with the greatest good humour; and as the water streamed from him at all points, as it were from a river god, and as he applied a brandy flask to his mouth, he said only at the intervals between his potations, "I am not quite so sure that your waders catch the most fish; gentlemen, I say I have my doubts of it."

William Scrope,
Days and Nights of Salmon-Fishing, 1843.

ADOLPHUS

It was 4 o'clock when I first saw Adolphus move. I call him Adolphus because I always give proper names to the animals with which I have to do, and Adolphus is a most proper name. I have a squirrel that runs about one, called Beecham, and a dog named Carpenter, because when a puppy it was always doing odd jobs about the house.

At 4 o'clock, then, I was sitting on the bank beside the weir-pool when Adolphus announced his presence by bounding, rather clumsily, into the air. He was a large and well made fish, and as he was obviously in a kittenish mood I naturally took his advance as an invitation to play. Accordingly I leant back and picked up my rod, which lay on the grass behind me. I knew at once that if I rose to my feet in order to cast, Adolphus would see me and, probably, retire. Fish, I gathered from my host's conversation the night before, have strange notions of humour, and often behave like boors when one attempts to frolic with them.

I thought it wise therefore to show Adolphus that while I was quite ready to play with him I could not be expected to gambol or curvet. So I lit a cigarette and proceeded leisurely to examine the fly which my host had assured me would be most acceptable to Adolphus and his relations. It was what he had called a "Silver Doctor". Why, I do not know. It was nothing like a doctor—at least not a Harley Street one. Of course I know that some country doctors are a trifle uncommon in appearance, but for the life of me I was unable to discover anything even remotely medical in this fly. It didn't even smell of iodoform. However, my host had said it was "a good killing one", so I suppose that is why it was called a "Doctor".

Having preened the fly's plumage carefully, I raised my rod, swished out a sufficiency of line, and cast down-stream at about the spot where Adolphus had appeared. The current, which was very rapid, swung the fly round, and I amused myself by twiching my top-joint, so that the doctor looked just like a rather pretty little fish darting about. I knew Adolphus would be hugely amused when he saw it.

1924

After moving the, fly about for some minutes I cast again, rather nearer the bank this time. I am perfectly certain that I was doing nothing that could possibly have given offence, and my sole intention was to amuse Adolphus; yet before my fly had been in the water 5 seconds he re-appeared like a bolt from the blue, jumped right on top of it, and bit it savagely. Of course I was entirely unprepared, and as Adolphus had taken the doctor with him my reel gave the most appalling scream, and rotated at about, I should think, 2,000 revolutions per minute. The rod was jerked out of my hand, and if I hadn't made a quick grab at it as it rounded the bush beside me I verily believe Adolphus would have pulled it into the river.

Even my closest enemy could not say that I am a hasty tempered man, but this was really too much. For one thing, the river didn't belong to Adolphus, and I had a perfect right, being the guest of the man who owned the fishing for miles, to cast my fly wherever I liked. If Adolphus objected to it he could have gone to another part of the river. I know perfectly well that salmon never eat anything when they leave the sea, so the only possible reason why Adolphus bit the doctor was because he, Adolphus, was in a bad temper.

Accordingly I rose to my feet, set my teeth, and determined to show Adolphus that it was not for him to take liberties with my host's doctor. I am thankful to say that he had had the decency to leave the pool, apparently ashamed of what he had done; but unfortunately he had retained possession of the fly. So I was obliged to follow him down-stream, and as he was swimming rapidly and nearly all the line was off my reel I had to break into a dignified run. The ground was rather rough, and there were some small bushes on the bank, which made things rather trying. However, at last I came up with Adolphus. He had halted in a deep pool some quarter of a mile below the weir, and was sulking under cover of a rock. I should have thought it was for me to sulk, not him.

After waiting a few minutes to see if he had any decency left in him, I wound up my reel until the tip of my rod was over him, and then jerked the line. No response. I jerked harder. If I had had any doubts as to Adolphus's breeding they were amply confirmed now. Without a word of warning he suddenly shot towards my feet. There was an appalling crack, my rod—or rather my host's rod—parted in the middle, and 8 feet of it slid gracefully down the line into the water.

Adolphus now appeared to go quite mad. I should have thought that when he saw the top-joint, and portion of middle-joint, sliding down the line towards him he would have welcomed it as a diversion; but apparently the opposite was the case. He simply flew about the pool, and had he been out of the water I verily believe he would have barked like a dog. He tried to bite the top-joint the moment it touched his nose, but fortunately, as his mouth was already occupied by the doctor, he was unable to achieve this.

After some minutes he seemed to quiet down, and presently he came up to the surface and indulged in the rudest possible antics. A Neapolitan guttersnipe could not have behaved worse. I was so angry now that I determined to give him no quarter. So I reeled up strongly and pulled hard. Adolphus, who seemed penitent at last, swam hesitatingly towards me. I began to relent. . . . After all he was only a fish. . . . The reel stopped suddenly: I had wound too quickly and a loop of line was caught round it. I looked down and began to free it.

What precisely happened then I am unable to say, but I can well guess. Adolphus, being utterly evil at heart, and seeing that I had taken my eye off him and was otherwise engaged, suddenly shot out into the pool. I was standing at the very edge, in fact balancing myself on two loose rocks. So that when the rod was jerked suddenly I lost my balance. . . . Fortunately I was at the tail of the pool and the water was only 3 feet deep, but for a moment or two it was extremely awkward.

There are occasions when it is lawful for a man to lose his temper, and I think this was one of them. As soon as I could see and breathe I "yanked" at the rod, which was still in my hand. The line had got free and the reel screeched. I felt for the gaff slung at my back: it was *in situ*. I smiled grimly and reeled up. Adolphus came like a lamb. Now that I was close to him he seemed very large, rather fierce perhaps; and even as he approached I could see the evil in his eye . . . I felt for the gaff, released it, and grasped it firmly in my right hand . . . I was not afraid of him now.

This time I knew exactly what would happen. As soon as I leant forward to take hold of the top-joint, and portion of middle-joint, Adolphus would start his antics again, and, as I could not move for fear of walking into deep water, the game of give-and-take would go on *ad infinitum*—or at least until Adolphus got bored or released the doctor. So I determined to forestall him. Slowly I lowered the gaff into the water, and guiding the fractured end of the submerged middle-joint towards it, neatly gaffed it through the lowest ring. Adolphus seemed greatly relieved when I removed the top ring from his nose, and in gladness he went for a swim round the pool.

But he had yet to reckon with me. A fish like this is a danger to the river. I raised the gaff on high, and as he wallowed lazily within 4 feet of me, obviously meditating further evil, I suddenly smote him over the head with all my strength.

It was entirely successful. I confess I had a moment's compunction when Adolphus quivered, lay still, and then rolled stomach upwards; but he was much easier to gaff in this position. I towed him ashore and, after a little dentistry, recovered the doctor, who, I am sorry to say, was somewhat dishevelled.

Adolphus looked very lovely in death, very peaceful . . . very appetizing. *De mortuis* . . . I plucked some buttercups and laid them reverently upon him. He weighed 17 pounds.

Journal of the Flyfishers' Club, 1926.

AFTER TEN HOURS

It is now half-past three o'clock, and we are rapidly approaching Newburgh. The change of tide seems to make the fish frantic. We are never still for half a minute, and never cease wondering what his size must be if his strength is so enormous and so untiring. Finally, he decides on going up with the tide. The waves become embarrassing, and the boat is no longer easy to manage. A new fiend enters the fish, and makes him play the maddest pranks imaginable. We have for some time discussed the probability of his being a strong fish hooked foul, which would account for some part of his power; but when the waves are at the highest and the boat is blowing up the river close upon the fish, out he springs 2 feet into the air, a monster as large as a well-grown boy, with the line leading fair up to his snout. "Never land that fellow with a couple of trout-lines, or any other line," is the fisherman's verdict; and as if to confirm it a cry comes the next minute, "The line has parted!" Sure enough one strand has gone, owing to the constant friction of the wet line running through the rings for so many hours, and within 20 yards of the end of the line there is an ugly place 2 inches long, with only two strands out of three remaining. There is no longer a moment's safety unless that flaw is kept on the reel; and the necessity of pressing close to the fish leads Jimmy such a life as he will probably not forget. We are hungry and cold and somewhat wet; it is growing very dusk, and if we could not land him with 120 yards of line, how can we with 20? We have caught a Tartar indeed.

And now night comes on in earnest. . . . The clock at home strikes 7, and we hear our passenger groaning over the fact that they are just going to dinner. Lights peep out on the hillsides. . . . At length a measured sound of oars is heard, and a black pirate-like boat comes down upon us. We state our need. Can he take this gentleman down to the pier, and bring us back some food? "Na!" And that is all he will vouchsafe to say as he sheers off again. Soon, however, a more Christian boat appears, and with many complicated manœuvres, to keep the line clear of the boat in the dark, we trans-ship our friend about 8 o'clock, loaded with injunctions to send off food and a light. The light would be of the greatest service, for a frozen finger and thumb are not sufficiently certain indicators of the passage of the frayed portion of the line from the reel; and as the fish has never ceased to rush from one side to the other, frequently passing sheer under the boat, and requiring the utmost care to keep the line clear of the oars, we think almost more of the coming lantern than of the sorely needed food. It is an hour before the boat returns, with an excellent lantern, a candle and a half, a bottle of whisky, and cakes and cheese enough for a week. Before setting to work upon the food we attempt to put in execution a plan we have long thought of and carefully discussed. A spare rod, short and stiff, is laid across the seats of the boat, with the reel all clear, and a good salmon-line on, with 5 or 6 yards drawn through the rings. We wait till the fish is quiet for a moment or two under the boat, and taking gently hold of the line he is on, pass a loop of it through the loop at the end of the salmon-line. As if he defined our intention, off he goes at once, running the flaw off the reel, and costing us some effort to catch him up again. This is repeated two or three times. At last we get the loop through, get a good knot tied, snap the old line above the knot, and there is our friend careering away at the end of 100 yards of strong salmon-line, with some 7 or 8 yards only of the thinner line. When we examine the now innocuous flaw, we find it is 7 inches long, and half of one of the remaining strands is frayed through.

Time passes on as we drift slowly up the river towards Elcho. Ten o'clock strikes, and we determine to wait till dawn, and try conclusions with the monster that has had us fast for 10 hours. The tide begins to turn, and Jimmy utters gloomy forebodings of our voyage down to the sea in the dark. The fish feels the change of the tide, and becomes more demoniacal than ever. For half an hour he is in one incessant flurry, and at last, for the first time, he rises to the surface, and through the dark night we can hear and see the huge splashes he makes as he rolls and beats the water. He must be near done, Jimmy thinks. As he is speaking the line comes slack. He's bolting towards the boat, and we reel up with the utmost rapidity. We reel on; but no sign of resistance. Up comes the minnow, minus the tail hook. Jimmy rows home without a word; and neither he nor the fisherman will ever get over it.

G. F. Browne,
Off the Mill, 1895.

189

A SECOND TIME

"I'm in him!" Dick shouted, and as I leaped to my feet the biggest fish I have ever seen rolled over on the surface, hung there for a moment in full view, then sank out of sight. From the height at which I stood I could see his entire length. He was enormous, half as long again as a 30-pounder he looked. I shouted across to Dick: "That's a tremendous fish—the biggest I ever saw."

Thereupon, as if to show his power, he turned and proceeded down-stream at a steady pace, neither very fast nor very slow, but deep in the water and with a kind of irresistible force. Dick said afterwards that he had never felt anything like it. And here I must say that with all its thrills and turns of fortune there seemed to be throughout the fight an uncanny sense of the inevitable.

Fifty yards more were soon gone, but still the line continued to travel steadily out. Dick followed the fish down till the water was well above his waist and within 2 inches of his wader tops. A steady grip on the line made not the least impression, it still ran out. Any increase of pressure only caused an answering exertion of strength from the fish, which obviously had no intention of stopping its downward course. Over 100 yards of line were out, and Dick, unable to go any farther, was shouting frantically for the ghillie and the boat. A faint answering shout showed that he was not far off now, but could he be in time?

Unable to help, I had run down my bank to watch the fish's movements—he was now travelling faster. Then I saw the rod bend slowly right down to the water—a moment of tremendous strain—all the line was out, some 200 yards of it, an extra heave from the fish, the line broke at the reel, swished through the rings, and was gone. At that moment the boat arrived. Dick got in and they set off down-stream, Dick watching the water, gaff in hand, from the bows. I saw them consult, and wondered what they were at. A thrilling idea had come to them—the line was brand new and surely it would float; if so, it could be recovered! Down the river they drifted looking out for the line. At first it seemed a hopeless quest, but luckily the reach was a smooth one, and after some 5 minutes I saw the boat slow up and Dick actually hooked up the line from the water.

Now the threading of the line and the re-attaching of it to the reel. This too was successfully accomplished, thanks to the length of line out. Then came the crucial moment. Was the fish still on? Dick reeled in as fast as he could. Yard after yard came in without resistance—the line began to tighten—still there was no movement. Was it a rock? No, by Jove, he's still there—now we'll have him! But not yet. Annoyed by the pressure, the great fish once more recommenced his heavy downward course, and the boat followed him.

Some hundred yards below there is a deep rocky pool overhung by a great limestone cliff which is deeply undercut by the current. A nasty spot to play a big fish. If once he entered the unknown depths beneath the rock it would be all over. And for this he was obviously making, with a deliberate persistence that seemed almost like reasoned purpose. This was the unusual feature of the battle. I have often thought that if all fish behaved as this one did, salmon fishing would become wellnigh useless.

Dick did everything possible to stop him. As he said later, you might as well have been pulling on an ox; there was nothing to be done, and eventually he left the boat and attempted to get on terms with the fish from the shingle bank opposite to the cliff.

This he afterwards thought was a mistake, and I think it was, though I feel that nothing would have made any real difference. For a few moments it seemed as though he was holding his own, but suddenly the line cut the water in a magnificent curving run, the first turn of speed the fish had shown. Straight under the overhanging rock he ran, then, except for a dull scraping sensation, all movement ceased. The line was immovable. Five minutes passed, then quite quietly the line came away cut clean through well above the cast.

So this mighty fish was lost a second time. A terrible blow, though, as Dick says, he never felt confident that he would bring him to the gaff.

What did he weigh? We often wonder. No great fish was picked up afterwards, as in the case of the Wye fish estimated at between 60 pounds and 80 pounds. But at a conservative estimate he was certainly well over 4 feet long.

G. D. Luard,
Fishing Fortunes and Misfortunes, 1942.

Although I had with me one of your 14-feet Salmon Rods, I used only during my visit to Grimersta one of your 9½-feet Gold Medal Trout rods, without the steel centre, and your tapered casts Medium Lake and Heavy Lake.

In 2 consecutive days' fishing, ten salmon were landed, of the following weights: 5½, 6, 6, 7, 7, 8½, 9, 11½, 15, and a Cock Fish of 28 pounds, making a total for the 2 days of 103½ pounds; the largest salmon took 1½ hours to bring to the net, and 70 per cent of the catch were fresh-run.

Letter quoted in Hardy Brothers Catalogue, *1937.*

BLACK DOG

Salar slept. The water lightened with sunrise. He lay in shadow. His eyes were fixed, passively susceptible to all movement. The sun rose up. Leaves and stalks of loose weed and water-moss passing were seen but unnoticed by the automatic stimulus of each eye's retina. The eyes worked together with the unconscious brain, while the nerves, centres of direct feeling, rested themselves. One eye noticed a trout hovering in the water above, but Salar did not see it.

The sun rose higher, and shone down on the river, and slowly the shadow of the ledge shrank into its base. Light revealed Salar, a grey-green uncertain dimness behind a small pale spot appearing and disappearing regularly.

Down there Salar's right eye was filled with the sun's blazing fog. His left eye saw the wall of rock and the water above. The trout right forward of him swam up, inspected that which had attracted it, and swam down again; but Salar's eye perceived no movement. The shadow of the trout in movement did not fall on the salmon's right eye.

A few moments later there was a slight splash left forward of Salar. Something swung over, casting the thinnest shadow; but it was seen by the eye, which awakened the conscious brain. Salar was immediately alert.

The thing vanished. A few moments later, it appeared nearer to him.

With his left eye Salar watched the thing moving overhead. It swam in small jerks, across the current and just under the surface, opening and shutting, gleaming, glinting, something trying to get away. Salar, curious and alert, watched it until it was disappearing and then he swam up and around to take it ahead of its arc of movement. The surface water, however, was flowing faster than the river at mid-stream, and he misjudged the opening of his mouth, and the thing, which recalled sea-feeding, escaped.

On the bank upriver 15 yards away a fisherman with 14-foot split-cane rod said to himself, excitedly, "Rising short"; and pulling loops of line between reel and lowest ring of rod, he took a small pair of scissors from a pocket and snipped off the thing which had attracted Salar.

No wonder Salar had felt curious about it, for human thought had ranged the entire world to imagine that lure. It was called a fly; but no fly like it ever swam in air or flew through water. Its tag, which had glinted, was of silver from Nevada and silk of a moth from Formosa; its tail, from the feather of an Indian crow; its butt, black herl of African ostrich; its body, yellow floss-silk veiled with orange breast-feathers of the South American toucan, and black Macclesfield silk ribbed with silver tinsel. This fly was given the additional attraction of wings for water-flight, made of strips of feathers from many birds: turkey from Canada, peahen and peacock from Japan, swan from Ireland, bustard from Arabia, golden-pheasant from China, teal and wild duck and mallard from the Hebrides. Its throat was made of the feather of an English speckled hen, its side of Bengal jungle-cock's neck feathers, its cheeks came from a French kingfisher, its horns from the tail of an Amazonian macaw. Wax, varnish, and enamel secured the "marriage" of the feathers. It was one of hundreds of charms, or materialized river-side incantations, made by men to persuade sleepy or depressed salmon to rise and take. Invented after a bout of seasickness by a Celt as he sailed the German Ocean between England and Norway, for nearly 100 years this fly had borne his name, Jock Scott.

While the fisherman was tying a smaller pattern of the same fly to the end of the gut cast, dark stained by nitrate of silver against under-water glint, Salar rose to mid-water and hovered there. Behind him lay the trout, which, scared by the sudden flash of the big fish turning, had dropped back a yard. So Salar had hovered 3 years before in his native river, when, as parr spotted like a trout, and later as a silvery smolt descending to the sea, he had fed eagerly on nymphs of the olive dun and other ephemeridae coming down with the current.

He opened his mouth and sucked in a nymph as it was swimming to the surface. The fisherman saw a swirl on the water, and threw his fly, with swish of double-handed rod, above and to the right of the swirl. Then, lowering the rod point until it was almost parallel to the water, he let the current take the fly slowly across the stream, lifting the rod tip and lowering it slightly and regularly to make it appear to be swimming.

Salar saw the fly and slowly swam up to look at it. He saw it clear in the bright water and sank away again, uninterested in the lifelessness of its bright colours. Again it re-appeared, well within his sky-light window. He ignored it, and it moved out of sight. Then it fell directly over him, jigging about in the water, and with it a dark thin thing which he regarded cautiously. This was the gut cast. Once more it passed over, and then again, but he saw only the dark thinness moving there. It was harmless. He ignored it. Two other salmon below Salar, one in a cleft of rock and the other beside a sodden oak log wedged under the bank, also saw the too-bright

Salmon flies (from H. Cholmondeley-Pennell, Fishing, *1885).*

thing, and found no vital interest in it.

The fisherman pulled in the line through the rod-rings. It was of plaited silk, tapered and enamelled for ease of casting. The line fell over his boot. Standing still, he cut off the fly and began a search for another in a metal box, wherein scores of mixed feathers were ranged on rows of metal clasps. First he moved one with his forefinger, then another, staring at this one and frowning at that one, recalling in its connection past occasions of comparative temperatures of air and river, of height and clearness of water, of sun and shade, while the angler's familiar feeling, of obscurity mingled with hope and frustration, came over him. While from the air he tried to conjure certainty for a choice of fly, Salar, who had taken several nymphs of the olive dun during the time the angler had been cogitating, leapt and fell back with a splash that made the old fellow take a small Black Doctor and tie the gut to the loop of the steel hook with a single Cairnton jam-knot.

Salar saw this lure and fixed one eye on it as it approached and then ignored it, a thing without life. As it was being withdrawn from the water a smolt which had seen it only then leapt open-mouthed at a sudden glint and fell back, having missed it.

Many times a similar sort of thing moved over Salar, who no longer heeded their passing. He enjoyed crushing the tiny nymphs on his tongue, and tasting their flavour. Salar was not feeding, he was not hungry; but he was enjoying remembrance of his river-life with awareness of an unknown great excitement before him. He was living by the spirit of running water. Indeed Salar's life was now the river: as he explored it higher, so would he discover his life.

On the bank the fisherman sat down and perplexed re-examined his rows and rows of flies. He had tried all recommended for the water, and several others as well; and after one short rise, no fish had come to the fly. Mar Lodge and Silver Grey, Dunkeld and Black Fairy, Beauly Snow Fly, Fiery Brown, Silver Wilkinson, Thunder and Lightning, Butcher, Green Highlander, Blue Charm, Candlestick Maker, Bumbee, Little Inky Boy, all were no good. Then in one corner of the case he saw an old fly of which most of the mixed plumage was gone: a Black Dog which had belonged to his grandfather. Grubs of moths had fretted away hackle, wing, and topping. It was thin and bedraggled. Feeling that it did not matter much what fly was used, he sharpened the point with a slip of stone, tied it on, and carelessly flipped it into the water. He was no longer

fishing; he was no longer intent, he was about to go home; the cast
did not fall straight, but crooked; the line also was crooked. Without
splash the fly moved down a little less fast than the current, coming
thus into Salar's skylight. It was like the nymphs he had been taking,
only larger; and with a leisurely sweep he rose and turned across
the current, and took it, holding it between tongue and vomer as
he went down to his lie again, where he would crush and taste it.
The sudden resistance of the line to his movement caused the point
of the hook to prick the corner of his mouth. He shook his head to
rid himself of it, and this action drove the point into the gristle, as
far as the barb.

A moment later, the fisherman, feeling a weight on the line, lifted
the rod-point, and tightened the line, and had hardly thought to
himself, *salmon*, when the blue-grey tail of a fish broke half out of
water and its descending weight bended the rod.

Salar knew of neither fisherman nor rod nor line. He swam down
to the ledge of rock and tried to rub the painful thing in the corner
of his mouth against it. But his head was pulled away from the rock.
He saw the line, and was fearful of it. He bored down to his lodge
at the base of the rock, to get away from the line, while the small
brown trout swam behind his tail, curious to know what was
happening.

Salar could not reach his lodge. He shook his head violently, and,
failing to get free, turned down-stream and swam away strongly,
pursued by the line and a curious buzzing vibration just outside his
jaw.

Below the pool the shallow water jabbled before surging in broken
white crests over a succession of rocky ledges. Salar had gone about
60 yards from his lodge, swimming hard against the backward pull
of line, when the pull slackened, and he turned head to current, and
lay close to a stone, to hide from his enemy.

When the salmon had almost reached the jabble, the fisherman,
fearing it would break away in the rough water, had started to run
down the bank, pulling line from the reel as he did so. By thus
releasing direct pull on the fish, he had turned it. Then, by letting
the current drag line in a loop below it, he made Salar believe that
the enemy was behind him. Feeling the small pull of the line from
behind, Salar swam up into deeper water, to get away from it. The
fisherman was now behind the salmon, in a position to make it tire
itself by swimming up-stream against the current.

Salar, returning to his lodge, saw it occupied by another fish, which his rush, and the humming line cutting the water, had disturbed from the lie by the sodden log. This was Gralaks the grilse. Again Salar tried to rub the thing against the rock, again the pull, sideways and upwards, was too strong for him. He swam downwards, but could make no progress towards the rock. This terrified him and he turned upwards and swam with all his strength, to shake it from his mouth. He leapt clear of the water and fell back on his side, still shaking his head.

On the top of the leap the fisherman had lowered his rod, lest the fly be torn away as the salmon struck the water.

Unable to get free by leaping, Salar sank down again and settled himself to swim away from the enemy. Drawing the line after him, and beset again by the buzzing vibration, he travelled 100 yards to the throat of the pool, where water quickened over gravel. He lay in the riffle spreading away from a large stone, making himself heavy, his swim-bladder shrunken, trying to press himself into the gravel which was his first hiding place in life. The backward pull on his head nearly lifted him into the fast water, but he held himself down, for nearly 5 minutes, until his body ached and he weakened and he found himself being taken down sideways by the force of shallow water. He recalled the sunken tree and it became a refuge, and he swam down fast, and the pull ceased with the buzz against his jaw. Feeling relief, he swam less fast over his lodge, from which Gralaks sped away, alarmed by the line following Salar.

But before he could reach the tree the weight was pulling him back, and he turned and bored down to bottom, scattering a drove of little grey shadows which were startled trout. Again the pull was too much for him, and he felt the ache of his body spreading back to his tail. He tried to turn on his side to rub the corner of his mouth on something lying on the bed of the pool—an old cartwheel—again and again, but he could not reach it.

A jackdaw flying silent over the river, paper in beak for nest-lining, saw the dull yellow flashes and flew faster in alarm of them and the man with the long curving danger.

Fatigued and aching, Salar turned down-stream once more, to swim away with the river, to escape the enemy which seemed so much bigger because he could not close his mouth. As he grew heavier, slower, uncertain, he desired above all to be in the deeps of the sea, to lie on ribbed sand and rest and rest and rest. He came to rough water, and let it take him down, too tired to swim. He bumped into a rock, and was carried by the current around it, on his side, while the gut cast, tautened by the dragging weight, twanged and jerked his head up-stream, and he breathed again, gulping water quickly and irregularly. Still the pull was trying to take him forward, so with a renewal by fear he turned and re-entered fast water and went down and down, until he was in another deep pool at a bend of the river. Here he remembered a hole under the roots of a tree, and tried to hide there, but had not strength enough to reach the refuge of darkness.

Again he felt release, and swam forward slowly, seeking the deepest part of the pool, to lie on the bottom with his mouth open. Then he was on his side, dazed and weary, and the broken-quick-silvery surface of the pool was becoming whiter. He tried to swim away, but the water was too thick-heavy; and after a dozen sinuations it became solid. His head was out of water. A shock passed through him as he tried to breathe. He lay there, held by line taut over fisherman's shoulder. He felt himself being drawn along just under the surface, and only then did he see his enemy—flattened, tremulant-spreading image of the fisherman. A new power of fear broke in the darkness of his lost self. When it saw the tailer coming down to it, the surface of the water was lashed by the desperately scattered self. The weight of the body falling over backwards struck the taut line; the tail-fin was split. The gut broke just above the hook, where it had been frayed on the rock. Salar saw himself sinking down into the pool, and he lay there, scattered about himself and unable to move away, his tail curved round a stone, feeling only a distorted head joined to the immovable river-bed.

Henry Williamson,
Salar the Salmon, 1935.

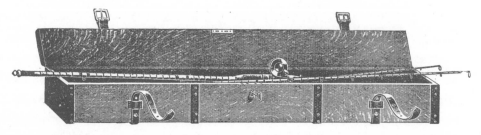

1912

TROUT

The trout makes the angler the most gentlemanly and readiest sport of all other fishes.

William Lauson

1898

PRACTICAL HINTS ON FLY FISHING FOR TROUT, ETC.

Fly-fishing for Trout is perhaps one of the most enjoyable sports practised on the waters of this country, and he who has not been educated to the true enjoyment of it, has suffered a great loss.

In the perfect casting and delivery of the fly, there is the same enjoyment as is experienced by the clever shot or billiard player, who prides himself on the true and perfect working harmony of hand and eye. But this is all the comparison, for besides the pleasure of perfect casting and eager expectation, there is all the excitement of stalking and ultimate capture, while the great uncertainty of the latter, adds not a little to the charm. Then if we take into consideration, that the angler is necessarily something of an entomologist and a naturalist in general, we may fearlessly say, that angling is perhaps the most truly enjoyable sport a man can indulge in.

To proceed to such a general description and direction as may be of some little use to the tyro, we may first observe that he should confine himself to a single-handed rod, of from 9 to 12 feet, according to the water to be fished. Two-handed rods were once commonly used for this class of fishing, more especially on wide rivers, but are now almost things of the past; as the shorter and lighter rods, working with finer tackle, gain in dexterity and delicacy of delivery, more than they lose in area of water under control. It is most important that the rod should be correctly balanced with a suitable reel and line. This should be carefully seen to, as no one can make good work with badly matched tools. The advice and assistance of some older hand should be asked in this matter.

To make an ordinary overhead cast correctly, the tyro should begin with a gut line not more than 2 yards long and with two flies. Supposing then the rod and line correctly balanced, and mounted with a suitable gut line and flies: he should draw off from the reel as much line as once and a half the length of his rod, holding the end fly between the finger and thumb of the left hand, grasping the rod a little above the reel with his right, and waving it gently a few times, until he gets the required momentum to carry out the line, when he should release the fly, making at the same time a cut with the rod, over or in line with the spot he intends his flies to alight, care being taken in doing this, that the point of the rod should not be allowed to drop further than at right angles to himself. He will do well at first to fish down-stream, as should he not have made the first cast correctly, the stream will put the matter right, and float the line and flies out straight. Then he should raise the point of the rod gently upwards, in order to get as much line clear of the water as possible, and also to give the flies a little life-like motion before making the back stroke; in fact all but the flies should be clear of the water. Then with a smart stroke back over his head, slightly inclining the rod point to the left, he should lift his line clear behind him, at the same time avoiding all elbow work, as much as possible, and without allowing the rod point to go back further than an angle of 45 degrees to the body. Having done this, a moment's reflection will tell him, that as the line went back in a curve, it will take an instant to straighten after the rod was thrown back into the required position. This is very important, as the line should exactly have time to straighten out before making the return cast. If he does not, it is possible he will hear a slight crack, signifying that the flies have gone.

1898

Bear in mind, that the throwing the flies back correctly is as important as the laying them straight and fine across the water. Now it
only remains to drive the line and flies forward, by smartly bringing
the rod down into a horizontal position again, and in doing this, he
should aim at a point, say 2 or 3 feet above where he intends the
flies to fall (as they should not be thrown at, but above), so that
they may alight softly on the water. Now if he studies these directions
correctly, there are three movements and a pause. 1. Raise the rod
point in order to get as much line clear of the water as possible. 2.
Make the backward sweep, then pause until the line gets time to
straighten, but not so long as to allow the flies to drop and catch the
grass, &c. 3. Make the cast as described over the place intended. It
is very simple and yet we have seen amateurs very much troubled
and in despair, simply because they had not tried in a simple and
systematic manner to attain the art.

*For fly-fishing only, the most convenient length is from 10 to 11 feet; but if the angler wants a rod suitable
also for worm and minnow-fishing, as I do, I recommend a rod of 12 feet. My 12-foot cane-rod throws
minnow and worm beautifully, and although I have used it for two seasons in all sorts of weather, it is
as straight as ever it was.*

Letter quoted in Hardy Brothers Catalogue, *1888.*

Having in some degree mastered this, he may let out a little more
line, about a yard at a time, until he finds he can fairly command
the water he is fishing, but on no account more than is absolutely
necessary.

He must now choose where and how he will fish, and in this only
experience will guide him, keeping in view that the wind at his back
is an advantage, and that he should always fish up and across
stream; never (unless unavoidable) down.

We will suppose the seat of his intended sport is on one of our sharp
gravelly north-country streams. Begin at the bottom or tail of the
pool, and fish all the likely parts across and up-stream, wading
gently and fishing every yard of likely water to the neck of the
stream. As soon as a fish is hooked, it should be brought down past
the angler, and played in that part which has been fished, so as not
to alarm the other feeding fish. Of course where the water runs quick,
he will require to make frequent casts, as the stream so quickly
carries the flies down. Use as short a line as possible. It is often a
very deadly plan to let the flies sink a little, and simply be guided by
the running line, striking when it stops.

The idea of fishing up-stream is this: The fish lie with their heads
up-stream, and do not see the angler until his flies have well covered

them; secondly, they take the drowned fly in a perfectly natural manner, as it floats down the stream, and, lying with their bodies in a direct line from the rod, are much more liable to be hooked. Fishing down-stream, although easy and often adopted by anglers from the bank, is a very poor business, and six fish will be missed for every one hooked. Let your maxim be, "Fish up and fish fine". The foregoing hints only apply to wet-fly fishing; the instructions to casting, however, hold good for either wet or dry fly. The art of dry-fly fishing we cannot in the small space at our disposal go into, and would refer those anxious to learn this, the highest branch of the angler's craft, to such works as Mr. Halford's *Floating Flies and How To Dress Them* and others of a like nature.

The Split-Cane with Steel Core makes a beautiful light trouting rod. The length of mine (made by HARDY BROTHERS) *is 10 feet 7 inches in length when put together, and the weight 10 ounces. I can cast about 22 yards with it, on a still day, on level ground. The correction of stiffness and swishiness leaves, to my mind, absolutely nothing to be desired.*

H. Cholmondeley-Pennell,
Salmon and Trout Fishing.

H. Cholmondeley-Pennell's trout rod (1898)

Besides throwing the fly, there is a great art in striking and hooking the fish. When a fish is seen to rise, the rod point should be smartly raised with a motion of the wrist only, care being taken not to do this in any degree harshly, as a very little, in fact the mere tightening of the line, is sufficient to fix so sharp an instrument as a small fly hook, in the mouth of the fish; and in this he must be careful, as the momentary excitement generally causes young anglers to strike too hard, and the consequence is a smash. The object of striking is simply to fix the hook before the fish has time to discover his mistake, and prevent his blowing out the fly from his mouth, which if left to himself he would generally do.

Having hooked your fish, it now remains to land him, and here much discretion must be used. Small fish may generally be dropped into the net as soon as you can shorten line sufficiently, but if large, say over ½ pound, caution must be used. Keep a firm strain on him at all times, and if he rushes wildly off do not attempt to stop him, but the moment he eases at once commence to put on more pressure, and in a few minutes, if you are fortunate enough to hold and keep him away from snags and the like, he will be exhausted. Then by winding in your line, and advancing the butt of the rod and so using its flexibility as a safety spring, he may be brought sufficiently near to be dropped into the net, after which he should be at once killed by a blow on the head. Fish killed at once after landing are always

The Halcyon spinner (1886)

better for table, and besides it is more humane.

Much depends on the correct choice of a rod for this work. Small wooded streams are easiest fished with 9 to 10-feet rods, but fairly open ones require a somewhat longer weapon. The correct thing is $10\frac{1}{2}$ feet or 11 feet, certainly nothing over $11\frac{1}{2}$ feet. It should be sufficiently fine in the point so as not to break the finest gut in striking just a little hard, and the other parts should be in proportion, so as to carry the top without the least top-heavy feeling.

It is almost impossible to describe the correct rod, as balance is a very subtle thing, and more a practical than a theoretical one. Our choice for all round fly-fishing, spinning a light minnow, or one of our "Halcyon" spinners on fine tackle, is one of our $10\frac{1}{2}$ to 11-foot cane-built steel centre rods that will tackle a 5 or 6 pound fish if required.

Hardy Brothers Catalogue, 1888.

1907

ON TROUTING
WITH THE FLY

When you are approaching a pool which you intend to fish, if the water is clear do so carefully; you must recollect that the trout see you much more readily if you are on a high bank than if you are on a level with the water. For this reason keep as low down as possible, and always, if the nature of the ground will admit of it, stand a few yards from the edge of the water. If there is a ripple on the water you may meet with good sport in the still water at the foot of the pools, but if there is no wind, it is useless commencing till you come to where the water is agitated. If you do not intend fishing the lower part, do not walk up the side of it, as by so doing you will alarm the trout in that portion, and they may run up to the head of the pool for shelter, and frighten the others; but always come to the edge of the pool at the place where you intend to begin fishing. If the water is very low and the sun bright, it may be advisable to kneel in fishing a pool, in order to keep out of sight, and you must avoid allowing your shadow to fall upon the water above where you are standing.

First, as you approach, fish the side on which you are standing with a cast or two, and then commence to fish the opposite side, where you are to expect the most sport. For this reason you should always keep on the shallow side of the water, as the best trout generally lie under the bank at the deep side. After having taken a cast or two on the near side, throw your flies partly up-stream and partly across, but more across than up, from where you are standing. You should throw them to within an inch of the opposite bank; if they alight on it so much the better; draw them gently off, and they will fall like a snow-flake, and if there is a trout within sight they are almost sure to captivate it. In this way your flies will fall more like a natural insect than by any other method.

Once I killed in 10 days 800 trout. I consider this was due in a great measure to the excellence of the rod.
Letter quoted in Hardy Brothers Catalogue, *1912.*

After your flies alight, allow them to float gently down-stream for a yard or two, taking care that neither they nor the line ripple the surface. There is no occasion for keeping them on the surface, they will be quite as attractive a few inches under water. As the flies come down-stream, raise the point of your rod, so as to keep your line straight, and as little of it in the water as possible; and when they have traversed a few yards of water, throw again about a yard or two higher up than where your flies alighted the previous cast, and so on. Unless the spot looks exceedingly promising, you need not cast twice in one place if you do not get a rise, but if there is any quick turn in the water where there is likely to be a good trout, we frequently cast over it six or seven times in succession, just allowing the flies to alight when we cast again. Where the current is strong, the trout may not see the fly at first, and so we cast repeatedly to make sure; and we have frequently, after casting unsuccessfully half a dozen times over the same place, caught a good trout at last. Move up the pool as quickly as you can, first taking a cast or two straight up on the side you are on, and then fishing the opposite side, and so on, until you finish the pool. Although it is about the edges of the pool you will generally get most trout, the main current must by no means be neglected; indeed, in it you will frequently capture the best fish. By fishing in the way we have described, throwing a yard or two farther up every cast, the flies may be brought in a wonderfully short space of time over every foot of water where a trout is likely to be.

The rod arrived safely. Its action is to my mind perfect. On Wednesday last I had my first day at the trout, 20½ brace, and can only say I could have gone on for 48 hours without stopping.
    Letter quoted in Hardy Brothers Catalogue, *1907.*

Streams should be fished in exactly the same manner as pools; fishing the side you are on straight up, and the opposite side partly up. All quiet water between two streams, and eddies behind stones, should be fished straight up, and the flies just allowed to remain sufficiently long to let the trout see them; and in fishing such places, care must be taken to keep the line out of the current. It is more difficult fishing streams than pools, as it requires greater nicety in casting; and on account of the roughness of the water it is not so easy to see a trout rise.

In fishing still water with no breeze upon it you should wait until the motion of the line falling has subsided, and then draw the flies slowly towards you, as, if they were allowed to remain stationary, the trout would at once detect their artificial nature.

Casting partly across and partly up-stream, for a variety of reasons, is more deadly than casting directly up. The advantage of having a number of flies is entirely lost by casting straight up, as they all come down in a line, and it is only the trout in that line that can see them; whereas, if thrown partly across, they all come down in different lines, and the trout in all these lines may see them. In casting across, when the flies light, the stream carries them out at right angles to the line, and they come down the stream first, so that the trout sees the flies before the line; whereas, in casting straight up, if a trout is between the angler and the place where his flies light, the line passes over it before it sees the flies, and may alarm it.

The moment the fly alights being the most deadly of the whole cast, it is obvious that the oftener it is repeated the better, and therefore the angler should cast as frequently as possible, always allowing the flies to remain a few moments, in order to let the trout see them;

but there is not much danger of casting too often, or even casting often enough, as the angler's arm will quickly rebel against it.

Rivers which can be commanded from bank to bank, either by wading or otherwise, constitute by far the most agreeable fishing; but if the river is so large that you cannot reach the opposite side, you must look for sport on the side you are on. And in this case, though you should neglect no spot where a trout may be lying, fish most carefully the part of the pool where the shallow merges into the deep, and where the current is moderately strong; fishing it in the same manner as you would do the opposite side, and always as you go up taking a cast or two straight up, as close to the edge as possible.

On all occasions cast your flies about a yard above where you think the trout are likely to be found, as if on alighting it attracts their attention, there is much less chance of their discovering its artificial nature at that distance. For the same reason, if you see a trout rise at a natural fly throw above it, and in general it will meet the fly half-way. If a trout rise and you miss it, cast again, and continue doing so until it ceases to rise; a small trout will frequently rise four or five times in succession; but the large well-conditioned fish are more wary, and if they miss once or twice will sometimes decline returning, however temptingly, you may throw your flies.

W. C. Stewart,
The Practical Angler, 1857.

1886

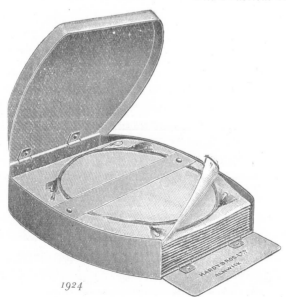

1924

1898

DRY FLY FISHING FOR TROUT

The great success of and the large demand for our "Houghton" dry-fly specialities is very gratifying, and it is a pleasure to feel that our efforts have satisfied the present needs of the advanced school of dry-fly fishers. Without doubt dry-fly fishing is becoming deservedly more popular, and is rapidly extending in the North of England and Scotland, not only in river fishing but also on lochs. In Ireland it is not unusual to see the "dry-flyer" successfully at work, and in Wales also the trout have reason to fear his skill; in addition on the Continent, in America and the Colonies the dry-fly is now a popular method. There is little or no cause for wonder at this. On most rivers the angler frequently reaches a quietly flowing pool, or a glassy glide at the head of a stream, where the upright split-wing floater, fished dry, is the lure par excellence; indeed, if properly presented to a rising fish in any such situation it is nearly certain to prove successful. But it must not be forgotten that after all it is not the fly but the angler that succeeds; and he must be fitted out properly before he can proceed successfully.

We would emphasize the fact that an ordinary wet-fly outfit is not suitable for dry-fly fishing; a special build of rod, a special make of line, a suitable reel, and a very evenly tapered cast are absolutely necessary if the angler wishes to become an expert—of course, the flies must be dressed to float. We have been asked so often by would-be dry-fly fishermen to give a few practical hints on the art of manipulating the "floater", that we make no apology for doing so. We have already expressed our thanks to the experts who have been good enough to approve of the appliances manufactured by us; to the beginner only, "who wants to know", do we address these remarks.

Briefly, then, the art of dry-fly fishing is to present a fly that floats —and floats perfectly—to the notice of a rising fish in such a manner that it is mistaken for the natural *ephemera* which is hatching out, and in the result is accepted as such by the fish. To lure *Salmo Fario* successfully after this manner it is necessary that the angler should have skill; be very observant; have the patience of Job, and, beyond all, be properly equipped for the task.

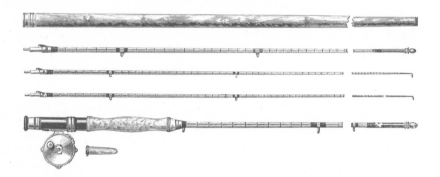

The Crown Houghton, a 9-foot 9-inch all-rounder (1907)

The rod must be built in such a manner that the utmost amount of strength, combined with the necessary pliant action, is contained in its $9\frac{1}{2}$ feet or 10 feet dimensions. The great strain and the wear and tear that are inevitably brought about by the continued process of drying the fly, necessitates the use of the best material, and the employment of thoroughly experienced workmen in the manufacture of a rod for this style of angling. Our "Houghton" pattern, No. 546, H, is specially made for the work, has quick action, and plenty of driving power in the butt; the tops are made extra heavy to obtain the maximum lifting power so that the heavy line can be neatly picked off the water (a very important point); and withal its action is so beautifully pliant, that one can fish with it all day without tiring. "Bridge" rings are, in our opinion, the best. It is advisable to "shoot" the line so that the fly alights in the desired spot. The reel must be capable of easily holding 35 yards of specially made line, and be of the "contracted" pattern, *i.e.* narrow but with a large drum, to enable the angler more quickly to wind up his line should a fish bolt towards him.

1888

Equal in importance to the rod is the line. Its 35 yards must be made from the very best silk obtainable, and waterproofed in such a manner that the dressing searches every fibre by a process that leaves the line round and perfectly pliable. When fishing, the line has to be fairly driven in the desired direction, and even with a perfect rod this would be impossible if the line were not equally suited to the purpose. Weight is therefore necessary, and yet the portion of line near to the fish must be very fine. This difficulty was surmounted by the introduction of tapered lines, which are admitted to be a great improvement upon the old level ones. In our opinion the degree and weight of the taper must be decided by the rod. A line that suits one style of rod admirably is quite unsuited to another. We recommend the angler to test the line on the rod he intends to use with it; when the average length of line with which he generally fishes is extended, the action of the rod should be fully developed. If the line is too heavy the rod will soon tell him so. We guarantee our "Corona Superba" and "Tournament" lines to be exactly suited to our rods.

Next in importance is the cast, every length of which should be tested carefully; it should taper regularly from the same size as the fine end of the reel line to finest drawn (or as fine as the angler dares to use): a perfect line, with cast attached, should taper regularly from the thickest part of the reel line to the finest end of the cast next to the fly. . . .

For our present purposes we must suppose our would-be dry-fly fisher has some preliminary knowledge of fly-fishing, and knows that when dry-fly fishing he must only use one fly. . . . Here are a few useful hints: 1—Never start to practise dry-fly fishing down-stream —you have all the ground to go over again when you start to fish up-stream, and fish up-stream you must if you wish to become a successful manipulator of the "floater". 2—With the heavier line you will be surprised at first the extra amount of casting power you have—do not overdo it; let the rod do its work, and be it your business to direct and control the line. After a while you will find that your arm, the rod and line, and your eye work in unison; next you will discover that you have no thought for rod or line and only eyes for the fly and the fish—now you are getting on! but you are not an expert until you can, as it were, *feel the fly* at the end of your cast and put it in front of a fish in such a manner that even an epicurean trout cannot refuse it. 3—Always pick the line very carefully off the water, or you will scare the fish equally as much as though you had made a fearful splash when casting. 4—To dry the fly (and always dry it well) whisk it through the air a few times, *i.e.*, make a few false casts; in this process be as careful as though you were really making a cast, it is grand practice. 5—Never let the fly alight upon the water until you are sure that it will settle down where intended! rather make another cast. 6—After a cast the line should extend itself straight out in front of you, but in the event of the reel line coiling or being drawn beneath the surface study it not; so long as the fly floats in the right direction let well alone. Always watch the current; and cast in such a manner that the reel line causes as little drag upon the fly as possible, really it ought not to cause any drag; rest assured that if the artificial does not float down with the current in a like manner to the natural fly you have a poor chance of creeling a wary trout.

Where to fish, how to hook, play and land the fish we have explained earlier. We would merely add here that when dry-fly fishing, the steady flowing pools and glassy glides should occupy most of the angler's attention, although the rough streams should by no means be passed over. We will conclude our remarks by giving our readers two very sound pieces of advice that were vividly impressed upon us by a past master of the art many years ago. 1— Let the fly float well over and behind the fish before picking it off the water for a fresh cast; very frequently a fish will let the fly pass him, and then ultimately turn round and ravenously rush at it. 2— Beyond all, when you go a dry-fly fishing "study to be quiet".

Hardy Brothers Catalogue, 1907.

1888

DRY FLY OR WET?

In treating of the advantages of dry-fly over wet-fly fishing, I am most desirous of avoiding any expression which should tend to depreciate in any way the skill exhibited by the experienced and intelligent followers of the wet fly. They require not only most undoubted judgment of the character of water frequented at various times of the day and season by feeding fish, not only a very full knowledge of the different species and genera of insects forming the

food of the fish, not only a full perception of the advantages of fishing up-stream under one set of conditions and of fishing down-stream under others; but, in addition to all this, great skill in placing their flies accurately in the desired position, and allowing them to drift down in a natural manner and without any drag or check over the precise spot they wish to try. There is far too much presumption of superior scientific knowledge and skill on the part of the modern school of dry-fly fishermen, and I should be the last to wish to write a line tending to encourage this erroneous assumption of superiority, or to depreciate in any way the patience and perseverance, coupled with an intuitive perception of the habits of the fish, requisite for a really first-rate performer with the wet fly. The late Francis Francis said that "the judicious and perfect application of dry, wet, and mid-water fly-fishing stamps the finished fly-fisher with the hall-mark of efficiency". This sentiment is to my mind pre-eminently characteristic of its author, and worthy of repetition by any of his admirers in later times.

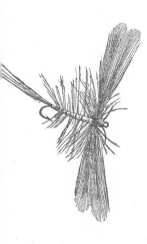

I was fishing at Bosworth Park the last week in November, and killed 7 brace of rainbows on my split cane rod, the largest weighing 3¾ pounds, and the smallest 2 pounds, and Mr. Scott declared it was entirely owing to the rod.

Letter quoted in Hardy Brothers Catalogue, *1907.*

Under certain circumstances the dry fly has in every stream great advantages over the wet, and in rivers where it is not generally used has the further advantage, that, from the fish being unaccustomed to see anything but the *natural* fly floating down cocked over them, they are altogether unsuspicious of the artificial, and take it with such confidence as to render their being hooked, if not their capture, almost a certainty. To define the circumstances specially suited to the dry fly is not difficult. When a fish is seen to be feeding on the surface, when the angler can ascertain the species of insect on which the fish is feeding, when he can imitate it, when he can present this imitation to the fish in its natural position and following precisely the course taken by the natural insect, and when he can carry out all these conditions at the first cast, so as to delude the fish before he has any suspicion of being fished for, the rising and hooking of the most wary trout or grayling is almost a foregone conclusion for the dry-fly fisherman.

ayflies (1888)

It must be remembered that the only possible means of establishing a satisfactory connection between the fish and the fisherman is the medium of sight. A fish's sight is much more highly developed than any other sense, it being questionable whether he has any hearing, or whether his power of smell with surface food is sufficient to guide him in discriminating between the natural and artificial fly. Hence keeping out of sight is a most essential point to study; in fact, as before said, the fish should be hooked before he has any suspicion of being fished for. On the other hand, where no rising or bulging fish are to be seen, and whence it may be inferred that the fish are not taking surface food at all, the conditions are favourable for the use of the sunk fly. Even under these conditions it will some-times occur that the floating fly is more efficacious than the wet.

F. M. Halford,
Dry Fly Fishing in Theory and Practice, 1889.

The rod was fitted with all the improvements referred to before, viz., the small agate rings and the screw winch fitting. I used it for 3 consecutive days, killed a considerable number of trout on it, and expressed to Mr. Hardy the opinion, that it is to my mind the best dry fly rod I have ever handled.

F. M. Halford,
The Dry Fly Man's Handbook.

THE SUNK FLY
ON CHALK STREAMS

The Halford dry fly rod (1912)

There are those who wax indignant at the use of the wet-fly on dry-fly waters. Yet it has a special fascination. The indications which tell your dry-fly angler when to strike are clear and unmistakable, but those which bid a wet-fly man raise his rod-point and draw in the steel are frequently so subtle, so evanescent and impalpable to the senses, that, when the bending rod assures him that he has divined aright, he feels an ecstasy as though he had performed a miracle each time.

G. E. M. Skues,
Minor Tactics of the Chalk Stream, 1910.

I have lost more than half a dozen over 4 pounds through the cast breaking in their terrific rush. Needless to say they were . . .'s casts and not Hardy's.

Letter quoted in Hardy Brothers Catalogue, *1925.*

UPSTREAM OR DOWN ?

Take that "upstream of down" question. Suppose you have a skilled exponent of either method arguing on each side. By listening quietly to their respective statements you will probably pick up a good many wrinkles as to the conditions in which the two methods do best, and also as to the ways in which each man makes his own method effective. There was a time—I will admit it—when I was one of the upstream disciples, and so convinced that if I saw a man fishing downstream I immediately set him down in my own mind as evidently a poor performer. But that was a long time ago, and since then I have angled in many waters, talked with and watched many anglers, and entirely lost my old attitude towards the downstream plan. At the same time, I have not lost my affection for upstream work, so I consider myself greatly the gainer. If one method does not succeed, to have an alternative method which may do better is decidedly a good thing. In the old days, if circumstances made upstream fishing impossible, it was a very half-hearted effort that I made in the other direction. Now I should be just as hopeful whichever way I was casting.

Of course there are different methods of fishing downstream. You can, if you please, cause your flies to behave very much as if you were fishing in the other way. By casting across with a little slack to your line you can cause them to float down unimpeded for a few yards. I fancy this method, which is well suited to big rivers and deep or difficult wading, is the one that the crack downstream men mostly employ. In principle there is little to distinguish it from the across-

and-up plan. But there are other ways of getting fish. You can work your droppers on the top, which is a pretty and sometimes a successful art, you can let your flies drag round in the stream, which rises fish well enough, though they do not always get hooked so surely as might be wished. You can cast your flies at an angle of forty-five, as in salmon fishing, and work them with movements of the rod-top. You can—if you come to a tunnel of bushes, a wide bridge, or similar otherwise inaccessible place—let a lot of line out on the stream and simply wind it back again, a plan which is often good for a trout or two.

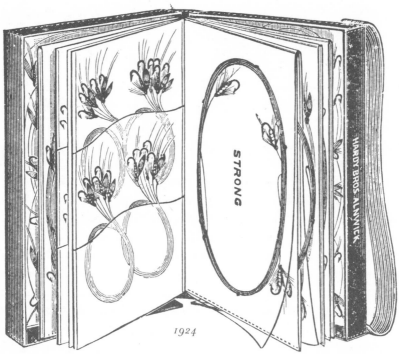

1924

In fact, when one comes to consider all the possibilities of the downstream method, it is clear that deliberate rejection of it would be to inflict a voluntary handicap on one's efficiency. There are occasions on which it is not only just as good as, but even better than, the upstream plan. One of these occasions which has impressed me forcibly of late years is the period when trout are not definitely taking. If you have been fishing up for some time without stirring a fin, it is always worth while to turn round and fish down. Cast your flies under the bushes or bank and work them out and across-stream with short draws of the rod-top, and it will be odd if you do not get a rise or two, and very likely in the same spots where the upstream method scored nothing. The movement of a fly fished in this manner may be unnatural, as some maintain, but it certainly has an effect on the trout, arousing curiosity at least, if nothing else. I do not know if wet-fly men at all commonly work their flies in this way—I rather think not—but the plan is well worth a trial by any one to whom it is new. I have owed to it many a brace of trout before the take has come on or after it has ended, which I am sure I should not have had if I had gone on plodding upstream.

One of the principal arguments of the supporters of the upstream method, as against the other, is that as trout lie with their heads to the current the angler is less visible to them when he comes up behind them. It is the sort of obvious benefit which I should never have dreamed of questioning but for an experience on a small mountain river during a period of dead low water and great heat one August. The stream was so fine and so clear that I found it impossible to cover the tails of the little pools even by the most cautious approach. Do what I would I could not get a fly to them without starting a *sauve qui peut* among the trout lying in the shallow water. They ran up into the pools, of course, and spread the alarm everywhere, so that, except for a chance with dry fly in certain places, it seemed hopeless to fish before dusk. But one day I tried fishing downstream, to see if it would be possible to get anything out of the stickles at the heads of the pools. And to my surprise I found that the fish were very much more approachable in this way. Indeed, at last I succeeded in killing some, though not many, and had to revise my ideas as to the invariable superiority of the upstream method on the score of visibility to the fish.

H. T. Sheringham, *Trout Fishing,*
Memories and Morals, 1920.

THE WAY OF A TROUT WITH A NYMPH

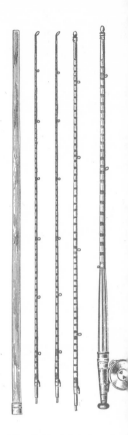

*The Halford Priceless dry f
rod. "Built from specially
selected bamboo, 10 feet
3 inches long, to a favourite
pattern in the possession of
F. M. Halford Esq." (189*

There are two states in which the natural nymph is taken by the trout—first, in the active larval stage, and second (and to the angler far more important) in the practically inert stage, in which the mature nymph arriving at the surface to split its final nymphal envelope and to emerge as a subimago often reaches them.

The active nymphs may be routed out and pursued by the trout from their shelter in weeds or silt. This may be done in water so deep as to afford no clue or opportunity to the angler. In shallower water it is apt to produce the evidence of activity known as "tailing", giving the angler a fairly precise indication where he may cast to his fish, but the opportunities thus afforded are few and the angler is handicapped by the fact that the natural nymph which the trout are pursuing are in one or other of their active stages and cannot be accurately represented in action.

Where trout are "bulging" in the correct sense of the word (i.e. rushing about over the weeds in comparatively shallow water pursuing nymphs which emerge from their shelter in weeds and making a bulge in turning as each nymph is captured), the nymph may be more or less active or it may be almost inert. In his chapter on "Nymphs and Bulgers" in *Fly Fishing: Some New Arts and Mysteries*, Dr. Mottram gives an interesting description of what he had observed on occasions when trout were bulging to nymphs. He writes:

> The nymph may be seen coming down-stream, but often diverging to one side or the other, at the same time rising slowly to the surface, the motion is quite slow and even, not in the least fast or jerky, and a "bulging" fish, although he is quiet in his motions, is obviously not chasing nymphs but moving now to this side, now to that, in order to meet the nymph coming down.

He regards the nymph at this stage as swimming—and I think he

is probably right, for I have often seen trout bulging furiously over weeds, as if the nymphs emerging from shelter were numerous, while the hatch of subimagines is scanty or almost non-existant; so that it seems as if there were occasions when the nymph emerged and if uncaptured by the trout, remained inactive enough to return to its fastnesses or to take refuge in others. Moreover, according to Dr. Mottram, the trout in these conditions is prone to take a dragging artificial nymph, a fact which rather suggests that he is in pursuit of nymphs of which some, at any rate, show a degree of activity.

There is another occasion on which the active nymphs may be taken, *viz.*, after weed cutting, when the nymphs, feeling their weed homes cut away from their stalks, seek shelter in bays and eddies under the banks—and are there found by the trout. Often, too, when cut floating weeds are coming down-stream, trout may be seen rising among them—undoubtedly taking the active nymphs which are deserting or drifting out of the cut weeds.

The commonest occasion known in which the trout feeds on the nymph on its way to hatch is when he lies in position under bank or run, poised to meet and accept without excitement or pursuit the mature nymphs brought to him helpless by the current. On such occasions it is often extremely difficult for the angler to detect whether the fish is taking nymphs or subimago, for there may be, and often is, a string of hatched duns coming over him on the same line of current as brings the nymphs. Yet quite frequently the fish will be found to be taking to the nymph to the exclusion of the winged duns, and that for hours at a time.

Dr. Mottram on his next page makes a distinction between the swimming nymph and the floating nymph which I call the inert nymph, and describes the way in which the fish takes the latter.

> The fish is taking just beneath the surface of the water nymphs which are floating down and about to burst their cases in order to change into duns.

He calls the fish thus feeding on floating nymphs, a "dimpling" fish in contradistinction from the "bulger", feeding on swimming nymphs. He adds a little later of the floating nymph: "In this position they are motionless, with legs and tail extended in the position of rest."

At times during a hatch of duns, trout, often large, may be seen questing about near the surface in mid-stream and taking the

Natural flies and stone fly creeper (from Dry-Fly Entomology, *1897).*

nymphs which are ascending from the river-bed as they find them, generally breaking or "humping" the surface when they effect a capture. And occasionally trout, when in the height of condition, may be observed hovering in the fastest part of the stream, not moving from one spot and intercepting just below the surface the nymphs on their way to hatch, and at times doing so without breaking the surface.

It will thus be seen that the occasions most favourable to the angler fishing to individual selected fish are those when he is taking the mature and, for the moment, practically inert nymph, on its way to hatch.

As a matter of fact, it does not seem to have been realized for many years after the advent of the dry fly, what a large proportion of the rising trout under banks, and indeed in the open (other than bulging) is to nymphs on their way to the surface to hatch, with the result that many a fish so rising has been vainly hammered by anglers with floating flies.

The due appreciation of *how* a trout is rising forms the very essence of fishing, whether it be with floating fly or artificial nymph—and it is often no easy matter. The late Colonel E. W. Harding in his invaluable volume, *The Flyfisher and the Trout's Point of View*, shows how the trout lying in wait with an upward gaze below a smooth surface is enabled to watch the reflection of the approaching nymph in the mirror made by the surface beyond the window through which he can see—and how, in order to keep the reflection in view of his upward gaze he has to come to the surface to meet the actual nymph as it and its reflection come together there.

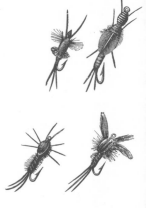

Artificial nymphs (1924).

G. E. M. Skues,
Nymph Fishing for Chalk Stream Trout, 1939.

THE EVENING RISE

Though I have seen many an evening rise and occasionally done right well, it passes my skill to greet a new one with calmness unless for some reason I do not particularly want to catch fish, which almost never happens. Usually I want to catch something very badly, because tea time has found me a shattered wreck with nothing in my creel. And my proceedings during the stages of the rise are too often as follows. The evening rise, as said, begins at 5 p.m. Its first portion consists of a few, very few, depressed fish making tiny dimples at nothing. As also said, I cannot catch these fish. I use a hackle red quill on a "short" oo hook, which I flatter myself is no bigger to a fish's eye than a ooo. I do not use it, though, till I have put a black smut on the new point, looked at it distrustfully, and then taken it off again untried. This custom is almost invariable. The mental process is something like this: "That is the sort of fish that wants a black smut. This is the black smut it wants. Good. But, come to think of it, does the fish want a black smut? Ought it to? The black smut is a thing for the daytime. It is true that the sun is burning a hole in my back, but this is the evening rise. No, a hackle red quill is what must go on." So it goes on, and as exactly as I can I have told why.

To continue, the depressed fish go on dimpling, "here a trout, and there a grayling", till about 6. By that time I have put a selection down (boasting, however, one short rise), and the others have gone down of their own accord, or by the laws of gravity. Then I go on to where, on a swift shallow, are what an ingenious friend calls the "decoys". These fish rise always, morning, evening, night, hail, snow, shine, or earthquake—at least, I believe so. They constitute the second period of the evening rise. On this shallow I always see two light-coloured duns, and I always say: "Ha! It's beginning." They are decoys, too. So I put on a ginger quill, and a pale watery, and a Wickham (which is so good for chance fish), and a sherry spinner, and one or two other things. The period ends with the decoy trout not quite so exuberant as they were and a winged red quill on my line.

I come now, having left the decoys, to the third period. This begins with me sitting on my basket at a bend in the stream favourable to observation, and saying to myself that the two light-coloured duns were one of Nature's accidents. I then tell myself that I shall do no good by wasting any more energy till the rise proper begins. The wise man sits on his basket, and takes the gut ends out of the eyes of flies which he has been changing. So, this decided, I spring up and rush feverishly to the top of the water to see if the evening rise is beginning there. As I go I change the red quill (which has not yet touched the water) for a blue upright. It is a fumbling business to change a fly as you hurry along, but it saves time perhaps. As I come back from the top of the water the blue upright is changed for a sherry spinner, because, of course, that is the fly that is going to do the trick when the fish begin. So the third period ends, with me sitting on the basket and a sherry spinner stuck in a ring.

The fourth period begins with me standing watchful at a bend of the stream, thoughtfully changing the sherry spinner for a blue upright, a fly in which I have the utmost confidence for evening work. It ends with me standing on the *qui vive* 100 yards higher up. I am, if you do me the honour to observe me, changing the blue upright for a Tup's Indispensable.

Now, at last, somewhere between 7.30 and 8, begins the fifth period. A rise, two rises, three rises, and there are flies of some sort, transparent things, dancing in the air. So I change the Tup for a blue-winged olive (which every one knows to be the evening fly for July), and proceed laboriously to put the fish down with it. I do not realize that I am doing so, of course. A series of mischances is attributed to unskilful casting, shyness of the fish, to anything you like. Presently the blue upright is given a trial, and it gains two or three short rises. The hackle red quill is of no effect. In a flash then comes the realization that the sherry spinner is, of course, the thing. It goes on, and has not the slightest result. Then I remember that those transparent things in the air were spinners. The flat-winged imitation ought to have been tried three-quarters of an hour ago, not now, when the spinner is all over.

So now we enter upon the sixth period, when the fish are really rising and the light is growing less. What are they rising at? The blue-winged olive. Am I keeping quite calm? No, I am putting on a sedge, and a black smut, and a red olive spinner, and a blue upright, and a Wickham, and a red quill, and a cochybonddu, and a coachman. And the fish are disdaining each with a deeper disdain, or being terrified of each with a greater terror, according as is their mood.

The seventh period begins with a slackening of rises as the fish find the blue-winged olives petering out. Precisely as the rise ends I remember what is the fly, and get it on to the cast somehow in the gloom. Looking along the path of light towards the west, by good luck I see a quiet dimple, at a sedge of course. The blue-winged olive reaches the spot, is taken (because darkness covers many sins), and the miserable little hook fails to hold the 4-pounder, for which I have

1898

yearned all the season. A good, sensible sedge on a No. 4 hook, and the fish would have been mine. That sedge is put on now at last with the aid of a match, but it is too dark to see any more. So ends another evening rise.

H. T. Sheringham,
Trout Fishing Memories and Morals, 1920.

A WARWICKSHIRE TROUT

I have never captured a record fish but I have caught two "notable" fish, one a trout and the other a tench. The trout came out of a brook in Warwickshire where no trout were supposed to be, but I afterwards found out this supposition had been cleverly bruited abroad by those whose lands adjoined the brook. The stream was certainly unprepossessing to the uneducated eye. It was very narrow, much overgrown with bushes and the banks patrolled by bulls. The latter, I have no doubt, had been placed there by riparian owners. But what are such trifles to a small boy? Any active and healthy boy is a match for a bull if he keeps his head, and as for keepers and farm bailiffs . . .

When I was about thirteen years of age I went to stay one spring with my grandfather, who, in his day, had been a keen fisherman. He had a coachman named Dickon, who wore a glass eye, always an object of morbid fascination to the young. Dickon had lost his eye one winter afternoon when he was chopping wood, a chip flying up had almost gouged it out.

But I digress. One spring morning I was with Dickon in his harness-room watching him polishing the brass fittings to a collar. I remember that harness-room very well, it smelt of saddle soap, leather, horses, and, of course, Dickon. The combination of all four odours was not unpleasing to my juvenile tastes as I sat swinging my legs on a high stool.

The conversation turned to fishing. "Ah," said Dickon, polishing away at a buckle, "there *are* trout if you knows where to look for 'em. Didn't Mr. Free used to get up at five in the morning when he stayed here, and go out and catch them?"

"Trout?" I asked incredulously.

"Aye, trout. Good 'uns too!"

"Where did he go?" I asked.

"Why, Pedder's Mill, of course."

"But the Commander told me that there were *no* trout there!" I exclaimed. (The Commander being the chief "riparian owner".)

Dickon smiled and went on polishing. That was enough. I would go to Pedder's Mill as soon as I could get my tackle together.

The next day I developed a roaring cold in the head. But despite this, and managing to conceal my malady from adult eyes, I set off soon after breakfast with my trout rod, neatly dodging my grand-father who was talking to Dickon by the coach-house.

It was a wild April morning, grey and blowing hard, with oc-casional showers. Though the wind was cold it was one of those days when you feel the spring everywhere, you hear it too, and smell it.

I reached Pedder's Mill and had barely rigged up my tackle in the shelter of the hawthorns by the old mill pool (they were speckled all over with bursting green buds and a thrush had built a very new emerald nest in the heart of one of them) when the miller up at the mill opened the hatch and the still water at my feet became alive with thundering turmoil, dead leaves appeared and drowned sticks turned over and over in the muddy maelstrom.

Then came the miller and ordered me off. I went out on the road, walked down it for a quarter of a mile and rejoined the brook.

I lay low under a willow stump until I saw the Commander come down the drive in his neat trap, complete with cockaded coachman, and then began to fish. Soon a man appeared up by the Dower House kitchen garden fence, and bawled at me at intervals. I took no notice for a time until he began to purposefully climb the fence. Bailiffs and bulls are best left to themselves. He meant business so I stood not upon the order of my going.

These interruptions were tiresome and this latest interference made me impatient. I made another détour and came upon the stream again. Here, under a pallisade of alder trees I at last got my fly on the water and fished the brook down for some two hundred yards without the sign of a rise. Then the stream took a sharp turn to the left in a sort of elbow.

Under the far bank, the current was swift and the fly tittupped round on the ripples and was engulfed. The reel sang as a big fish made upstream and I had to follow. He made for a biggish pool some twenty yards above and there we fought it out for twenty minutes. I had no net (the very young do not carry nets) and I had to play my fish right out and beach him on the shingle at the pool head.

He was a beauty and I took no chances with him; he was practically drowned when I towed him ashore and fell upon him, a trout of three and a half pounds.

The battle won I wrapped it up in dock leaves and put it in my pocket, though the tail flapped under my right arm. I regained the road and almost at once heard the sound of a fast-trotting horse. It was as I had feared, the Commander was returning.

I raised my cap respectfully, and then I heard the clatter of hooves mingle and stop as the trap was pulled up. The Commander was a red-faced man, clean-shaven, of course. He glowered at my rod. I endeavoured to keep my right side turned from him lest he should see the "tell-tale tail". I wished the ground would open and engulf me but at that moment Providence took a hand. There came again the sound of trotting hooves and just as the Commander was about to cast aside his carriage rug and descend upon me, no doubt with the object of searching my small person, there swept round the corner my Grandfather, likewise in his trap, with Dickon beside him. Under the confusion of the meeting I bolted through the hedge and ran all the way home.

Now, by hook or crook, I had made up my mind to have that fish "set up". As bad luck would have it my grandmother met me in the drive and I foolishly showed her my trout, telling her I was going to have it stuffed.

She said nothing, probably because she knew I was a determined young devil, but when my grandfather returned, having calmed the the Commander, she told him I was going to have my big trout "stuffed".

"That trout will be eaten here!" he thundered, and, as I was afraid of my grandfather, I said no word. Next day I was due to leave for home and without saying anything to anyone I raided the larder, procured my trout and wrapped it up in paper, posting it off from the post office e'er I left for the train.

1886

In the queer way grown-ups have, the trout was forgotten in the business of seeing me off to the station and on the way thither I confided in Dickon what I had done, and he gave his unqualified approval. That is why that three-and-a-half pound brook trout still surveys me as I write these lines, superbly mounted in an ebony framed case, a pleasant reminder of boyhood's triumphant victory over elders and betters, and an aldermanic fish.

"B.B.",
Fisherman's Folly, 1924.

EXACT IMITATION

"It is very neceſſary to take notice as you walk by the river, of the particular ſort of Fly that the trouts leap at, then catching one of them, and having a bag of materials for that purpoſe, try how far art can imitate nature, and tho' you miſs at first, yet by diligent obſervation and experience, you may ſoon arrive at perfection, and take a particular pleaſure in Fly-making."

Thus spake Charles Bowlker of Ludlow, who died in the Year of Grace 1779. They are brave words, and they go to the root of the whole matter. We will never arrive at perfection—no one will—and we may never take a particular pleasure in Fly-making, but we miss a great deal if fishing for us be no more than the casting of a meaningless amalgam of fur, silk and feather over a rising trout.

All else has changed: Bowlker's rod, reel, line, and horse-hair cast belong to the dark ages, but his fundamental principle, that we must deceive the trout with a representation of its natural food, is as true to-day as when he enunciated it 160 years ago.

It is odd that our gentle art should engender heated discussion, recrimination, hatred and spiteful speech, but we may remember that even Christians hate one another for the love of God, and that men have gone to the stake for their beliefs. So judge them by their writings, the purist would pile the faggots high o'er the chuck and chancist, and the wet-fly bigot would not stop short at the semi-submersion of the dry-fly fanatic.

Among the fishermen one meets there are two distinct trends of thought—one, that the exact imitation of the natural fly is necessary for success: the other, that any attempt at imitation must be so imperfect, that it does not matter much what one fishes with, if the size, shape and colour be not too outrageous. For my own part, I think that the latter view is wrong, though on many occasions it has its justification. Those who hold it, and fish and catch fish with one favourite fly throughout the season, are as a rule dexterous fishermen, and the fly they fish with is a generalized imitation of a fly which is often on the water. Often this fly is a Red Spinner, a Tup's Indispensable, or a Sedge. Trout are fond of Spinners, and they take them even during a hatch of duns in the day, as if they remembered their agreeable flavour from the meal of the early morning or of the previous evening. Tup's Indispensable represents a light coloured Spinner, a light Olive, a Pale Watery dun, and if wet, a light bodied nymph. There are 360 varieties of Sedge, and there cannot be many hours of the day when one is not on the water. Others, who fish with a fancy fly, argue, and argue with some justice, that the contents of a trout's stomach generally are such a mixed bag that the trout will take anything with some semblance of an insect, and they quote with approval Marryat's classic answer that it was the "Driver" and not the fly which was catching fish.

It is those who fish on difficult rivers, where the trout are educated and hard fished, who feel that success depends on something more than on accurate casting. Sometimes, even on these rivers, trout will take anything, but time and again they will have nothing but a close imitation of the fly. Feather and silk can never reproduce the beauty and delicacy of nature, but they can furnish a passable deception to the short-sighted vision of the trout.

At the very outset of my dry-fly fishing I was convinced once and for all that there are occasions when the fly can be imitated perfectly —from the trout's point of view—and that they refuse anything but the perfect imitation. It was what scientists call a controlled experiment of such an unequivocal kind that it left no room for doubt. Until 1896, I had never fished with anything but the wet fly, nor on any rivers except the Tweed and its tributaries, but before going to Scotland that summer I had been shewn the use of the dry fly on the Anton. One day in August I was fishing with the usual cast of wet flies when I came to a pool where the trout were rising steadily. I rose no fish until it occurred to me to take off all the flies except the tail fly and to fish it dry. Straightway, in five successive casts, I caught five good fish. As I removed the fly from the last trout which I had caught, I saw that the gut was frayed at the neck, so I threw it away and took out another attached to a new piece of gut—I had no eyed flies in those days. The fly was an Olive, tied with a seagull's wing, ginger hackle and green wool body, and I had none of quite the same pattern, though several near it. To my surprise, I did not catch nor even rise a fish with it. I tried every fly in my book, but caught no more, though the rise went on as gaily until I left the river in despair 2 hours later.

I may say that I hastened to the local tackle-maker to lay in a large stock of this pattern, as I did not tie my flies then, but I never met with the same success with it as on the first day. I think that the explanation is that the Blue-Winged Olive, which hatches out so freely on the Tweed in August, is a difficult fly to imitate. The body changes in colour from olive to orange, and the wings vary so much in shade, that for some hours or days one pattern is most killing, and then loses its virtue, and I have noticed that sometimes it seems the more attractive when it is rather the worse for wear, as it was on this occasion.

Since this day, especially when there has been a strong hatch of one particular kind of dun, I have so often found the fish taking one fly and one fly only, and have so often with my imperfect imitation of that fly been able to catch them, that I am convinced that the more closely we adhere to Bowlker's principles the more we enhance our pleasure and our success.

Journal of the Flyfishers' Club, 1930.

FLY FISHING IN A FLOOD

On the Tweed last summer the long drought ended with July, and in the Peeblesshire hills rain fell every day in August. I do not know if the Tweed be an exception or not, but our best fishing in the summer months is often to be had at the height of a flood. When the spate is at its highest, and the water is so thick that one cannot see beneath the surface, there is good sport with the dry fly. I used to think that this might be explained by the fact that the river below Peebles is

1924

often so much discoloured by the effluent from the mills that the trout had acquired the habit of rising under these conditions, but this year I fished for the most part above any source of pollution, and I found that the trout fed readily when the water was thick from undissolved mud.

One knows the ominous silence that comes to a river in flood. The cheerful sound of the rippling stream is lost and gives place to the noiselessness of smooth swift-gliding water. This is the time when the sagacious local angler comes forth with worm and salmon roe, and makes baskets in the quiet eddies and backwaters, but it is also the time when in certain pools on the Tweed fish can be caught with the dry fly. How they see the fly I do not know, but they do see it, and very few flies go down untaken. Accurate casting is necessary, as the trout will not move far from their stations, and the surprising thing is that they still show discrimination and will not rise at anything except a passable imitation of the natural insect. Their seeing the fly is independent of any condition of light, as they rise as well on a dull, rainy day as in bright sunshine.

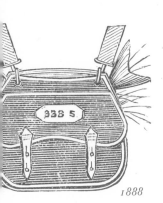

1888

I had a good instance of this kind of fishing last summer in early August. The Tweed at Dawyck was in yellow flood on a mild cloudy day with heavy showers. Three of us went out, two to fish with worm, and I to wait until I saw something rise, as I am resolved to fish with worms no more. The nervous system of the worm may not be very sensitive, but mine has become so since I was a boy. I watched my friends fish down-stream and catch a few trout, until we came to the pool below the Crown Bridge. It is about 200 yards long, with a good stream on the north and slack water on the south bank, and in this slack water, close to the side, trout were rising at the few Willow Fly which were drifting down. There were not many of them, but every one was taken. I had no imitation of the fly, and I fished with a small Red Spinner. I caught seven good trout while the rise lasted, but I rose and ran many more, and I am sure that, if the trout had been rising at a fly which I could have imitated, I should have been much more successful. I was surprised at the number of short rises and at the number of fish which were so lightly hooked that they escaped, as when fishing under similar conditions in the past I had always found that feeding fish rose without hesitation and were firmly hooked. During all other spates I had fished below Peebles, and had always found a hatch of Olives, a fairly easy fly to imitate, but my Red Spinner was no imitation of the Willow Fly on which the fish were feeding. It says a good deal for the vision of the trout that they were able to see so clearly in such an opaque medium, and a great deal for their intelligence that they made so few mistakes.

Journal of the Flyfishers' Club, 1930.

IRON BLUE

If I was to be limited to one fly for the rest of my life I would scrap all the others and stick to the iron-blue quill. It is not merely a Test fly, for I have caught a 2-pound trout with it in a little Scottish burn, casting it dry on chance up-stream into a likely place. There used to be a superstition that the iron-blue was a bad-weather fly and only useful in a thunderstorm, but my experience is that it is the best of them all on glass-smooth water in bright sunshine. In fact, it is often the only fly they will take in such conditions, and it is certainly the only thing they will look at when they are smutting. If you pick up a smut and examine it closely you will see that it has the identical metallic blue-black colour of the iron-blue. It is quite probable that the trout look on them as the smaller and larger edition of the same fly. This is borne out by experience. Everyone knows the "fisherman's curse", which in spite of its diminutive size monopolizes the whole attention of the fish when it is coming down. They treat everything else with silent contempt, and suck down the tiny smuts greedily. The iron-blue is the only fly of regulation pattern which they will take in these circumstances.

The most fast and furious week-end I ever had was on the late Col. Grove-Hills's water on the Kennet at Ramsbury at Whitsuntide in 1921. We arrived there at luncheon-time on the Saturday, and were on the water about 3. From that moment till I took down my rod on the Monday night there was a steady rise of fly, which never stopped even for half an hour. It was more than steady, it was brilliant. It was a "May-fly" rise of duns. There were gingers and olives and pale-waterys, floating down in crowds. But the fish were taking no notice of them. They were picking out the iron-blues every time. During the whole of those 3 days I never changed my fly once till the sedges and blue-winged olives came on in the evening. It is a commonplace to see the iron-blues on the water in dark blowy weather, but on this occasion the heat was almost tropical—we were burnt as black as coals by the Monday—and there was not a breath of wind, and yet they wanted nothing but the iron-blue for breakfast and luncheon and dinner, and often for supper too.

This does not apply merely to the Kennet or the Test or the Bourne, but to trout-water anywhere. The big Black Forest trout would have the dark-blue dun or nothing. If your fish is a big one, it does not matter whether he is a Rooshian or a Prooshian or a Frenchman or an Englishman; he would rather have the iron-blue at any time in any weather. I do not mean that you cannot catch them with others, but if you have to stick to one, or pin your faith to one for the rest of your life, then stock your box with iron-blues.

H. Plunkett Greene,
Where the Bright Waters Meet, 1924.

THE BOTTLEBRUSH FLY

Of the five or six superlatively good trout fishermen whom I know well only one is not a fly-dresser, and that one knows exactly what he wants when he gets his flies. I suspect him of having at any rate passed his apprenticeship in the art in earlier days. Most of us, however, who cannot tie flies are not quite sure what we want, and in consequence we get a great many things that we do not want. I possess an incredible number of abominable productions which call themselves flies, purchased at various times in foolish faith that they might come in handy. This is bad enough, but it is much worse that one or other of these monstrosities will sometimes in the most insolent manner prove itself capable of catching fish when other more respectable patterns have wholly failed.

One of the most scandalous instances of this occurred on the Penydwddwr some years ago. It was at the end of April, and we had been having a grievous time owing to the wintry weather and lack of fly. Our united catches had for some days barely found us in breakfast, and we had got into the habit of going out each morning

Fly minnows (1924).

K

without any hope of better things. One morning I started thus handicapped (and more, for I was afflicted with a chill as well), and flogged aimlessly down-stream with the usual assortment of flies and the usual lack of result. Then something induced me to put on the Bottle-brush. I have always thought of it as the Bottle-brush because it has no other name and deserves none—had rather; it is now no more. This creature was two sizes larger than anything else in my book and was an unpleasing brown thing with an inordinate quantity of stiff stark hackle and no wings. It was exactly like a bottle-brush in shape. Supposed to be a wet-fly it would have needed a small paternoster lead to make it sink. I never met with a pattern I disliked more on sight. Well, I dragged this thing about the river in a half-hearted way, and presently a trout hurled himself upon it. I basketed him, and soon afterwards another, and more followed until I had amassed sixteen of excellent size. Then the disintegration of the bottle-brush was complete—it was badly tied as well as horrible in appearance—and thereafter no more could be done. But I had the best basket for quality, that I ever achieved in that small river. The sixteen compared favourably with the threes and fives that the other anglers produced at tea time. And it was all due to a fly which I should never have dreamed of putting on had I not been dispirited and unwell.

H. T. Sheringham,
Trout Fishing Memories and Morals, 1920.

1907

LOCH FISHING

It is now admitted that to describe the loch as the "Duffer's Paradise" is an abuse of terms. Lakes differ as much as rivers, and though there are lochs in which no great skill is required to kill fair baskets, there

h flies (1898).

are others which make as great a demand upon the intelligent use of skill as any river. Our angling fathers used to consider a breeze essential to sport on lakes; now our ideas are different, and, by the use of fine tackle and improved gear, there is no sort of condition under which trout and sea trout may not be killed with the fly in lakes. Into the history of this change, it is unnecessary here to enter.

The principle on which the modern loch fisher proceeds is, that loch trout worth catching must be treated with precisely the same respect as is shown by the river fisher for his quarry. Regard must be had for the cunning, the moods and habits of the fish, and the loch must be treated as a large still pool in a river. It is a mistake to suppose that preserved or almost virgin waters holding large trout can be fished successfully by the "duffer" or by the man of skill who declines to study their peculiarities, and employs the same methods, uses the same flies, and generally "fishes in the same way" in all sorts of lochs, in all states of water, wind and weather, and at all seasons of the angling year, times of the day, and moods of the fish. The real secret of success in loch fishing, apart from mere manual skill, lies in an *intelligent study of the conditions*, in leaving no method untried, and "in using the head" freely and fully. Unless you are an opportunist and cultivate the faculty of observation and deduction you will miss half the charm of loch fishing, and your successes will be limited to "good days".

In the matter of the proper rod or rods for loch fishing for trout, sea trout, and salmon, one is necessarily forced to take refuge in a generalization, and within certain limits the proper rod varies with the angler, for all anglers do not possess the same strength and the same temperament. As I have said elsewhere, "go to a good rod maker who also is an experienced angler, trust him, and do not grudge the initial expense". Let him choose the rod best suited to your personal peculiarities. Any rod with which you cannot cast continuously for a day is too heavy for loch fishing. Use is not everything in a rod but it counts for much, and it is better not to be under any necessity to change your rod when you pass from brown trout to sea trout fishing. For this reason a first-class split-cane rod of from 11 to 11½-foot, will be found to exactly fulfil all the requirements of a rod suitable to every sort of fly-fishing from a boat in lochs. For an angler who confines himself to trout fishing, or who prefers like the writer to use one rod for both brown and sea trout, there cannot possibly be a better rod, and there is certainly no

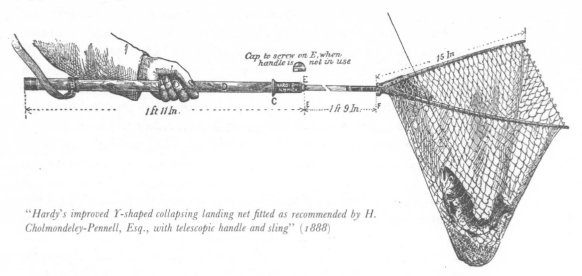

"Hardy's improved Y-shaped collapsing landing net fitted as recommended by H. Cholmondeley-Pennell, Esq., with telescopic handle and sling" (1888)

cheaper rod of the same quality, than the cane-built rods of Messrs. Hardy Brothers. For fishing in lochs I never use any other rods, and I have never fished with any rods which gave me the same satisfaction, the same sense of security (a great gain), and the same pleasure as an 11-foot one of this class which I possess. In 12 days with one of these rods in a weedy loch holding good trout I killed ninety-three fish running from 1½ pounds to 2¾ pounds and landed in 6 days almost every fish that rose. The conditions were of the most varied kinds, from dead calm and hot sun to a gale of wind and rain.

The reel is important and it should be one of the quick winding ones, *i.e.*, much contracted and with regulating check, called the Hardy's "Perfect", for this reason. Fish so often on being struck run towards the boat that you must wind very quickly. Besides, in general use a reel of this sort saves a great deal of labour in winding up, as with the number of turns you can do the same work—a great saving certainly.

As to tackle for loch fishing, the finer you fish, the better will be your sport; though here again, as in the matter of rods and "the stiffness" of your reel, a great deal depends upon the temperament of the angler. In any case every angler should endeavour to fish as fine as he dare, and as the varying conditions compel him to fish. Flies should vary in size and pattern with the lake and with the day. It is quite unnecessary to use large flies in any lake either for brown trout, sea trout, or salmon, and, as a general rule, flies dressed on three sizes of hook (Nos. 8 and 9 Limerick and 4 sneck bends) will

satisfy all the conditions. Flies imitating surface flies should be used as top droppers, while those imitating subaqueous insects should be used as tail and middle flies.

The angler should have a very large landing net and the best known to the writer is Hardy's "Collapsing" net, the grilse or salmon size. The shaft should be long and strong and the angler should land his own fish. The reel and line must balance the rod.

As a rule loch trout must not be struck too quickly. The secret of success is to wait until the fish is "felt", though every rise must be treated on its merits. Large loch trout are generally as "slow" takers as sea trout, and this is particularly true of good fish rising in a calm or a very light breeze. To determine to strike late generally results in the angler schooling himself to exercise the necessary restraint, which prevents too quick or too hard striking—faults to which the loch fisher is peculiarly liable. Sea trout cannot be struck too late, and the angler is always the most successful who determines *not to strike at all*. He rarely "misses" large fish and he is ready for all sorts of fish, from a ½ pound "brownie" to a 6 or 7 pound sea trout. In playing large loch and sea trout, as well as salmon, the great aim of the angler must be to keep the fish under control and parallel with the boat. In open water it is very easy to follow a fish and to "play" him with the boat, but in lochs with reed beds delicate coaxing is often necessary to persuade the fish into the open, when all his attempts to get away from the boat may be met by judiciously heading him off. In landing a good fish the stock of the net should be

The Loch Ordie Flies which you have tied for me are beautifully made and have given every satisfaction. I have tried them on bad days with good results. For general use, the smaller fly is sufficient for the purpose, but in very rough weather or late at night, the big fly is effective, and people need not be afraid to use it. I have only used it on large Highland lochs, but I feel sure it would be equally effective on big rivers. So far, I have found it quite 50 per cent better than the ordinary wet fly in all weathers and in all lights, but especially towards dark.

The best way to use it is to dope the fly and cast a fairly long line left or right from a drifting boat. Let the fly settle, then gently raise the point of the rod, when the wind will blow the fly across the water. Keep the rod still a moment, then raise it slightly towards you, and repeat the process, etc. The fish chase the fly when moving, and invariably take it when it is still and floating. They always rise high, and are rather apt to try to drown it, and this means they must take it when the line is slack. This is of no moment, as it is fatal to strike too quick. If there is too much slack, it is easy to draw in a little of the line.

The fly is an adaptation of an American Salmon Fly, and is the result of some study of its effect on trout.

The Duke of Atholl,
quoted in Hardy Brothers Catalogue, *1937.*

brought under the elbow and lie along the arm. This gives leverage in lifting. The strain at the last moment should be even and steady. The boat should be suffered to come slowly back on the fish, and the net allowed to glide under him.

Fly-fishing for salmon in lakes does not call for separate treatment. In most lochs frequented by salmon the fish may be taken with the same flies, and landed on the same "gear" as sea trout. The same rod and reel may, on a pinch, be used for all three fish, salmon, sea trout, and brown trout, and it is for this reason that the writer recommends all loch anglers to use Hardy's built cane rods of from 11 to 11½ feet.

Hamish Stuart,
Hardy Brothers Catalogue, 1911.

BLOW-LINE FISHING
FOR TROUT

The dry-fly fisherman who "stalks" trout in such rivers as the Test, the Itchen, the Darenth, or the Kentish Stour, views with undisguised horror the use of natural baits for trout. Your angler who "swears by" feather, fur, and silk, is ungenerous if he views with contempt the operations of him who fills his basket by the skilful manipulation of the natural fly, minnow, or the humble worm.

Far be it from us to suggest that rivers such as those which we have mentioned, should be fished otherwise than with the artificial presentment of the delicate dun or the dainty quill-gnat, that for the time is on the water. We are not of those who would ruthlessly deplete, with minnow or with worm, the chalk streams of the south of England. In countries such as Ireland, however, where the water that is available to the angler can be computed by scores of square miles, the use of natural baits is as sportsmanlike and as honest as it is legitimate; and we are content to treat with indifference the sneers of those who decry any form of fishing other than the one they themselves prefer to pursue. As the natural drake jauntily dances over the rippling surface of an Irish lough, and the expectant angler eagerly awaits the appearance of the tell-tale rings that announce a rise; as the trout sucks down the delicious tit-bit, and upon finding himself hooked, with a mighty dash and a glorious plunge rushes out the gossamer line to the delightful music of the reel; as the fish is carefully played and handled to the net, and the lid of the basket agreeably creaks in welcome to the scaly captive, we are at peace with all men, even the "dry-flyer".

Now, let us suppose that our angler is to angle in Ireland, and that he has decided to give natural bait a trial. Should he arrive in the Emerald Isle when the "drakes" are hatching out, his basket should frequently be filled with heavy fish; for, beyond all doubt, the yellow drake and the grey drake are the most deadly natural baits for trout. In fact, when they are on the water, the fish will seldom take any other; and those artful trout which, at ordinary times, refuse natural or other baits—no matter how wily be the angler, or how adroit his methods—fall to the superior attractions of these large and luscious lures. Yellow drakes, especially, seem to be irresistible. It is necessary that an ample supply of "drakes" should be available to the angler, and this is assured by the employment of local lads. A few shillings judiciously expended in the right direction will have the desired result. Take care that your flies are fresh: those caught in the early morn of the day on which they are to be used are by far the best.

"Drakes", "daddy long legs", "stone-flies", and "blue-bottles", are all most successfully fished by means of the "blow-line". The outfit for the "blow-line" consists of a very light stiffish rod, about 16 feet long; from 80 to 100 yards of the finest gossamer pure silk line; a winch, the check of which runs very smoothly; a fine gut cast, 3 yards long, and a supply of specially made hooks. All being in readiness, our boatman rows us out to a favourite "drift" on the lough where we are about to fish, and then a couple of "drakes" are very carefully placed upon the hook—handle your lure as though you loved it—some yards of line are drawn from the winch, the rod is held in an upright position, and, the wind being at our back, wafts the bait straight out in front of us some 6 yards. As soon as the light line is fairly extended, the top of the rod is lowered, and the

1888

"drake" alights on the surface of the lough as lightly as thistle-down. Not long is it allowed to dance upon the wavelets. There is the unmistakable rise of a trout, and the fly disappears; very gently is the line tightened—it is suicidal and quite unnecessary to *strike* a trout when fishing with extremely delicate tackle; the angler need merely tighten on the fish:—there is a rush, a plunge, and soon we are busy playing a grand specimen of the Irish lake trout.

When the "drake" season is not on, other flies must be used in their stead. Other insects that frequent the lough may be manipulated after the same manner. We have had good sport in August with the "daddy". In fact, fishing with the "daddy" is a second edition of the "drake" fishing, not so fast and furious perhaps, but still often affording great sport. Should all else fail, we, with some confidence, fall back upon the natural minnow, and if light spinning tackle be used in conjunction with delicate flights, it is seldom that the minnow does not score, especially during the months of September and October, when the 5-, 6-, and 7-pounders are on the look-out for such tempting meaty morsels.

Hardy Brothers Catalogue, 1907.

THAMES TROUTING

Of all Thames fish the trout is gamest, and is prized most by Thames anglers. Small wonder that this is so, for trout of 10 pounds weight and upwards have been taken, while 7-, 8-, and 9-pounders are comparatively common. If the angler resides in the neighbourhood of London he will find grand fish close at hand, while an hour's journey from the metropolis will enable him to run his bait over some of the largest trout to be found anywhere in the Thames. To fish from the magnificent weirs controlled by the Thames Conservancy a permit is necessary, which costs but 10 shillings per annum; and, as the trout season lasts from 1st April to 10th September, inclusive, no one need grumble at this small outlay.

Thames trouters chiefly fish with the spinning or live bait, using bleak, minnows, gudgeon, or small dace, and relinquishing the fly as almost useless for the larger fish. The rod is by far the most important part of the outfit. A Thames trout rod should be carefully constructed of the best possible materials, it has to "give" to heavy, quick travelling, plunging fish; it must be supple enough to allow the use of fine tackle, yet with plenty of power to stand the strain; not too heavy, though with sufficient weight and substance to enable the angler to master fish in very heavy water. The rings should be upright, hard, and of good-size, as a freely-running line is indispensable. The "Wheeley 'Thames' Trout Rods", are peculiarly suitable for the work, and are the results of much careful study and patient observation. We need only say that sportsmen who have used them report them far in advance of anything hitherto made; and perfect for this or any kind of light spinning for trout, &c. The winch should be at least 4-inch, a centre-pin with check; and we advise the angler to use at least 150 yards of line, which should be a fine plait, soft-dressed, some prefer an undressed line, but if so it should be greased, as it is important, especially in live-baiting, that the line should not bury itself too deeply in the water. A 2-yard cast is generally of sufficient length, though one of 3 yards may sometimes be advantageous in clear water, or when fishing the shallows. We prefer a fixed liphook, and not less than three triangles for spinning, but two is better for live-baiting. At least two swivels should be used on the spinning trace, and one when live-baiting in a weir. For open water live-baiting, except where the stream is very swift, a swivel is not necessary. Always avoid, as much as possible, the use of anything that will make a show in the water.

Spinning is conducted in the ordinary fashion, and we cannot recommend any method but that of throwing direct from the winch, as most places suitable for the capture of Thames trout are full of obstructions at foot, and in many situations the foothold itself is of a very limited nature, being sometimes the cross beam at a weir head, and here our new patent "Silex" reel is the proper thing. The leads on the trace must, of course, be adjusted with regard to state of water, locality, &c. As a rule, more fish are killed by live-baiting than by spinning; as the live-bait can be worked so quietly and into such difficult places. A tapered float of plain cork is used when live-baiting; the line runs through it and the float is adjusted to any required depth by means of a peg. The float is not employed to indicate a run, as in pike fishing, but simply to show the position of the bait, and to keep it at a certain depth. The live-bait can be worked behind boulders, stumps, &c., in places where the spinner cannot possibly fish, this accounts, to a great extent, for the more frequent practice of live-baiting during recent years. A deep landing net, with a strong and large hoop, is preferable to a gaff, for the fish are well worthy of preservation, and as a trophy for an angler's hall or smoking room, we know of nothing to beat a well set up Thames trout. The trace should be of the very best undrawn gut; the thickness and colour depend greatly on the state of the water.

It may safely be stated that many of the fish caught are "known" fish, *i.e.*, fish whose feeding times and places have been carefully studied. Many Thames trout feed with wonderful regularity within a radius of a few yards, and almost at the same times during each day. This is well known to experienced Thames trouters; and the watching of the fish becomes most fascinating, while it needs but little imagination to realize what capital sport an 8- or 10- pound fish can afford in a vast weir, the depth of which may be 30 feet under or near the main runs of water. For really exciting play we advise the angler to fish the weirs, as open stream fishing is comparatively tame work.

Hardy Brothers Catalogue, 1907.

SPINNING FOR TROUT, ETC.

The use of the Natural Minnow on such streams as are devoted to the dry fly is a thing strictly forbidden. We have, however, known it permitted where it was desirable to reduce the number of big trout, who, having passed the age of rising to a fly, had become cannibalistic, so that their removal was a thing to be desired. Generally speaking, however, spinning the minnow is considered quite sportsmanlike, and although it must be admitted that it takes a fairly heavy toll of the best trout, yet it does a certain amount of good by removing old fish, who, as we have already remarked, rarely take anything but their smaller brethren.

There are two classes of spinners. In the first place, there is the man who occasionally spins with his fly rod; in the second, there is the man who believes in being perfectly equipped for the work, and who is content to go out with his spinning rod only. In this short article we will refer only to the occasional spinner and his methods, treating the second form in the following article.

A word first as to the rod. The angler who *occasionally* indulges in spinning and is provided with one of our 10½- or 11-foot steel centre fly rods may make this do, at the same time it is not the correct thing. True he may have a shorter top which makes it more suitable, but this only improves an unsuitable rod, and is far short in action and efficiency to a properly constructed spinning rod. In trout as well as in salmon fishing, we prefer to take out two rods. Being intended for different purposes they are quite distinct in their action, and thus each is more perfectly adapted for its particular purpose. A rod which has to combine the perfect properties of a spinning and a fly rod is an impossibility; and although we frequently make them to order, as, for instance, a powerful fly rod to be used at times with a minnow; the result must always be an imperfect rod for either purpose. Where, however, one fishes without an attendant, the second rod must be dispensed with, and the best use made of the fly rod.

Cautiously approaching the stream, so as to keep out of sight as much as possible, our angler draws as much line off the reel as the length of his rod, then taking the bait in his left hand, and bending by pressure the top of the rod about 2 feet towards him, with a motion of his right arm, he swings the bait as far as he can across the top of the stream. He must now work the bait by a rapid motion across and then straight up the side of the stream, until within a few feet of where he stands. When a fish is seen to take the bait he should pause until it turns before striking.

Streams are the only places he need attack, every part of which should be carefully covered. In the roughest water at the very throat of the stream he will often find the largest trout. The trace should be about $1\frac{1}{2}$ yards long, and sufficient swivels to spin the bait freely should be carried.

Hardy's "Ariel" tackle, the "Wee Minnow" Spinner, Wobblers and Spinning Tackles are all good for Natural Minnow, but our angler is insufficiently equipped, however, if he does not also carry a few small Phantoms, Devons, &c., which he may use in flooded water, or on occasions where it is impossible to get a supply of Natural Minnows.

1898

The greatest advance which has so far been made in reels for bait casting is seen in the No. 2 "Silex" model.

Everyone who is fond of spinning for trout *must* have one of these reels. They are also the best combined fly and spinning reel in existence. For float-fishing they are superb. In fact for any kind of fishing, and for all-round work, no other reel approaches them.

The art of casting a minnow up-stream in clear water fishing is not generally known or practised, and although somewhat difficult to attain, no one need despair of a certain amount of success from the first. It is better, when possible, to wade, so as to get behind the fish. This method may also be practised in fishing from the bank by casting obliquely up and across stream. The splash caused by a minnow falling into the water will not scare trout, but the sight of the angler, clumsy wading or the movement of the rod, will at once effect this. Therefore, keep the rod's point down, and cast as near as you can in a line parallel to the water. Do not cast directly into the centre of the stream, but rather to the side of it. Reeling in must be done quickly, otherwise you will be unable to strike effectively. An excellent position for this work is where the bank is high, and forms a background.

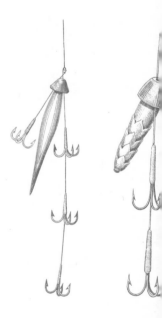

Mounts for dead baits (1886)

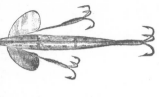

Hardy's Excelsior spinner (1888)

Trout will often follow and seize a minnow even when lifting for a fresh cast. A very fine well-dressed line is a *sine qua non*.

A porter-coloured water is best for spinning for trout, and under these conditions the work is comparatively easy, as the general method is to cast down and across, and allow the minnow to re-cross the current and then travel up the side. A trace of $1\frac{1}{4}$ yards to $1\frac{1}{2}$ yards is quite long enough. If using a bait without lead in the body, a lead is necessary on the trace. If a small anti-kink lead be used, it prevents twisting of the fine line.

Hardy Brothers Catalogue, 1894.

SPINNING FOR TROUT AND SEA TROUT

Spinning for trout, etc. with a light and correctly balanced outfit is as attractive and sporting a method of angling as dry-fly fishing itself and demands quite as much, if not more, skill and we recommend a choice from the following outfits:

Rod: The 'Hardy-Wanless' 4-lb.
Reels: No. 1 or 2 'Altex'.
Lines: 'Monofilament' to 7 lbs.
Anti-kinker: Non corrodible, ball-bearing swivel.

The usual method is to cast square across, or slightly downstream, and wind in fairly quickly, but we personally find that to vary the angle of the cast from straight upstream to square across, and straight downstream is much more successful . . .

We have seen as far as four to five fish chasing the bait at one time, and eventually one would take it, and when a fish takes a bait spinning in this manner, he is generally well hooked. We advise varying the speed of winding in the bait. We find, when possible to obtain them, that freshly killed baits are the best.

Do not imagine because you are using a very light rod and fine line that you cannot handle fairly large fish. We have with it on odd occasions killed fish up to 10 lbs, and are quite sure that larger could be successfully handled. The combination is so perfect and the action of the rod so designed, that the fine line and trace, will stand the strain when the rod is nearly doubled. We do, however, advise a frequent examination of the end of the line, and the breaking off of all not up to strength. There is an excessive amount of wear and strain on a fine line with this style of fishing.

Hardy Brothers Catalogue, 1960.

THE COLLAGH

It was late one evening, as we were starting out to fish "the flat", that Dick remarked, "We must have a night with the collagh soon."

I wonder how many fishermen would have known what he meant, for I believe that even now night fishing of this kind is a form of sport confined to certain localities in Ireland and Wales. I certainly knew nothing of it then, and said so, whereupon Dick explained.

The collagh, pronounced "colley", which is Irish for the stone-loach, is well known as an excellent spinning bait for salmon. Being soft and succulent, it is also a favourite food of the trout. But owing to this fish's protective colouring and self-effacing habits amongst the stones of the river bed, the trout must be put to considerable trouble in finding and capturing them. It may be that this is the reason why when presented under entirely unnatural conditions in the dark, and on the surface, it sometimes proves irresistible, particularly to large fish. . . . The outfit is extremely simple, a fairly long stiffish rod—a yard or so of medium-lake gut, and at its end a No. 1 or 2 salmon hook with a small liphook whipped on just above it, and no lead. That is all. No! two things I have forgotten, a dozen small collaghs or loaches, less than the size of your little finger. These, by the way, should be kept alive in a wooden box leaded to make it sink and pierced with holes, such a box in fact as is used for sand-eels by sea fishermen, the box being sunk in a suitable spot in the river and attached by a chain or strong cord to a post on the bank. Note that for this type of fishing the collagh must not spin, and therefore when mounted it must be perfectly straight without kink or bend.

The other essential now-a-days is a good torch.

In Wales, I believe, a big "lob-worm" or "blue-head" is used, and I have sometimes wondered whether the "lob" in lobworm was not originally derived from this method of fishing. The procedure is as simple as the tackle. Choose a deep smooth pool, one of those places which is useless by day except in a wind, and take your bearings carefully, so that you will not step into it in the dark. Then standing as near the edge as possible, and with as much slack line in your left hand as you can manage to get out with the light bait, swing or lob out your collagh as far as you can and draw it steadily along the surface towards you. So long as it does not spin, it does not matter if it makes a wake, in fact this seems to be what attracts, and if there is a big trout on the move, ten to one he will take it with a rush.

It is astonishing what large objects trout will attack, particularly at night. Once in Yorkshire I caught a perfectly formed and full-grown trout not as long as my little finger on a $1\frac{1}{2}$-inch devon. On another occasion, when fishing the Lambourne late, with a sedge, I caught a trout of nearly 2 pounds which on being landed disgorged a large shrew-mouse.

The biggest trout I ever saw landed on the collagh at night was caught by Dick. Three of us were camping out one August above a familiar bridge on a river in County Cork. In the far corner is a fairly deep hole, and the minute the collagh landed in it there was a splash and a mighty pull. The trout weighed just under $2\frac{1}{2}$ pounds, a very big fish for our rivers.

*   *   *

In a later book Luard described how he subsequently tried out the collagh on a lake at night. The occasion comes when Luard and his fishing companion, X—, are challenged by two fellow guests at an Irish fishing hotel to bet on the outcome of the next day's fishing. Luard accepts, on condition that the day's fishing should last until midnight. Later and privately, he explains his scheme to X— . . .

"A collagh at night!" exclaimed X—— "I don't know what you mean."

Then I explained how in rivers, by dragging a collagh or minnow without spin over the surface of the deep still pools at night, really big trout might not infrequently be induced to rush from their lairs and be caught. X—— not being Welsh or Irish and so never having come across this strange form of fishing looked his astonishment. "Of course," I added, "it is a very slender chance and to tell the truth, I have only once tried it on a lake and then not seriously or for long, but on that occasion I did hook several trout, though I landed none, and my boatman was as astonished as you seem to be."

An angling match on Loch Leven, 1862 (Mary Evans Picture Library)

"The essential thing is an absolutely calm night and the darker the better. Now the weather is obviously improving and if we are lucky, tomorrow night may be what we need. So before I go to bed I intend to tie some fairly large bait-hooks for the purpose. Then there is the question of minnows. Collaghs are probably not easily obtainable, but I saw some very large minnows yesterday near the boat-house, and I can't see why they should not do as well. It may be a complete failure but anyway it will be an interesting experiment."

"Well, I'm game for anything," said X——, with a grin, "especially if it helps us to down those two blighters," and off he went to bed.

It did not take me long to tie four suitable hooks with small lip-hooks at their heads onto stout lake-gut, and then I too went to bed.

Next morning on coming down to breakfast which we had ordered for 8 o'clock, I saw at once that the breeze had shifted from the west and that the day promised to be fair. Our rivals were not yet stirring. In fact as I passed his door on my way down, I heard the large man snoring like a grampus. We had the start of them anyway. All would now depend on the trout and luck.

By 8.30 we were off in my car and Denny our boatman, whom I had warned to be early as it was our last day, was ready waiting for us.

Greetings over—"We shall want a lot of big minnows today," I said to him and handed him the muslin net which I usually carry with me. Three dozen were soon caught and placed in two jam jars I had borrowed for the purpose. Then having put up our rods, we set off. . . .

As yet there was no sign of our adversaries. We put out a couple of trolls, and as we rowed steadily along, I told Denny of the bet and asked him whether if the night was suitable he was prepared to stay out really late.

He looked up at the sky—"It should be a fine night anyway," he said. Then he grinned all over his face—"Sure sorr—we'll bate them two —— all to blazes," and he spat over the side. Evidently they had not made a good impression.

Then I explained my plan for trying the minnow at night. It seemed he had heard of the method but had never tried it, and he was all eagerness to do so.

After a short pause, "It will be in the deeps you'll be trying it," he remarked with a query in his voice. "Its there the big ones do lie." "Yes, that's right," I said, "It's the western end will be the best," he went on, "and there's other places too I know of."

At that moment there was a screech from the reel of one of the trolls and X—— seized the rod. Far back a very respectable trout jumped in the air and was gone.

"Bad cess to the blagiard," muttered Denny, "he'd av weighed a pound and a half anyway."

When we had nearly reached the point about the middle of the lough where we intended to begin fly-fishing—the other troll had a pull. This time all went well and our first trout of the day, weighing 1 lb. 10 ozs., was soon in the boat.

The breeze was fitful, and the sun bright, but now and then as one of the numerous white clouds passed over its face the water was pleasantly ruffled.

Just as we were beginning I looked back across the shining expanse of the lake and noticed some movement round the distant boat-house. Our adversaries had arrived.

The trout rose fairly well at intervals but at the end of two hours we had only caught five average fish. What the others had done we had no idea. About lunch time however they passed within hail and we learned that they had four, so we had a lead of one. After lunch the breeze began to die away, and except for a faint ripple here and there most of the lake was a glassy calm in which the trees and white cabins on the shores, were almost perfectly reflected.

We therefore took it easy for a while on the sunny grass slope where we had lunched and I confess that I had a very pleasant twenty-minutes' snooze.

About three o'clock some clouds blew over, and in the breeze which they created we caught three more trout, none of them large.

Then we trolled for a while as the other boat was also doing and got two more, one a nice fish of nearly 2 lbs.

And so the afternoon wore on without much success—but one thing looked certain; whether for fly or for our projected experiment with the minnow, the night would be calm and fine.

At 6.30 p.m. we rowed back to the boat-house, whither our adversaries had already gone and on the way picked up another trout of 1½ pounds. The fact is, we were curious to know how we stood and what the others had caught. On arrival we found that they had nine to our ten, so the half-hour they had lost at the beginning of the day had not made much difference. The real tug-of-war was yet to come. Having finished our evening meal of sandwiches, under some pleasant trees at a little distance from our rivals, to avoid unwanted conversation with them, we set out once more.

The light was failing fast, and on the smooth surface of the water, now ruddy in the afterglow, a few rings showed that the evening rise had begun. We pulled down the lake at a good pace, this time without the trolls, for we were determined to arrive first and so have control of the deeper water at the western end, always the best in the late evening, and also with a view to our trial with the minnow. As we went we changed over to stouter casts mounted with fair-sized "rails", as sedges are called in Ireland.

There Denny stopped the boat. The evening rise seemed to have petered out. Except for an occasional ring far out in the middle, not a fish moved. So we just sat and waited for something to happen. For a quarter of an hour we continued thus—the glow died away; the water turned a sort of pearly grey, and I was beginning to think it was going to be an "off" night, when Denny quietly remarked to X—— "There's one sorr to your right." X—— made a hurried cast. "A little further out sorr and you'll cover him," added Denny. X—— cast as he was bid and as he slowly drew the flies a good trout a little above the average rose, was hooked and eventually landed. Then it was my turn, with a similar fish, but they were rising poorly and after we had caught four and lost one or two more, the rise ceased.

By this time it was pretty dark—and we were beginning to wonder what the other boat was about and what they intended to do, when suddenly there was a sound of oars and they loomed up close upon us from behind a promontory of rushes. "Well, what luck?" boomed the voice of the big man out of the darkness. "We've not done too badly—we've got seven more since we saw you. I'll bet we're ahead."

"Yes, you are so far," I replied, "but——"

"So far! So far!" he exclaimed irritably—he was I suspect thinking of his whiskies at the Inn. "Why it's nearly 9 o'clock—surely we can call it a day?"

"Oh, we can't leave it at that," I replied, "we must have one more shot."

There was a pause and some low-toned discussion in the other boat. All the while I was hoping most anxiously that our persistence would not induce them to stick it too, for the last thing we wished was for them to see anything of our future procedure. Then the big man's voice boomed out once more across the intervening water:

"All right—we're for home. I think you're damn fools to stay out—the whole thing's over—and listen, I'll bet you another 10 bob you don't do any good."

There was an obvious undercurrent of annoyance in his voice, which irritated me. "Done," I said, "good night," and they rowed away into the darkness, the sound of the oars becoming gradually

fainter and fainter as they went.

"Well, thank God they're gone," I exclaimed, but not too loudly, for sound carries on water, "We probably are 'damn fools' as he said, but at any rate now we can get going on the great experiment."

Each of us had a fairly stiff rod ready, and by the light of a torch we soon had a couple of minnows mounted. Whilst doing so I once more explained to X—— that he must cast out as far as he could and draw the minnow slowly along the surface.

Denny manoeuvred the boat over the deepest spot and for 5 minutes we continued casting without anything happening.

Suddenly there was a splash. "Glory be!" exclaimed Denny in astonishment. "Damn!" said X—— "I missed him—I snatched it out of his mouth—and a big fish too," and he drew in the minnow and examined it. "Torn to shreds," he remarked—and then "I never would have believed it." His voice trembled with excitement.

"Never mind," I said, "thank Heaven it works." He put on another minnow. Another 5 minutes passed. Another splash again to X——'s rod—this time the fish was firmly hooked.

"It's a big fish too," he added—"I can't do much with him." For a few moments the trout cruised deep, near the boat, then there was a prolonged screech from the reel, and far away in the dark, there was a "slop" as he leaped and fell back. After that run the fight was soon over and Denny netted a lovely trout which looked like weighing every bit of 3 pounds.

All this while I had continued casting, but my interest being concentrated on the hooked fish, without paying much attention. Suddenly there was a violent wrench at my rod, and more by luck than skill, I too was fast in a big fish. On feeling the hook he leaped high in the air, and then ran and ran, so that had not Denny followed him with the boat, every inch of line would have gone and he would probably have broken me. As it was, half my backing was out when I got control again. Knowing my tackle was strong, I now put on all the strain I dared, for precious time was passing, but for some time with little effect. At last however the trout began to circle the boat in smaller and smaller rings—Now his tail occasionally broke the surface as he attempted to plunge once more into the depths. At last however he turned towards the boat and by good fortune I was able to run him right into the capacious net which Denny had waiting. Four pounds if it was an ounce.

All this rowing about had rather disturbed the water where we were, so Denny took us to another deep spot nearer the middle of the lake.

Here X—— got another which appeared to be over 2 pounds, and I one of about $1\frac{1}{2}$ pounds after just touching two others. Then we packed up and went home, more than content.

X—— was enthusiastic. Denny rowed for a long time in silence. He still seemed to be a little dazed. About half way to the boathouse he suddenly remarked: "Sure if an angel from Heaven had told me I wouldn't have believed it—them great trout leppin' up out of the depths that way—and God knows what they take it for," and he relapsed once more into ruminative silence. After a moment, "Look now, Denny," I said, "promise you'll say nothing about how we fished tonight—say it was just a question of the right fly at the right time. We don't want all the world to be trying it, and besides, I don't know, but possibly your master might not approve."

"As to that you can be aisy in your mind, sorr—not a word of the truth will I say. All the same," he added—and I could just see the gleam of his teeth as he grinned—"it's myself would like to be trying it one of these nights."

Five minutes later we arrived at the boat-house, packed up our rods and tackle and placed the eighteen trout on a bed of grass in the boot of the car. Then we said goodbye to Denny—who, I need hardly say, received not only a handsome tip, but 10 shillings extra, as representing the last bet the big man had made.

It was after midnight when we arrived at the hotel, but our adversaries were still up. Looking through the window we saw that they were imbibing copious whiskies and sodas as usual. They had, we felt certain, awaited our arrival, in the sure hope of crowing over our defeat.

Before meeting them, however, we carried our catch through to the kitchen to weigh the five largest. And now, with plenty of light, we saw what really lovely fish the big ones were. The largest weighed $4\frac{1}{4}$ pounds. X——'s biggest just over $3\frac{1}{2}$ pounds, and the other three, 2 pounds 1 ounce, 2 pounds dead, and 1 pound 11 ounces.

Then having laid them out on the flags of the big larder, alongside the opposition catch, we went to seek our rivals.

"Don't look elated, whatever you do," I said to X——, as he was preparing to open the door of the lounge, "I want to give them a shock"—and it was clear from the first remark the big man made on seeing us enter that we had not given ourselves away by our expressions.

"Oh! here you are at last," he exclaimed rather thickly—"We've been waiting for hours. No good I suppose from your looks. Where's my 10 shillings?" and he chuckled.

"As a matter of fact," I replied, "we did get one or two more—but we did not count yours in the larder, so we'd better all go and have a look at our catches. That will settle it." I tried to speak casually, but I saw a slight gleam of suspicion come into his eye. Then he heaved his bulk out of his deep chair and they both followed us into the larder.

I turned on the light. It was a dramatic moment. "Good God!" muttered the big man, as his eye fell on the two biggest fish. The stocky one merely gaped. Then—"Some damned trickery about this," he growled, but without much conviction.

"Oh no!" I said, "just a question of sticking it out and luck combined." Back in the sitting-room the big man gave us a queer look and shook his head, but they paid up their 30 shillings without demur. Then we all went to bed.

Next day we departed. We heard later that on the following night which was fine, they stayed out till nearly midnight and had some success—a couple of fish over 2 pounds, but nothing like our biggest.

G. D. Luard,
Fishing Fortunes and Misfortunes, 1942, and
Fishing, Fact or Fantasy? 1945.

DROP MINNOW TACKLE

This is, without exception, the most deadly system of fishing for trout, perch and pike that can be practised. So deadly is it that we have heard south-country anglers call it poaching—a view we certainly do not hold, although we can quite see the desirability of not permitting it in waters where the fish are scarce.

It is not very well known in the South of England, but in the North it is much practised; and as the fish taken by this method are generally large, the baskets are often heavy.

Our new tackle consists of two treble hooks and one single, tied to a piece of gut, at the end of which is a fine tapered round lead, with a brass wire running through it, which forms the eye to which the gut is attached.

Drop-minnow mount (1886)

To Bait.—Hold the minnow between the forefinger and thumb of the left hand, and taking the tackle in the right, push the lead well into the minnow. Turn the hooks up and fix them in the side with the single hook through the tail.

This mode of fishing is well adapted for taking large fish in deep water, and is fished as follows:—Use about 2 yards of line from the point of the rod; drop the minnow gently in by the side of a bush, keeping well out of sight, and work it up and down by letting it drop about 2 feet and drawing it up again to within a foot of the surface of the water. Keep on repeating this sink and draw motion until you feel your fish, when, steady your rod, give him time to turn, strike gently but firmly, and you will be pretty certain to secure him.

In this style of fishing, which is generally over high banks, between trees or from a boat, a landing net is indispensable.

Hardy Brothers Catalogue, 1888.

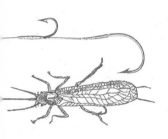

The "Creeper" Tackle, baited and unbaited

The Creeper is a larvae of the Stone-Fly (Phryganea), *and is found under stones in shallow water by the edges of rough streams. If the stones are gently lifted the Creepers may be easily secured, and should be placed in a box with a perforated lid. We generally place some damp moss in the bottom. It is a very deadly bait during May and June, and should be fished same as worm up stream, care taken not to flip the bait off in casting.*

Hardy Brothers Catalogue, *1888.*

WORM FISHING

This style of fishing has its charms as well as any other, and although we quite agree with those who protest against it, as it is permitted on some waters, *i.e.* (from early Spring till late in the Autumn), yet an angler would feel very stupid after walking several miles to the seat of his intended sport to find the water was too heavy, or the sun too bright for fly-fishing, and he minus his worms. Indeed we should never think of going out for a day's sport without a few from July to August, more especially when the weather is bright and the water clear and low. They are easily carried, and make sport more of a certainty.

Your fly-rod, if good, will answer the purpose quite well. The cast line should be 6 feet or more in length, according to the state of the water. The hooks best adapted are (as single hooks) our new pattern Needle Point, and our Special Round Bend Fine Wire, which are made in three sizes. As a two-hooked tackle, Captain Ilderton's pattern is good in bright water, and certain in hooking. Our Stewart Worm Tackle, made with fine eyes instead of whipping, is certainly for bright water, as a Stewart Tackle, the best extant.

Lead in some form is required in order to steady the line; more or less may be applied at the discretion of the angler, when by the waterside he ascertains the rate of the current, &c.

The worms which are best for trout-fishing are the marsh-worm, red-worm, button-worm, and the brandling. The last two kinds we recommend. All these worms should be scoured, a process which consists of starving them in damp moss neither too wet nor too dry for 3 or 4 days before use. Worms that are wanted for immediate use will be scoured in the following manner:—To a gallon of water add a tea-spoonful of common salt, wash the worms in the water for a few minutes, and then wash in clean water, and put them in damp moss, in an appropriate bait box or canvas bag, adding a little Bole Armenian, finely powdered, which will greatly improve their colour and appearance.

Fishing with the worm is practised by obtaining all the apparatus described. The angler then with his wading boots on, if he uses them, quietly wades into the water; or, if preferring *terra firma*, he keeps as much as possible out of sight of the fish upon a part of the bank suitable for his purpose, and below the water to be fished. The worm should in all cases be cast up-stream and suffered to float down again for reasons which will be clear enough, when explained as follows:—
1. The trout always lie head-up stream, and, therefore, do not see the angler so well below them as above; 2. The bait floats gently down without injury, which must be done to it if dragged against the stream; 3. In hooking the fish the barb is much more likely to hold in this way than if struck in the line of the axis of his body; and fourthly, the water is not disturbed by the wader till it has been

already fished. The angler swings or casts his worm gently as far up-stream as he can, using as long a line as he can easily manage, and no more, and suffering it to float down with the stream, until within a short distance of where he is standing, when it should be lifted and recast. When a fish is felt to bite or lay hold of the worm, wait a few seconds until he has done nibbling; and the moment he is running off with it, strike smartly but tenderly with the wrist—with Stewart tackle strike as soon as you feel the fish—not with the whole power of the arm, and proceed to land your fish with as little delay as possible. In striking, the point of the rod should be lowered as near the surface of the water as possible, and the stroke made in the opposite direction to which the fish is going.

These rules will also apply to shade fishing, with the exception of the hooks, which must be Nos. 6 to 8. The principal baits are as follows:—Dung Beetles, Grasshoppers, Natural May Fly, Caddis Fly, Bumble Bees, Blue Bottle Flies, and many Larvæ, or Grubs, the principal of which are Flesh Maggots, Caddies, Caterpillars, Wasp, and Dock Grubs.

Hardy Brothers Catalogue, 1888.

IN DEFENCE OF SALMON ROE

The first instance I shall bring forward with respect to the attractive power of this bait, I find jotted down in my angling note-book, as occurring on 24th November, 1837. The piece of water fished on was the lower extremity of a short side-stream on the Teviot, about a mile from Kelso, a spot which, in the summer season, was wont to be clear and shallow, and, in consequence, not plentifully stocked with trout. Immediately below, lies a succession of rapid streams, extending onwards above 200 yards, and then terminating in a large pool or dam.

Having taken up my stand at the margin of the small snatch of water above described, I commenced operations about 2 hours before noon, concluding them a short while after 3 o'clock, during which moderate interval I captured no fewer than 11 dozen of trout, many of them about a pound in weight, and along with these, a clear bull-trout weighing about 5 pounds. Nor, on leaving off, had I nearly exhausted the apparent contents of the spot; I say apparent, for it was evident to me, both from their scarcity at the commencement, and the gradual increase of the trout in number as I continued to fish on, that they approached the bait, as it were by a trail, from various quarters further down; some from the rapid streams immediately below, but the greater part undoubtedly from the pool in which these terminated, and which, at that advanced season of the year, formed, unless induced to leave it by some exciting bait like the one then employed by me, their natural haunt.

Another instance, of later date, which I shall mention, occurred at Teviot-foot, not very far distant from the scene of action already spoken of, on the 16th October, 1844. The water, on this occasion, was only slightly swollen, and far from that state which is generally held in estimation by roe-anglers; nor, indeed, was the paste used by me of the best quality, being fabricated, not from the roe of the salmon, but that of the bull-trout, and in consequence very inferior, both as respected colour and flavour. I commenced angling precisely at 8 o'clock, A.M., and left off, my bait being wholly exhausted, at 10 minutes before 1, the whole period of time occupied by me extending to nearly 5 hours. The number of trout captured was in all 212, several of them weighing 1½ pounds. I hooked and played also two bull-trout, or large whitlings, but owing to the undersize of my hooks, or some other cause, they made their escape. As on the former occasion, the fish, when I was compelled for want of bait to abandon the sport, were still in feeding humour, more eager indeed, and ravenous than during any other portion of the forenoon. The spot I occupied, on the above-mentioned day, lies at a distance of 300 yards from the junction of the Teviot with Tweed, and as the varieties of the common or parr-trout inhabiting the two rivers are quite distinct, the one from the other, in external appearance, I was at no loss to specify and assort them. I came accordingly to the conclusion that, at the fewest, two-thirds of the fish captured by me

belonged to Tweed, and that these, owing to the attractive qualities of the salmon-roe, had traced their way up to the bait, some of them, I have no doubt, out of Maxwheel pool, situated at the distance of ½ mile from the spot in question.

It were easy, did I choose it, to inflict upon the reader a detail of similar occurrences, all tending to prove the wonderful virtues possessed by the salmon-roe in gathering and concentrating trout, but the two instances above related are quite enough for my present purpose. They demonstrate the instinct of the fish to pry out its favourite food; they disclose to us that, for this end, it is gifted by nature with the most delicate perceptions; and more, they make us aware of the great extent of damage done during the spawning season, to the deposits of the salmon, by the depredations of the common trout. It is solely upon this last-mentioned ground, that I take my stand, when palliating the use of the salmon-roe as an angling bait, in certain rivers and seasons. I am of opinion, that in large waters frequented by salmon for the purpose of spawning, and also on their tributaries, the moderate employment of it in a salted state, acts powerfully in diverting the attention of more than one species of prowler from the natural ova or deposit, a very large proportion of which is every year consumed, as well upon the redd of the fish itself as when carried down below it; moreover, I can conceive it to be of great benefit to the breeding and increase of the *salar* or salmon proper, were it made allowable, by an amendment introduced into the various acts of parliament regarding our Scottish salmon fishings, to capture, by means of this bait during the close season, that species of fish which is well known under the designation of bull-trout. There is not, I am convinced, among the finny tribe, an enemy to the ova and incipient spawn of salmon more rapacious and destructive than this very fish; nor is it one, as is well known, remunerative as a marketable article to the tacksman or proprietor of fishings. It is seldom taken from our rivers in good and edible condition, ascending them in large quantities only during close-time; and at the commencement of the open season, continuing to haunt them, in the shape of a hungry and good-for-nothing kelt; thus, not only tampering with and preying upon the undeveloped deposit, but committing unmeasured havoc among the infant fry.

Thomas Tod Stoddart,
The Anglers' Companion, 1847.

TODAY AND YESTERDAY

The slanting rain was falling across the Hampshire landscape, and four men had sought shelter in a little round fishing hut on the banks of the famous Houghton fishery. Outside the crystal Test flowed placidly by, its surface dimpled by rain drops. The only living thing visible was an occasional dab-chick which, as it called to its young in the reeds, gave quaint jerks with its tail at each note, a sort of combined orchestra and conductor, the beak providing the music and the tail the *bâton*.

Inside the hut there was perhaps more of interest, though the occupants were not a little depressed by the hopelessness of the position. The oldest man there was Francis Francis; the youngest, and he was delightfully young in those days, was myself; while the between-men were my dear old friend Halford, and one who was probably the wittiest and cleverest Hampshire fisherman of that or any other century, G. S. Marryat.

I suppose I could fix the date by painfully searching through old diaries and other documents, but it was long, long ago, before even "Red Spinner" was Angling Editor of the *Field*, or "Detached Badger" had produced any of his monumental works on Dry Fly Fishing. The day is particularly fixed on my memory, apart from the meeting with these notable fishermen, because it was my introduction to the use of the dry fly on Hampshire streams, though I had used it successfully for some time on my own water on the Lambourn.

Poor Francis was nearing the end of his life; the dreadful throat malady from which he suffered had almost deprived him of the power of articulation. Now and again with effort he could make himself understood, but the only thing I heard him say distinctly was during a discussion on the merits and demerits (if there be any) of the use of the floating fly, when he suddenly jerked out the remark, somewhat dismaying, having regard to the company, "I wish dry-fly fishing had never been invented."

Presently the clouds broke, the landscape brightened, and we all strolled out to look for a rising fish. Francis Francis was using a big, double-handed rod; one which, nowadays, we might almost consider heavy for grilse fishing. Marryat and Halford had their short, powerful rods, rather heavier perhaps than they would be using to-day, but not greatly different. I recollect the weight of their lines struck me as being remarkable, for my earliest experiences had been with the old-fashioned and now almost forgotten plaited undressed lines of silk and horsehair in the streams of Devonshire, Ireland, and the Black Forest, and fly fishers generally were only just beginning to use oil-dressed lines.

Nineteenth-century trout anglers
(*Mary Evans Picture Library*).

Here and there fish were rising. I was told that the wet fly was absolutely no use on the Test, notwithstanding which, as we were crossing the little wooden bridge, I banged down a silver sedge on a rippling shallow, and a large trout came at it with a splashing rise, missed it, and refused to come again. Since those days I have often noticed that sedge is a good fly in the daytime late in the season, and was quite pleased to see the point alluded to in Halford's latest work which gives the improved dressing of a limited number of patterns. I remember that I had an almost new split cane rod on that day, which, by substituting a short handle for the ordinary butt, became converted from an 11 ft. 6 in. rod into a most useful 9 ft. 6 in. dry-fly rod. It had been built to my own ideas. Marryat expressed great approval of it, and subsequent facts proved the correctness of his opinion, for it was the finest rod I ever had, and it only came to final grief two years ago when striking a white trout on an Irish lake, close to the boat, it broke in half. Even then I had it spliced and put in order for old times' sake, but, as bad luck would have it, left it in a train in Norway last summer, and that was the end.

But to return to this old-time day on the Test. Somehow or other the fish, though rising, would not take. Francis Francis went home; Marryat disappeared—I know not where; and Halford, telling me it was "no use," went into the Mill House to tie flies. I am afraid it was unsociable, but I hardly liked to spend any moment of the first day on such a famous river as the Test, indoors, so I begged him to let me keep out and see if after all I could not get hold of a fish. A little later on I saw two grayling feeding on the hollow below the weir pool formed by the waste water hatch, and after trying them in vain with a dry fly, I put a little apple-green bodied dun with ashen coloured hackle and wings, and fished them wet, or shall I say semi-dry, and, lo and behold! I got the brace and took them up to the Mill House joyfully. I really think my dear old friend thought I had done something unsportsmanlike in not sticking to the dry fly. I remember his kindly endeavour to raise me in his own estimation by a careful explanation that, though I was fishing wet, I was really fishing dry, as flies dressed in the manner in which mine was dressed would not sink. One might write a most interesting note on what is a wet fly and what is a sunk fly—because in truth there is a very good deal of difference —but not on this occasion. It was a happy and notable day in my life as a fisherman.

More than twenty years have passed, and the changes which have taken place in the meantime are many and important. The fly rod has been enormously improved. Little weapons are now made which are less than half the weight of those used at the time I have been writing of, and with a line too heavy for their strength, a fly can be cast across the wind or even against it almost as accurately as with the very heavy lines which were considered necessary when dry-fly fishing was in its early youth. Then there are the delightful agate rings by which we can shoot an extra yard or two of line. Gut hanks are now sold in far greater lengths and infinitely more carefully prepared than they used to be, and better gut casts are made up. There are very few tackle makers of repute who cannot offer one a 15 or 22-inch hank of gut. The paraffin bottle has lightened our labours and lengthened the life of many a rod. The fish culturist has come into existence all over the kingdom. In the days that I have written of, I can only remember Howietoun and Andrews of Guildford. There have been vast improvements in the dressing of flies, due most of all to Halford, and later to G. E. M. Skues. The eyed hook has been improved in its manufacture, and come into general use, except for what I may term the finest forms of wet-fly fishing; and in the management of fisheries we are yearly making big strides towards perfection. Lastly, because most recently, we have a new cult, introduced by G. E. M. Skues, another old friend of mine, the main feature of which, I think, may be described as the scientific use of the wet fly, introducing in particular representations of the nymphs of the lesser ephemeridae. The dry-fly man is only interested in the duns and their spinners after the wondrous metamorphosis has taken place. There should be no rivalry between these sects. There is, as a matter of fact, a large school of men, with whom the present writer associates himself, who admire the knowledge and skill required in the use of both methods and endeavour to practise them.

John Bickerdyke, *in the Journal of the Flyfishers' Club*, 1918.

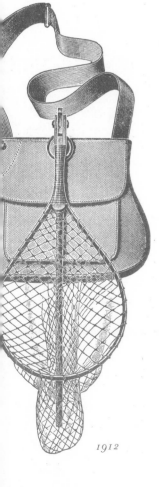

1912

THE HUMORIST

The beat below was divided from ours by a wire fence across the stream, and the big fellows had a way of taking up their positions either under or immediately above the wire. Apart from the gamble as to which side you would find them, or whether they would creep up or drop back, there were the intense excitement of getting your fly straight across the stream and the palpitations of the heart which go with terror of the drag and the sight of your enemy dropping slowly back with his eye cocked suspiciously at that little dun that moves in such a funny unorthodox way across his nose. Six inches did it; if he receded that much you were a poacher. But sometimes you were rewarded. I remember following one of these jibbers on his backward course with curses and fist-shakings, having wasted a futile perspiring $\frac{1}{2}$-hour over him and as I leaned exhausted against the wire a better than he swam slowly past me up-stream, brushing my waders as he went, wagged his way with great deliberation to pleasant casting distance, took up position, rose and obligingly swallowed my fly as soon as I asked him to. It was the most hospitable apology for the other's bad manners. . . .

There were two fish there which I never forgave. One was a 3-pounder, who rose regularly in the open 100 yards or so below the hut. I must have hooked him a dozen times in the various days I was there, but I never got him near the net. He was such a consistent riser that I was positively indignant when at last he sulked and would not come up any more. We were so intimately associated that I looked upon him as my private property, always on hand to provide me with a prize-fight, and when one day I arrived and found he was gone—for I never saw him again—and realized that some poacher with a hackle fly had robbed me of him, I regretted that I was only a guest of the club.

The other fish was a big, hilarious, salmon-like humorist who lay with his tail against a stump under the far bank half-way between the little fall and the shallows. He was exceedingly good-looking, and he knew it: also the fly invariably dragged 6 inches before it reached him, and he knew that too. I have never seen a fish more acutely, and yet comfortably, aware of that acid test than he. He sucked in the non-draggers and fairly shook with laughter at the draggers. Nothing put him down. He was as safe as a house with that infernal little swirl acting as policeman. When I think of the hours I wasted over him, without once rising him, even with a late sedge, I grind my teeth.

H. Plunkett Greene,
Where the Bright Waters Meet, 1924.

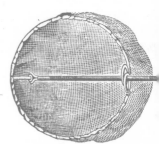

Dry fly requisites: a 3¾-fly-catching net and a lea[ ] knee-pad (1912)

COARSE FISHING

Viator: Now it is at the place, almost. A bite. Strike! Well done, indeed.
Now ye have her.
Piscator: I shall have, bye and bye, I hope.

The Arte of Angling.

GENERAL ANGLING

Coarse Fishing has a subtle charm of its own; there are many weedy
depths, quiet pools, and prolific swims stocked with pike, roach,
dace, bream, carp, gudgeon, bleak, and eels, that exert a certain
influence over the harried business man, who has succeeded in
snatching a few brief hours from the inexorable call of trade or
professional duties. At that season of the year when coarse fishing is
at its best, the country side is clad in its russet autumn mantle: the
rivers pursue their smooth, calm course, through delightful dreamy
districts, presenting at each bend, reach, and pool, some new attraction for the angler and the admirer of charming colour tints, and
sylvan scenery.

The rods we specially make for this class of fishing are very light,
in two or three joints, and 10½-foot to 12-foot long. A 3¼-inch reel
should be fitted, with about 40 yards of finest silk line. To this
should be fixed the trace of 3 yards of fine gut, carrying the float and
suitable hook.

Ordinary trout traces are excellent. The length to be used depends
entirely upon the depth of water you are fishing.

Of paramount importance are the roach-fisher's hooks. Those
principally used are Nos. 9, 10, and 11, <i>short shank</i>, round bend, and
Nos. 8, 9, 10, 11, and 12, crystal bend.

The best colour for the float is a dull deep black, except the extreme ½-inch of the top which should be white. Four, five, or six floats of different sizes should be included in the outfit, so that more or less shot can be attached to the line to suit the swim operated upon; the float in use should be so shotted that only the white tip appears above the surface of the stream.

One lead only should be squeezed on as close to the hook as 2 inches, the others fixed upon the line from 10 to 15 inches above the hook. Tight-line fishing, when the angler fishes from the bank, necessitates the use of a seat of some kind, and we recommend the use of what is termed a seat basket.

Of the various baits more or less useful in roach-fishing, worms, gentles, caddis, and other grubs rank second, for beyond doubt the principal bait is paste, and the angler must be careful to have the bait perfectly sweet and clean. Paste made from an arrowroot biscuit is very popular with some roach fishermen, but we prefer to utilize bread 1 day old. When at the water-side take a piece out of the middle of the loaf in a square shape, about as big as a large walnut, place it in a piece of clean white rag, and dip it into the water, then press all the water out and proceed to knead until quite smooth, solid and white. The piece you put on the hook should be about the size of a pea, and as round, and so placed on the hook that the point is just at the outside of the round.

The next consideration is the ground-bait, and this consists of bread and bran well soaked. Imagine then the angler at the river

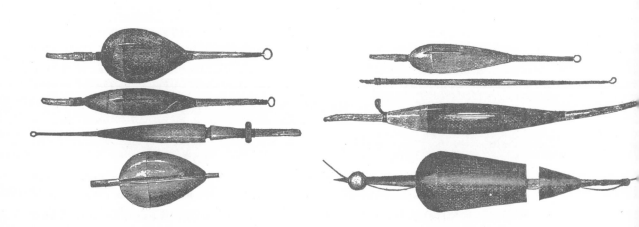

An assortment of floats (1888)

side preparing to fish a swim. The rod has been put together, and the line is attached. The depth of the swim is first to be ascertained, and for this purpose a plummet must be used. The plummet is attached to the hook, and the rod extended over the surface of the stream. The plummet is quietly lowered into the water, and the exact depth ascertained at each part of the swim. The float is so adjusted that the bait just trips the bottom of the river. The hook bait is next put on, then we prepare to fish and ground-bait the swim at one and the same time.

A small piece of ground-bait is squeezed on the line round the single shot that is about 2 inches from the hook; the ground-bait and hook bait attached to the line are carefully lowered into the water at the top of the swim. As the stream carries down the line the ground-bait gradually flakes off, and is deposited on a tiny trail along the bottom of the river.

Should the float steady, stop, or slightly move to one side, it indicates a bite, and the rod is instantly and smartly raised by a turn of the wrist, the hook is driven into the mouth of a fish which soon after you are busily playing. Tire the fish out well, bring your quarry to the net, disengage the hook, and proceed as before. A skilful angler can strike and hook a roach 25 yards away.

Hardy Brothers Catalogue, 1902.

1898

PIKE FISHING

Without doubt pike fishing ranges very high in the coarse fishing world, and if "the fell tyrant of the liquid plain" is sought after in an artistic manner, and the tackle used is as fine as the size and nature of the fish permit, the sport he provides is by no means to be despised.

The most sportsmanlike methods of angling for pike are spinning and paternostering. The rod should be light, and stiff in the hand, and develop sufficient action in use to produce some little spring when a cast is being made or a fish is being played. The winch should be of such a size as to hold the 80 or 100 yards of line used, and have an adjustable check so that the angler when spinning can either do so directly from the reel (Nottingham fashion) or by coiling the line in the hand or on the ground (Thames style).

Traditional Nottingham
reel with star back (1894

The line should not be less than 80 yards (100 yards are not too many) in length, and be made from the best pure silk, plaited. Opinions differ as to whether a pike line should be dressed or not; but a soft and pliable dressed line is undoubtedly the better. The spinning trace can be of either twisted or single gut, or steel wire. It should have a small loop or swivel at the end next to the reel line, and at the other end a hook-swivel or loop of sufficient size to enable the angler to attach the flight of hooks; $1\frac{1}{4}$ yards is a convenient length for a pike spinning trace. There are various forms of leads, but whichever one is adopted it should be of such a pattern as to be easily attached to and detached from the line. Never adjust the lead too close to the bait (2 feet is near enough). Should a flight be used that is fitted with a belly lead, of course the trace lead is dispensed with (and this is what we prefer).

Of the legion of different patterns of flights our "Crocodile" tackle is to be preferred. Whatever the flight used may be like, too much care cannot be taken in baiting it; handle your bait so that few, if any, of the scales are displaced; some prefer to cut the fins and tail off, as they prevent the bait spinning as it otherwise would do. So far as artificial baits are concerned, we can only say that we make many patterns, all of which have something to recommend them, and refer our readers to those pages which contain particulars of what we consider to be the best. In passing, we would remind our readers of the vast importance of having their tackle mounted in the very best manner; nothing is more annoying than to lose a good fish through the trace breaking or the hooks drawing; all our flights and artificial baits are mounted on material which is the best procurable, the hooks are tested, and they are bound with silk that has really been waxed. With a short description of the different methods of manipulating the tackle we have described, we will conclude our remarks on spinning for pike.

What is known as the Thames style is perhaps the easiest, and any reel may be used, but if the angler desires to avoid entanglement and annoyance we cannot too strongly urge the necessity of learning to cast from a "Silex" reel. Grasp the rod in the right hand well above the winch, and rest the end of the butt against the hip: with the left hand draw sufficient line from the winch to reach the desired spot; this line can be coiled on the ground if the bank is free from anything likely to be picked up by the line, and thus cause a foul when the cast is made, or—and this is to be preferred—it can be worked around the fourth finger and thumb *crosswise*. Next let out line from the top of your rod to about half the length of the rod, and with a swinging motion get some spring into the rod; now propel smartly (but not with too much force) the bait in the desired direction, allowing the line to travel from the ground through the hand or from the distended thumb and finger as the case may be; lower your rod as the bait travels through the air so that the line has a perfectly free and straight course. It is well worthy of note that the right instant to let go the line when making a cast, is when the bait reaches the extreme backward point in the act of swinging: attention to this will materially assist the beginner. When spinning for pike, the bait should travel regularly through the water, and not be worked by fits and starts, and in addition it is best not to spin too fast.

When the angler feels the tug at the end of the line which so surely denotes that a fish has "struck" the bait, he should instantly tighten on the fish and drive the hooks firmly home; and then proceed to play him in the usual manner. The less hurry you are in the sooner you will probably bring him to the gaff.

The Nottingham style of casting, *i.e.*, direct from the winch, is far the best. One or two matters we may as well emphasize: Never cast with too much force. More "tangles" are caused through too much "powder" being put into the cast than from any other cause. After making the cast when winding in the line, be very careful to see that it is evenly wound upon the barrel of the winch; directly you strike a fish put your fingers on the drum of the reel to serve as an extra check.

Paternostering for pike, especially from a boat, is a delightful method of pursuing *Esox Lucius*; it is much better style than the ordinary method of live-baiting, besides being more sportsmanlike, and, in our opinion, more deadly. So much ground can be covered and varying depths of water are so much better got at by means of the paternoster which we will next describe. To $1\frac{1}{4}$ yards of stout salmon gut is attached a single hook on fine gimp (the hook should be very square in the bend to allow the bait to open and shut its mouth). To the end of this salmon gut is attached a piece of fine gut about 12 inches long, carrying the lead, which is pear-shaped, and varies according to the size of bait being used. To bait, place the hook through the lips of the bait. You are now equipped, and with this tackle you can search every likely hole. When you feel a fish strike your bait, wait for a minute or so, and allow him to travel a bit if he wishes to, paying out the line so that there is no drag. Remember that the single hook is in the lips of your bait, and that a pike always seizes its prey across the middle. Presently your quarry will turn the bait head first down its throat, and as he does that he will give the line a vicious tug: now is the time to drive the hook home. Should the pear-shaped lead hang up while you are playing the fish, the fine gut will easily break and you will only loose the lead.

The new "Swallow Tail" (1907).

The orthodox style of live-baiting with a float needs no description; we may remark though that the line for this purpose should be very fine, and that all lines are the better of a rub with red-deer fat or "Cerolene" each time of using. The whole secret of striking a fish when live-baiting is that your line should float perfectly; further, when a line does float the bait is not so easily distressed, and, consequently, lives longer and "works" better. Of the various live-bait hooks, we are inclined to favour the "Jardine" snap, and we have no particular choice of floats, they are all "much of a muchness". We strongly recommend the use of a short salmon gut collar, say 1 yard in length, above the hook, and in addition a single swivel attached is of service. Our live-bait tackles are complete and carefully fitted and tested. Be sure and draw in all your slack line before striking a fish or you will be liable to strike the water only.

Until we manufactured our drop minnow tackle of suitable size for pike, trolling with a dead bait was little less than an abomination; but with this tackle it is no longer unsportsmanlike.

One of the most important tackles for pike angling is the "Jardine" dead snap. We have no hesitation in asking anglers to give it a trial, feeling confident that they will be glad they did so.

Hardy Brothers Catalogue, 1894.

USE HIM AS THOUGH
YOU LOVED HIM

"HARDY'S MULTUM IN PARVO"
SPINNING & PRAWNING TRACE.

1924

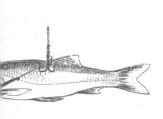

And thus use your frog, that he may continue long alive:

Put your hook into his mouth, which you may easily do from the middle of *April* till *August*, and then the frogs mouth grows up, and he continues so for at least 6 months without eating, but is sustained, none but he whose name is Wonderful, knows how: I say, but your hook, I mean the arming wire, through his mouth, and out at his gills, and then with a fine needle and silk sew the upper part of his leg with only one stitch to the arming wire of your hook, or tie the frogs leg above the upper joynt, to the armed wire; and in so doing, use him as though you loved him, that is, harm him as little as you may possibly, that he may live the longer.

And now, having given you this direction for the baiting your ledger hook with a live Fish of frog, my next must be to tell you, how your hook thus baited must or may be used: and it is thus. Having fastened your hook to a line, which if it be not 14 yards long, should not be less than 12; you are to fasten that line to any bough near to a hole where a Pike is, or is likely to lie, or to have a haunt, and then wind your line on any forked stick, all your line, except ½ yard of it or rather more, and split that forked stick with such a nick or notch at one end of it, as may keep the line from any more of it ravelling from about the stick, than so much of it as you intend; and choose your forked stick to be of that bigness as may keep the Fish or frog from pulling the forked stick under the water till the Pike bites, and then the Pike having pulled the line forth of the clift or nick of that stick in which it was gently fastened, he will have line enough to go to his hold and pouch the bait: and if you would have this ledger

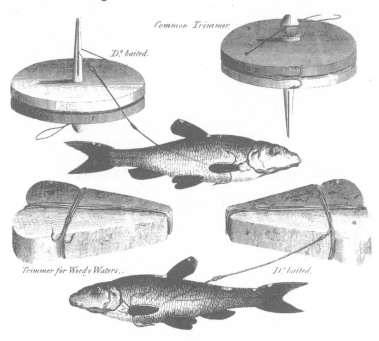

Common Trimmer.

D.º baited.

Trimmer for Weedy Waters..

D.º baited.

Pike trimmers (from a nineteenth-century engraving)

SNAP HOOKS (and TRIMMERS.

bait to keep at a fixt place, undisturbed by wind or other accidents which may drive it to the shore side, (for you are to note, that it is likeliest to catch a Pike in the midst of the water) then hang a small Plummet of lead, a stone, or piece of tile, or a turf in a string, and cast it into the water, with the forked stick, to hang upon the ground, to be a kind of Anchor to keep the forked stick from moving out of your intended place till the Pike come. This I take to be a very good way, to use so many ledger-baits as you intend to make trial of.

Or if you bait your hooks thus with live Fish or Frogs, and in a windy day, fasten them thus to a bough or bundle of straw, and by the help of that wind can get them to move cross a *Pond* or *mere*, you are like to stand still on the shore and see sport presently if there be any store of *Pikes*; or these live baits may make sport, being tied about the body or wings of a *Goose* or *Duck*, and she chased over a *Pond*: and the like may be done with turning three or four live baits thus fastened to bladders, or boughs, or bottles of hay or flags, to swim down a River, whilst you walk quietly alone on the shore, and are still in expectation of sport.

Izaak Walton,
The Compleat Angler, Part I, 1653.

OF THE LUCE OR PIKE

The Pike is of a long and roundish Body, has a plain, smooth Head, is covered with small Scales, of a whitish colour, the Body is sprinkled on both sides with Yellowish Spots, the young ones are more green, the upper and lower Jaw are full of Teeth, and three Rows of Teeth upon the Tongue; he's the Tyrant of fresh-Water-Fish, and reckon'd a longer liver than any other Fish, except a Carp; he is very chargeable to his Owners; the chief of his Subsistence being upon other Fish, even those of his own Species; he will bite at a Dog or any other Creature he sees in the Water, of which many Instances might be given. A very particular one I shall relate as follows: My Father catcht a Pike in Barn-Meer, (a large standing Water in Cheshire) was an Ell long, and weigh'd 35 pounds which he brought to the Lord Cholmondley; His Lordship ordered it to be turn'd into a Canal in the Garden, wherein were abundance of several sorts of Fish; about 12 Months after his Lordship draw'd the Canal and found that this overgrown Pike had devour'd all the Fish, except one large Carp that weighed between 9 and 10 Pounds, and that was bitten in several places; the Pike was then put into the Canal again together with abundance of Fish with him to feed upon, all which he devoured in less than a Year's time, and was observ'd by the Gardiner and Workmen there to take the Ducks and other Water-fowl under Water; whereupon they shot Magpyes and Crows and throw'd them into the Canal, which the Pike took before their Eyes; of this they acquainted their Lord, who thereupon order'd the Slaughterman to fling Calf's-bellies, Chicken's-guts, and such like Garbage to him to prey upon, but being soon after neglected he dyed, as suppos'd for want of Food. It is the general opinion that no other Fish will associate themselves with this Water-Tyrant, for he always swims alone, and is the most bold and daring of all our fresh-water Fish, knowing no other pleasure, as we conjecture, than Prey or Rest.

OF THE SPAWNING TIME

He spawns but once a Year, which is usually about the end of February or beginning of March, at which time he goes out of the River into some Ditch or Creek, and all the while the Spawner is casting her Eggs the Milter hovers over her, but never touches her: The best of those Fish are those that breed in Rivers, and the Female much preferable to the Male: Their chief Season is from May 'till Candlemas; his feeding is generally upon Fish or Frogs, there being a great antipathy between him and them; sometimes he feeds upon Pickerell-weed.

THERE ARE FOUR WAYS OF TAKING A PIKE

The First is with a Ledge's bait, which is a bait fix'd to a certain place; it is best to have your Ledge's-bait living, whether it be a Fish or Frog, and to keep them alive the longer, observe this method: If it be a Fish, as a Roach or Dace, which are I think most tempting (tho' a Perch lives longest upon the Hook) having cut off his Fin on the back, which may be done without hurting him, make such incision between the Head and the Fin, as you may put the Arming Wire of your Hook into it, taking care to hurt the Fish as little as may be, and so carrying the Wire along his back into or near his Tail, between the Skin and the Body; draw out the Wire at another Incision near the Tail, then tie him about with Thread, but no harder than just to hold him to the Wire to avoid hurting the Fish; some use a Probe to open the passage for the more easie entrance of the Wire, but without so much trouble a little Experience will make you perfect in this matter: When your bait is a Frog, it may be either a Water or Land Frog; chuse the Yellowest you can get, for that the Pike likes best; and between the Months of May and August' they are most beautiful: To preserve him long alive, manage him thus, put your Hook in at his Mouth and out as his Gills, then with a fine Needle and Silk sow the upper part of his Leg with one Stitch only to the arming Wire, (or if you tie his Leg fast above the upper Joint will do as well. Having thus prepared your Ledger-bait either with a Fish or a Frog, fasten your Hook to a Line, which must be 12 or 14 Yards at least in length, then fix the Line to some Bough or other rest next to the Water, near to the Hole where you guess the Pike to be, then wind up your Line on a forked Stick with a notch in one end to keep your Line fix'd to the length you design, that when the Pike comes he may the more easily run off with the remaining part of the Line to his Hold, in order to swallow the bait.

THE SECOND WAY OF TAKING A PIKE

Is what we call taking them at Snap; for this purpose your Rod must be at least 12 Foot in length, very strong and taper but not too heavy, with a substantial Loop at the end to put your Line to, which must be as long within a Foot as your Rod: When you bait for the Snap you must make a hole in the Fish's side you intend for the bait as near to the middle as you can with the point of your Hook or Probe, put in your armed Wire and draw it out at the Fish's Mouth, then sow up his Mouth. When you Fish thus for the Pike, before you strike let him run a little, and then strike contrary to the way he takes: It is best to use a double Spring-hook in this sort of Fishing, being much preferable to any other, and never fails: This manner of Angling is only proper to be practiced in March, for then the Pike is sick and bites shie.

1898

THE THIRD WAY OF TAKING A PIKE

Is by snaring of haltering; and the chief time of the Year for this is from March to July, and in the hottest part of the Day, when the Fish appears, as they all do towards the top of the Water: When you have spied a Pike, fix your Eye stedfastly upon him without looking off, which will make him the quieter, and have your Snare with you ready fix'd after this manner: Take a strait taper Pole, that is stiff and strong enough, but not too heavy, of about 4 Yards in length;

fasten it to the lesser end a small piece of hard twisted Whip-cord about a Yard long, more or less according to the depth of the Water, and the other End fasten to a well Nealed Brass Wire, made into a Noose or Snare like a Hare Gin; or let it all be of Nealed Wire and no Cord, then having open'd the Noose wide enough to flip over his head without touching him, let it down with your Pole into the Water even in depth with the Pike, 2 or 3 Yards before him, and guide it very gently towards his head, fixing your Eye full upon him till you have put the Snare over his Head and Gill-Fins, but no further; Then immediately with a strong Jerk upright, hoist him instantly to Land Keeping your Eye as much as you can on the Pike, will cause him to look upon you the more and mind the Snare less: Be sure your Pole be not brittle or rotten: Thus you may halter other Fish, as Trouts, Eels, Carp and Tench.

THE FOURTH WAY OF TAKING A PIKE

Is by Trolling, and very pleasant: The Lines and other Tackle for this purpose are now so accurately and exactly made, and so commonly sold, that I need not trouble you with a description of them: It is best Angling after this manner in a clear Water, and especially in a Windy-day: Some prefer a single before a double Pike-hook, and baiting with a Minnow as well to catch Pearch as Pike by Trolling: When you are compleatly fitted with all Materials, and your Hook is baited, cast your Fish-bait up and down in such places as you know the Pike frequents, letting him sink a considerable depth, before you pull him up again: When the Pike comes, if it be not sunk too deep, you may see the Water move, at least you may feel him; then Slack your Line, and give him length enough to run to his hold; whither he will immediately make and there paunch and swallow the Bait; thus let him lie till you see the Line move, when you may certainly conclude he hath swallow'd the Bait, and is ranging about for more; then with your Trole wind up the Line 'till you think it is almost strait, and with a nimble Jerk hook him and bring him pleasantly to Land. The Pike loves a still, shady and unfrequented Water, with a Sandy, Chalky or Clay bottom: His best biting time is early in the Morning or late in the Evening in a clear Water and gentle Gales: He takes all Sorts of Baits, except Flies, but the most principal are, large Gudgeons, small Roaches, and Daces, large Minnous, Bull-heads, Bleaks, (in July) young Frogs or Salmon-Smelts; some use fat Bacon in the Winter Months; a young Trout, Jack or Perch are also good: Take care that all your Fish-baits are fresh and sweet when you use them.

Charles Bowkler,
*The Art of Angling, c.*1746.

WHAT EYES HE HAS!

A friend of mine (sacred be his name!) of great repute for his dexterity with the rod, and celebrated for his agreeable and amiable qualities, as well as for his intelligence and various accomplishments, had this poetical facility of seeing what did not really exist in substance. A curious instance of this popular talent occurred at a friend's house in the country with whom he was staying. There was a fine piece of water in the park, well stored with fish, where he used to spend most part of the morning, rod in hand; so that his perseverance excited considerable admiration from the host, as well as from his guests. Not having been very successful, his ardour at length began to flag. It was a pity, for it is a pleasant thing to be excited. What was to be done? You shall see. A report was raised that there was an enormous pike seen in the water, about the length of a decent-sized alligator. He was said to have maimed a full-grown swan, and destroyed two cygnets, besides sundry ducks. At first he was no more believed in than the great sea snake, which encloses at least half the world in his folds. But after the lapse of a few days, the keeper came to the private ear of my friend, and told him that a *mortal* large pike was basking amongst some weeds, and could be seen plainly. "You are sure to cotch en, sir." He was rewarded for this intelligence, and exhorted to keep the important secret from the other visitors at the mansion.

When piscator, cunning fellow! thought that all were out of the way, employed in hunting, shooting, or some other occupation, he and John Barnes the keeper glided down secretly to the awful spot,

Frog, trimmer and pike (*from* The Book of the All-Round Angler, *1899*).

and they there descried the semblance of a fish so enormous that it was doubted if any thing less than a small rope could hold him. The sportsman was astounded—the keeper was not; for the said awful animal was nothing more than a large painted piece of wood, carved deftly by himself into the shape of a pike, painted according to order, and stuck in the natural position by means of a vertical prop, which could not be discovered amongst the weeds. It was too bad, really a great deal too bad; but tolerably ingenious, and beautifully deceptive. The gentleman approached with tact and caution, and the eyes of the fish glared upon him; as well they might, for they were very large and dazzling, being made of glass, and originally designed to be inserted in a great horned owl which the keeper had stuffed.

"What a prodigious fish, John!"

"Very perdigious indeed, sir."

"What eyes he has!"

"So he has, sir."

"I'll try him with a roach. There—it went in beautifully, and he did not move."

"No, he won't take it no how. Give him a frog; he seems a difficult fish."

Piscator did tender him a very lively one in vain; in short, he offered every bait he could possibly think of, running through all the devices and temptations he was master of. Cautious in his approaches, that the supposed fish might not see him, he always advanced to make his cast upon his knees, to the no small merriment of his friends, who were looking at him through a telescope from the windows of the mansion.

A nineteenth-century pike fly 1898

Well, thus he spent the whole morning; waiting, however, at times, for a cloud to intercept the sun-beams, and a breath of air to ruffle the surface of the water. When these came, he would set to work again with renovated hopes; till at last, tired and discomfited, he bent his steps homewards. On his arrival there, he was accosted on the very threshold by some of the guests.

"Oh! you have been fishing all the morning, I see; but what could make you stay out so long, and get away so cunningly with the keeper?"

"Why, to tell you the truth, Barnes (you know what a good creature he is) told me of an immense pike that was lying amongst the weeds at the end of the lake; he must be the same that swallowed the cygnets. I never saw so enormous a monster in fresh water."

Omnes.—"Well, where is he—where is he? let us look at him."

Host.—"John, tell the cook we will have him for dinner to-day. Dutch sauce, remember."

Piscator.—"You need not be in such a hurry to send to the cook, for I am sorry to say I did not catch him."

Host.—"Not catch him—not catch him! Impossible, with all your skill, armed as you are to the teeth, with roach, bleak, minnows, frogs, kill-devils, and the deuce knows what. Not catch him! Come, you're joking."

Piscator.—"Serious, I assure you. I never was so beat before, and yet I never fished better; but though I did not absolutely hook him, *he ran at me several times.*"

William Scrope,
Days and Nights of Salmon-Fishing, 1843.

It may interest you to know that in 1915 I bought one of your Silex spinning reels, which has been in constant use ever since, and with which I have taken over 1½ tons of pike (fish up to over 20 pounds). Letter quoted in Hardy Brothers Catalogue, *1937.*

A BET AT BLENHEIM

Several more remarkable tales were told, and then as it was getting late and I and Delaney and Roberts were making an early start next morning, the party broke up. We three were going to pike fish at Blenheim, and as we were going down the steps of the Club, talking and laughing, Delaney, who was extremely "cheerful", suddenly turned to Roberts and myself, saying, "Look now, I'll bet you an even bottle of whisky each, that I catch a greater weight of fish tomorrow than both of you together." Being in the humour we simultaneously answered "done".

Next morning, after a very early breakfast, Roberts and I met on Delaney's doorstep within a few minutes of the appointed hour. His big Lagonda was already at the door. It made short work of the distance and by 10.30 we were launched on the Blenheim Lake. It was fairly mild for the time of year, there were gleams of misty sun and a slight breeze.

We did poorly to start with, but live-baiting in the shallower water changed our luck with the small pike which abound there—Roberts and mine that is to say, and by 4 o'clock each of us had four of from 3 to 6 pounds. Then they went off the feed. Delaney had had no luck at all. Everything went wrong for him. Several of the fish he hooked got off and once he was even broken. I'm afraid we weren't very sympathetic and chaffed him not a little. He was uncommonly good-tempered.

At 4.30, as nothing was doing, we decided that it was a day, and suggested knocking off.

The weight of our united catch was now nearly 33 pounds, as against Delaney's two miserable Jack which weighed a mere 6 pounds between them.

Delaney, however, persuaded us to take one turn round the deeper part of the lake in the hope of catching something bigger.

He changed from live bait to a golden sprat, which he had ready mounted, and as soon as we were on the move he began casting and a very pretty caster he was. Roberts and I did not think it worth while, and leisurely began to pack up our traps.

For some time Delaney continued to cast without result, and I confess that somewhat unkindly we kept cheering him on with chaffing encouragement. Then he actually caught a fish of 5 pounds. We cheered ironically. The score now stood at 33 pounds to us against 11 pounds to him.

A few minutes later he hooked another, obviously quite small, and he reeled it in so fast to save time that it came swaying along the surface. We cheered again with much laughter in which Delaney joined. Suddenly, just as he was bringing it alongside, there was a terrific rush and flurry which threw the water in every direction—  an enormous head appeared, and with a jerk pulled the point of Delaney's rod into the water, a huge fish dashed off with the small pike in its jaws. That fish put up a tremendous fight and it was nearly dark when he was at last brought to the gaff.

By a miracle, one triangle had taken firm hold. He weighed 29 pounds, so Delaney won his bet after all, with a score of 43 pounds to our 33 pounds. You may be sure we did not grudge the whisky.

The big pike for many years adorned our Club room in a glass case.

G. D. Luard,
Fishing Fact or Fantasy?, 1945.

BARBEL FISHING

In the early part of the season barbel are principally found in the rough water—at weirs, for example; later on they frequent the heavier streams. They are ground feeders and seldom take food in midwater; on the surface never. Barbel swim in shoals, and the larger fish, as a rule, lie farthest up-stream. They are considered by many to be the strongest and gamest fish of any available to the bottom-fisherman, certainly there is no such thing to be done as hauling them out on fine tackle: 'tis an impossible task; they require to be patiently brought to the net if they are ever to be in the basket.

The barbel is a bold biter at times: and when a shoal begins to feed in earnest, a heavy basket may be looked for confidently: although difficult to capture at most times, anglers who have succeeded in landing some of these fish, agree that he is well worth the trouble and exercise of skill required to successfully fish for him. Probably the best days in which to fish for barbel are those which are dark and lowering: if it is bright weather you stand little chance of getting any fish until the sun is off the water—the nearer dusk the better your chance of sport.

Ledgering is the best style of fishing for barbel. The tackle should be fine, but strong: the rod light, with sufficient "play" to materially assist the angler in tiring a big barbel, and fetching him from the bottom. The Nottingham style of barbel-rod is advocated by many anglers: it is made with bamboo butt and middle joint, and green-heart tops, 12 feet in length. We make several patterns of these, and find that the favourite is made as described. The rings should be upright, of the "snake" pattern, or our patent "Bridge"; the latter, although a little more in price, are certainly worth the extra. The

preferable pattern of winch is our new Patent "Silex", or the Combined Fly and Spinning Reel, with adjustable check, but many anglers use an ordinary winch. From 50 yards to 100 yards of plaited silk line (undressed) should be used.

There are many patterns of leger: one that we can confidently recommend is made up as follows:—To 3 yards of fine natural gut attach a large crystal bend hook; some 12 inches from the hook a separate length of fine gut about 15 inches long is attached to the main cast, and at the extreme end of this independent length of gut is fastened a pear-shaped lead. Thus it will be seen that this tackle partakes of the paternoster somewhat. It has these advantages: the strike is directly on the fish, and not on the lead as is the case frequently when the orthodox leger is used: in the event of a "hang-up" the lead only is lost as the length of gut by which it is attached (being much finer than the main cast) breaks first, when a break does occur. We have seen this style of leger worked to much advantage. The ordinary leger is well known to our readers.

Fine and far-off float-fishing with a fixed float is a neat manner of negotiating the capture of barbel, and it is much practised on such rivers as the Trent. The depth in this case must be first ascertained, and the float so fixed upon the line that the bait just clears the bottom. A large porcupine quill or celluloid float is most suitable, and should be of sufficient size to carry a good lot of shot. The manner of fishing is much the same as for roach with running tackle; and here we would remind our readers that in this fine and far off fishing the reel line *must* float, and it is a capital dodge to occasionally rub it with red-deer fat.

When legering the line is held between the fore-finger and the thumb of the left hand, the least movement of the bait being then felt; care must be taken that the line is presented straight and with no loose link: if these things be attended to there is ample time to strike effectually. The extreme sensitiveness of touch in this respect if often a matter of surprise. The larger and more cunning of the fish will often attempt, especially when the hook is visible, to head the bait from the hook, and that, too, without seriously disturbing the line; the angler, however, if at all on the alert, will not fail to detect this, and strike before the act can be fully effected. When there is circumstantial evidence of an attempt at underhand dealing after this fashion, a very fine tackle with a strong hook of fair size should be baited with a couple of medium-sized worms, one being threaded above the other upon the line, allowing but the least possible freedom to their extremities. This done, throw in a few scraps of worms, cast your bait into the swim and strike at the second "knock" of a fish. .

Hardy Brothers Catalogue, 1894.

BAITING A BARBEL SWIM

Should the angler know where barbel lie, having chosen the swim, he will proceed to bait it, with about 1,000 fresh lob or dew-worms, coming to it at least 20 hours before he intends to fish it. He breaks each worm up into about four pieces, and casts the whole into the place he intends to fish. On the Thames, in order to keep the bait from straying too far, the worms are enclosed in huge balls of clay, and they bait the night before fishing; so that when they come in the morning, less than 12 hours after, they find the fish collected together, doubtless, but gorged with the worms so profusely provided for them, and so close to the place where the punt-poles are to be driven in, and the punt or boat fixed, that the fish, startled, even if they are hungry, get shy of the boat and retire to a distance. On the Trent they do not put the bait into clay, but let it scatter down the stream; and as they fish a long way from the stand or boat, as the case may be, the barbel are not alarmed. Whether the angler fishes from a stand on the shore, or from a boat, the *modus operandi* is the same. The object is to let the hook-bait travel over the whole distance along which the ground-bait has been scattered, dragging, like the ground-bait, slowly along the bottom. (For barbel, which are a ground-routing fish, the bait should always touch the bottom.) Coming then to the spot which has been baited, and having deter-mined the depth, let the bait drag slightly, and cast in some ten or a dozen broken worms in order to set the fish biting again—taking care, of course, to keep the bait as much in a line as possible with the spot which you have taken the depth of. . . .

The French fish using a short piece of whalebone or stick, of some 18 inches long, instead of a rod, and playing the fish, when hooked, with the hands. The tackle they use is of course stout. They weld up horse-dung with the clay ball, which is supposed to render it more attractive. I have seen a Frenchman make some very good takes of barbel in this way, with about 12 feet of water-cord, and the half of an old umbrella rib.

John Bickerdyke,
The Book of the All-Round Angler, 1899.

1898

The Angler at Large

No life so happy and so pleasant as the life of the well-govern'd angler.
Izaak Walton

THE DETERMINED ANGLER

DEAR SIRS,—Now that the nineteenth century has come to a close I may as well tell you what your rods, reels, etc. have done for me in it.

The number of the slain appears from my angling record to be as follows:—

> 560 salmon up to 32 pounds, considerably more than half of which have been killed (and gaffed by myself), with your single handed trout rods, trout casts, and small trout flies.
>
> 275 white trout up to $5\frac{3}{4}$ pounds.
>
> 20,066 Brown trout up to 4 pounds 14 ounces.
>
> 1,040 perch up to $1\frac{3}{4}$ pounds.
>
> 150 pike up to $10\frac{1}{4}$ pounds.
>
> Fifty-six eels up to $5\frac{1}{2}$ pounds, or a total of 22,157 fish.

Of the other coarse fish I have kept no record, but had I done so the total would have been considerably increased. Although I have tried your rods hard, for many a time they have been doubled up for nearly a couple of hours, they have stood well, and I believe them to be the best the world can yet show. Last year I had a heavy fish hooked above the tail with a small trout fly, on a 10-foot rod for 3 hours and 5 minutes before I got him to the gaff and the rod came quite straight again. On 5th August, 1895, while fishing in one of my lakes with your "Gem" $9\frac{1}{2}$-foot rod, a fine trout cast, and three No. 10 trout flies, I hooked at one cast, and successfully landed a salmon of $5\frac{1}{2}$ pounds, a white trout of slightly over 1 pound, and a brown trout of over 6 ounces. After bearing the strain for an hour and threequarters (I had to gaff the salmon myself), the rod came back as straight as ever. On 4th July, 1892, fishing the river in a heavy flood with one of your $14\frac{1}{2}$-foot rods, I hooked twenty-nine salmon of which I landed twenty-three. No breakage occurred.

I have great pleasure in testifying to the excellence of all kinds of tackle with which you have supplied me.

Hardy Brothers Catalogue, 1902

A BORDER BOYHOOD

It was worth while to be a boy then in the south of Scotland, and to fish the waters haunted by old legends, musical with old songs, and renowned in the sporting essays of Christopher North and Stoddart. Even then, thirty long years ago, the old stagers used to tell us that "the watter was owr sair fished", and they grumbled about the system of draining the land, which makes a river a roaring torrent in floods, and a bed of grey stones with a few clear pools and shallows, during the rest of the year. In times before the hills were drained, before the manufacturing towns were so populous, before pollution, netting, dynamiting, poisoning, sniggling, and the enormous increase of fair and unfair fishing, the border must have been the angler's paradise. Still, it was not bad when we were boys. We had Ettrick within a mile of us, and a finer natural trout-stream there is not in Scotland, though now the water only holds a sadly persecuted remnant. There was one long pool behind Lindean, flowing beneath a high wooden bank, where the trout literally seemed never to cease rising at the flies that dropped from the pendant boughs. Unluckily the water flowed out of the pool in a thin broad stream, directly at right angles to the pool itself. Thus the angler had, so to speak, the whole of lower Ettrick at his back when he waded; it was a long way up-stream to the bank, and, as we never used landing-nets then, we naturally lost a great many trout in trying to unhook them in mid water. They only averaged as a rule from three to two to the pound, but they were strong and lively. In this pool there was a large tawny, table-shaped stone, over which the current broke. Out of the eddy behind the stone, one of my brothers one day caught three trout weighing over seven pounds, a feat which nowadays sounds quite incredible. As soon as the desirable eddy was empty, another trout, a trifle smaller than the former, seems to have occupied it. The next mile and a half, from Lindean to the junction with Tweed, was remarkable for excellent sport. In the last pool of Ettrick, the water flowed by a steep bank, and, if you cast almost on to the further side, you were perfectly safe to get fish, even when the river was very low.

The flies used, three on a cast were small and dusky, hare's ear and woodcock wing, black palmers, or, as Stoddart sings,

> Wee dour looking huiks are the thing,
> Mouse body and laverock wing.

Next to Ettrick came Tweed: the former river joins the latter at the bend of a long stretch of water, half stream, half pool, in which angling was always good. In late September there were seatrout, which, for some reason, rose to the fly much more freely than seatrout do now in the upper Tweed. I particularly remember hooking one just under the railway bridge. He was a two-pounder, and practised the usual sea-trout tactics of springing into the air like a rocket. There was a knot on my line, of course, and I was obliged to hold him hard. When he had been dragged up on the shingle, the line parted, broken in twain at the knot; but it had lasted just long enough, during three exciting minutes. This accident of a knot on the line has only once befallen me since, with the strongest loch-trout I ever encountered. It was on Branxholme Loch, where the trout run to a great size, but usually refuse the fly. I was alone in a boat on a windy day; the trout soon ran out the line to the knot, and then there was nothing for it but to lower the top almost to the water's edge, and hold on in hope. Presently the boat drifted ashore, and I landed him—better luck than I deserved. People who only know the trout of the Test and other chalk streams, cannot imagine how much stronger are the fish of the swift Scottish streams and dark Scottish lochs. They are worse fed, but they are infinitely more powerful and active; it is all the difference between an alderman and a clansman.

Tweed, at this time, was full of trout, but even then they were not easy to catch. One difficulty lay in the nature of the wading. There is a pool near Ashiesteil and Gleddis Weil which illustrated this. Here Scott and Hogg were once upset from a boat while "burning the water"—spearing salmon by torchlight. Herein, too, as Scott mentions in his Diary, he once caught two trout at one cast. The pool is long, is paved with small gravel, and allures you to wade on and on. But the water gradually deepens as you go forward, and the pool ends in a deep pot under each bank. Then to recover your ground becomes by no means easy, especially if the water is heavy. You get half-drowned, or drowned altogether, before you discover your danger. Many of the pools have this peculiarity, and in many, one step made rashly lets you into a very uncomfortable and perilous place. Therefore expeditions to Tweedside were apt to end in a ducking. It was often hard to reach the water where trout were rising, and the rise was always capricious. There might not be a stir on the water for hours, and suddenly it would be all boiling with heads and tails for twenty minutes, after which nothing was to be done. To miss "the take" was to waste the day, at least in fly-fishing.  From a high wooded bank I have seen the trout feeding, and they have almost ceased to feed before I reached the water-side. Still worse was it to be allured into water over the tops of your waders, early in the day, and then to find that the rise was over, and there was nothing for it but a weary walk home, the basket laden only with damp boots. Still, the trout were undeniably *there*, and that was a great encouragement. They are there still, but infinitely more cunning than of old. Then, if they were feeding, they took the artificial fly freely; now it must be exactly of the right size and shade or they will have none of it. They come provokingly short, too; just plucking at the hook, and running out a foot of line or so, then taking their departure. For some reason the Tweed is more difficult to fish with dry fly than—the Test, for example. The water is swifter and very dark, it drowns the fly soon, and on the surface the fly is less easily distinguished than at Whitchurch, in the pellucid streams. The Leader, a tributary, may be fished with dry fly; on the Tweed one can hardly manage it. There is a plan by which rising trout may be taken—namely, by baiting with a small red worm and casting as in fly-fishing. But that is so hard on the worm! Probably he who can catch trout with fly on the Tweed between Melrose and Holy Lee can catch them anywhere. On a good day in April great baskets are still made in preserved parts of the Tweed, but, if they are made in open water, it must be, I fancy, with worm, or with the "screw", the larva of the May-fly. The screw is a hideous and venomous-looking animal, which is fixed on a particular kind of tackle, and cast up-stream with a short line. The heaviest trout are fond of it, but it can only be used at a season when either school or Oxford keeps one far from what old Franck, Walton's contemporary, a Cromwellian trooper, calls "the glittering and resolute streams of Tweed".

Difficult as it is, that river is so beautiful and alluring that it scarcely needs the attractions of sport. The steep banks, beautifully wooded, and in spring one mass of primroses, are crowded here and there with ruined Border towers—like Elibank, the houses of Muckle Mou'ed Meg; or with fair baronial houses like Fernilea. Meg made a bad exchange when she left Elibank with the salmon pool at its foot for bleak Harden, frowning over the narrow "den" where Harden kept the plundered cattle. There is no fishing in the tiny Harden burn, that joins the brawling Borthwick Water.

The burns of the Lowlands are now almost barren of trout. The spawning fish, flabby and useless, are killed in winter. All through the rest of the year, in the remotest places, tourists are hard at them with worm. In a small burn a skilled wormer may almost depopulate the pools, and, on the Border, all is fish that comes to the hook; men keep the very fingerlings, on the pretext that they are "so sweet" in the frying-pan. The crowd of anglers in glens which seem not easily accessible is provoking enough. Into the Meggat, a stream which feeds St. Mary's Loch, there flows the Glengaber, or Glencaber burn: the burn of the pine-tree stump. The water runs in deep pools and streams over a blue slatey rock, which contains gold under the sand, in the worn holes and crevices. My friend, Mr. McAllister, the schoolmaster at St. Mary's, tells me that one day, when fish were not rising, he scooped out the gravel of one of these holes with his knife, and found a tiny nugget, after which the gold-hunting fever came on him for a while. But little is got nowadays, though in some earlier period the burn has been diverted from its bed, and the people used solemnly to wash the sand, as in California or Australia. Well, whether in consequence of the gold, as the alchemical philosophers would have held, or not, the trout of the Glengaber burn were good. They were far shorter, thicker and stronger than those of the many neighbouring brooks. I have fished up the burn with fly, when it was very low, hiding carefully behind the boulders, and have been surprised at the size and gameness of the fish. As soon as the fly had touched the brown water, it was sucked down, and there was quite a fierce little fight before the fish came to hand.

This, all this, was in the olden time, long ago.

The Glengaber burn is about 20 miles from any railway station, but, on the last occasion when I visited it, three louts were worming their way up it, within 20 yards of each other, each lout, with his huge rod, showing himself wholly to any trout that might be left in the water. Thirty years ago the burns that feed St. Mary's Loch were almost unfished, and rare sport we had in them, as boys, staying at Tibbie Shiel's famous cottage, and sleeping in her box-beds, where so often the Ettrick Shepherd and Christopher North have lain, after copious toddy. " 'Tis gone, 'tis gone:'' not in our time will any man, like the Ettrick Shepherd, need a cart to carry the trout he has slain in Meggat Water. That stream, flowing through a valley furnished with a grass-grown track for a road, flows, as I said, into St. Mary's Loch. There are two or three large pools at the foot of each loch, in which, as a small boy hardly promoted to fly, I have seen many monsters rising greedily. Men got into the way of fishing these pools after a flood with minnow, and thereby made huge baskets, the big fish running up to feed, out of the loch. But, when last I rowed past Meggat foot, the delta of that historic stream was simply crowded with anglers, stepping in in front of each other. I asked if this mob was a political "demonstration", but they stuck to business, as if they had been on the Regent's Canal. And this, remember, was 20 miles from any town! Yet there is a burn on the Border still undiscovered, still full of greedy trout. I shall give the angler such a hint of its whereabouts as Tiresias, in Hades, gave to Odysseus concerning the end of his second wanderings.

When, O stranger, thou hast reached a burn where the shepherd asks thee for the newspaper wrapped round thy sandwiches, that he may read the news, then erect an altar to Priapus, god of fishermen, and begin to angle boldly.

Probably the troops who fish our Border-burns still manage to toss out some dozens of tiny fishes, some six or eight to the pound. Are not these triumphs chronicled in the *Scotsman*? But they cannot imagine what angling was in the dead years, nor what great trout dwelt below the linns of the Crosscleugh burn, beneath the red clusters of the rowan trees, or in the waters of the "Little Yarrow" above the Loch of the Lowes. As to the lochs themselves, now that anyone may put a boat on them, now that there is perpetual trolling, as well as fly-fishing, so that every fish knows the lures, the fun is mainly over. In April, no doubt, something may still be done, and in the silver twilights of June, when as you drift on the still surface you hear the constant sweet plash of the rising trout, a few, and these good, may be taken. But the water wants re-stocking, and the burns in winter need watching, in the interests of spawning fish. It is nobody's interest, that I know of, to take trouble and incur expense; and free fishing, by the constitution of the universe, must end in bad fishing or in none at all. The best we can say for it is that vast numbers of persons may, by the still waters of these meres, enjoy the pleasures of hope. Even solitude is no longer to be found in the scene which Scott, in "Marmion", chooses as of all places the most solitary.

> Here, have I thought, 'twere sweet to dwell,
> And rear again the chaplain's cell.

But no longer does

> Your horse's hoof tread sound too rude,
> So stilly is the solitude.

Stilly! with the horns and songs from omnibusses that carry tourists, and with yells from nymphs and swains disporting themselves in the boats. Yarrow is only the old Yarrow in winter. Ages and revolutions must pass before the ancient peace returns; and only if the golden age is born again, and if we revive in it, shall we find St. Mary's what St. Mary's was lang syne—

> Ah, Buddha, if thy tale be true,
>   Of still returning life,
> A monk may I be born anew,
>   In valleys free from strife,—
> A monk where Meggat winds and laves
> The lone St. Mary's of the Waves.

Yarrow, which flows out of St. Mary's Loch, was never a great favourite of mine, as far as fishing goes. It had, and probably deserved, a great reputation, and some good trout are still taken in the upper waters, and there must be monsters in the deep black pools, the "dowie dens" above Bowhill. But I never had any luck there. The choicest stream of all was then, probably, the Aill, described by Sir Walter in "William of Deloraine's Midnight Ride"—

> Where Aill, from mountains freed,
> Down from the lakes did raving come;
> Each wave was crested with tawny foam,
> Like the mane of a chestnut steed.

As not uncommonly happens, Scott uses rather large language here. The steepy, grassy hillsides, the great green tablelands in a recess of which the Aill is born, can hardly be called "mountains". The "lakes", too, through which it passes, are much more like tarns, or rather, considering the flatness of their banks, like well-meaning ponds. But the Aill, near Sinton and Ashkirk, was a delightful trout-stream, between its willow-fringed banks, a brook about the size of the Lambourne. Nowhere on the Border were trout more numerous, better fed, and more easily beguiled. A week on Test would I gladly give for one day of boyhood beside the Aill, where the casting was not scientific, but where the fish rose gamely at almost any fly. Nobody seemed to go there then, and, I fancy, nobody need go there now. The nets and other dismal devices of the poachers from the towns have ruined that pleasant brook, where one has passed so many a happy hour, walking the long way home wet and weary, but well content. Into Aill flows a burn, the Headshaw burn, where there used to be good fish, because it runs out of Headshaw Loch, a weed-fringed lonely tarn on the bleak level of the table-land. Bleak as it may seem, Headshaw Loch has the great charm of absolute solitude: there are no tourists nor anglers here, and the life of the birds is especially free and charming. The trout, too, are large, pink of flesh, and game of character; but the world of mankind need not rush thither. They are not to be captured by the wiles of men, or so rarely that the most enthusiastic anglers have given them up. They are as safe in their tarn as those enchanted fish of the *Arabian Nights*. Perhaps a silver sedge in a warm twilight may somewhat avail, but the adventure is rarely achieved.

These are the waters with which our boyhood was mainly engaged; it is a pleasure to name and number them. Memory, that has lost so much and would gladly lose so much more, brings vividly back the golden summer evenings by Tweedside, when the trout began to splash in the stillness—brings back the long, lounging, solitary days beneath the woods of Ashiesteil—days so lonely that they sometimes, in the end, begat a superstitious eeriness. One seemed forsaken in an enchanted world; one might see the two white fairy deer flit by, bringing to us, as to Thomas Rhymer, the tidings that we must back to Fairyland. Other waters we knew well, and loved: the little salmon-stream in the west that doubles through the loch, and runs a mile or twain beneath its alders, past its old Celtic battle-field, beneath the ruined shell of its feudal tower, to the sea. Many a happy day we had there, on loch or stream, with the big sea-trout which have somehow changed their tastes, and to-day take quite different flies from the green body and the red body that led them to the landing-net long ago. Dear are the twin Alines, but dearer is Tweed, and Ettrick, where our ancestor was drowned in a flood, and his white horse was found, next day, feeding near his dead body, on a little grassy island. There is a great pleasure in trying new methods, in labouring after the delicate art of the dry-fly fisher in the clear Hampshire streams, where the glassy tide flows over the waving tresses of crow's-foot below the poplar shade. But nothing can be so good as what is old, and, as far as angling goes, is practically ruined, the alternate pool and stream of the Border waters, where

The triple pride
Of Eildon looks over Strathclyde,

and the salmon cast murmers hard by the Wizard's grave. They are all gone now, the old allies and tutors in the angler's art—the kind gardener who baited our hooks; the good Scotch judge who gave us our first collection of flies; the friend who took us with him on his salmon-fishing expedition, and made men of us with real rods, and "pirns" of ancient make. The companions of those times are scattered, and live under strange stars and in converse seasons, by troutless waters. It is no longer the height of pleasure to be half-drowned in the Tweed, or lost on the hills with no luncheon in the basket. But, except for scarcity of fish, the scene is very little altered, and one is a boy again, in heart, beneath the elms of Yair, or by the Gullets at Ashiesteil. However bad the sport, it keeps you young, or makes you young again, and you need not follow Ponce de Léon to the western wilderness, when, in any river you knew of yore, you can find the Fountain of Youth.

From the Mary Evans Picture Library.

Andrew Lang,
Angling Sketches, 1891.

HIS FIRST TROUT

Henceforth, when I could escape control, I divided my time between the water and the meadows: in warm weather the water, in cold the land possessed me. Then I began to tamper with the minnows; and, growing more ambitious, after a sleepless night full of high contrivance, I betook me at early dawn to a wood near the house, where I selected some of the straightest hazel sticks I could find, which I tied together and christened a fishing rod: a rude and uncouth weapon it was. I next sought out *Phyllis*, a favourite cow so called, in order to have a pluck at her tail to make a line with. But Phyllis was coy, and withheld her consent to spoilation; for when I got hold of her posterior honours, she galloped off, dragging me along, tail in hand, till she left me deposited in a water-course amongst the frogs. The dairy-maid, I think, would have overcome this difficulty for me, had I not discovered that horse-hair, and not cow's tail, was the proper material for fishing lines; so the coachman, who was much my friend, plucked *Champion* and *Dumplin*, at my request, and gave me as much hair (black enough to be sure) as would make a dozen lines. For three whole days did I twist and weave like the Fates, and for three whole nights did I dream of my work. Some rusty hooks I had originally in my possession, which I found in an old fishing book belonging to my ancestors. In fact, I did not put the hook to the rod and line, but my rod and line to the hook. I next proceeded to the pigeon-house, and picking some coarse feathers, made what I alone in the wide world would have thought it becoming to have called a fly; but call it so I did, in spite of contradictory evidence. Thus equipped, I proceeded to try my skill; but exert myself as I would, the line had domestic qualities, and was resolved to stay at home. I never could get it fairly away from the hazel sticks; therefore it was that I hooked no fish. But I hooked myself three times: once in the knee-strings of my shorts, once in the nostril, and again in the lobe of the ear. At length, after sundry days of fruitless effort, like an infant Belial, I attempted that by guile which I could not do by force; and dropping the fly with my hand under a steep

bank of the stream, I walked up and down trailing it along: after about a week's perseverance, I actually caught a trout. Shade of Izaak Walton, what a triumph was there! That day I could not eat —that night I slept not. Even now I recollect the spot where that generous fish devoted himself.

William Scrope,
Days and Nights of Salmon-Fishing, 1843.

SIR FRANCIS CHANTREY'S FRIEND

The greatest feat I happen to have witnessed, in the way of killing salmon with the worm, was accomplished 6 or 7 years ago, on the Hemp-side Ford stream, close to Kelso, by a friend of the late Sir Francis Chantrey, who himself, on the occasion I allude to, was also engaged angling on the pool immediately above. Sir F. I understand to have been held in repute as a Thames fisher, and from the specimen I then witnessed of his skill in heaving the line, the perfect control he exhibited over his rod and tackle, I could at once perceive that he was no raw or undisciplined angler. Quite otherwise it was with his friend, who, although I make no question but that he had frequently, before then, disturbed the finny tribe, was evidently a very inferior craftsman, compared with the sculptor. The latter, however, notwithstanding that he plainly knew nothing or little of the habits of salmon, relied upon his own address and attainments, as a Cockney angler, to achieve something extraordinary. Accordingly, instead of chiming in with the approved practice of the district, he chose to resort, as a means of capturing the fish in question, to the mode of taking trout adopted on some of the English rivers, and actually plied Tweed with a tackle comprising nearly a dozen hooks and a whole string of pellets weighing almost a quarter of a pound, while the bait, in absence of a bleak or gudgeon, consisted of an entire parr or fingerling. This he pitched from him, by means of a long, stiff rod, to an extraordinary distance, not less certainly than 40 or 50 yards, allowing his line to spin out through the rings, and recovering it by the double action of his reel and hand, until the bait, having completed its course of transit, hung suspended midway betwixt the butt and top-piece. He then repeated, in a similar manner, the cast or heave out, causing the parr, as it returned towards him, to revolve with considerable speed and no doubt attract the notice of all the finny tribe within range of observation. I need not, however, state the result. The craziest salmon that ever cleft water would scarcely dream of showing snout to such a contrivance. At that season of the year especially, it was then about the end of autumn, there was not the smallest chance of obtaining even an offer, and unless the tackle should happen, by pure accident, to run athwart some spawning fish lying heedless on its redd, our distinguished sculptor might have ventured cast after cast, during a whole term of weeks, without being able to hit the features of a solitary grilse.

While Sir F. was thus employed attempting to reconcile the monarch of the rivers to the food of the freshwater tyrant, his friend Mr. W. had judiciously placed himself under guidance of T. Kerss the fisherman, who, as the water was small and the day clear, recommended the use of the worm in preference to fly. Acting according to Kerss's instructions, who stood at his elbow with the gaff-hook, Mr. W., in the course of two or three throws, had the satisfaction of fastening on a moderate-sized grilse. It was evident, however, that he had not been accustomed to deal with fish of great calibre, for no sooner was it hooked than he endeavoured, by a violent effort, to haul it directly to the edge—an act of temerity immediately repaid by the snapping asunder of his casting-line, and, of course, the escape of the fish. Being a dun grilse, the loss was by no means severe, and became speedily supplied by the capture of one in better condition. To this succeeded another, and after it a third. In short, within the course of two hours, Mr. W. landed no fewer than eleven fish, salmon and grilse, all within the distance of 100 yards from each other—an angling feat, under the circumstances of the case, seldom equalled. It may be proper to state that the fish were none of them in the primest condition.

Thomas Tod Stoddart,
The Angler's Companion, 1847.

AN ANGLER FROM LONDON

Thin and new were his shoes—new also was his jacket, new his waistcoat, and novel his pantaloons; but newest of all was his top-varnished salmon rod, turned out by Eaton: but he was shabbily thatched, his hat being worse than common. His flies, to all appearance, were made by the Turks—men forbidden by their religion to imitate any of the works of the Creation. As for the man himself, no one could look at him without being put in mind of Mantellini.

"Demnition fine pool, sir."

"Very fine indeed, sir; but you will never catch a fish where you are casting at present, because fish do not lie in that bare water."

Upon this our man faced round, put his forefinger to his nose, and, with an expression of sagacity and wisdom that I should in vain attempt to describe, said,

"Do you see anything green in my eyes, sir?"

It was evident such a person was not born to be instructed, but simply to be admired. My friend, therefore, left his rod upon the bank, and walked after him, cigar in mouth, to get some insight into his tactics. Arrived at a better part of the pool, he hooked a fish; and here it was curious to see the difference of opinion between a Cockney and one who had been bred to the sport. The Cockney was of a yielding disposition, and judged it advisable to let the fish have his own way; the result of which was, that he ran out an exorbitant length of line, and was going to a sort of whirlpool amongst the rocks.

"Hold him in, hold him in; if he gets to that eddy, you are done."

"Fine fish, sir, fine fish; fast hooked, sir. Do you see anything green in my eyes? I have an opinion of my own, sir."

"So has the fish. And now it is all over with you; for if you had nothing but a dried herring at the end of your line, you would never get it out of that mess. I hope you have another casting line, because you will never see that again."

"Fine fish, sir; fine rod, sir; fine line, sir; fast hooked, sir—fast hooked. Do you see anything green——"

He was stopped short in the sentence by an alarming rush of the salmon, who shot forward up the stream, and took out the whole of the line of the consenting party to the tune of 120 yards. Now it is a wholesome rule to make fast the end of the line, by running it through a hole in the cylinder of the reel, and tying some knots at the extremity to secure it; and as this rule is wholesome, so it has been practised time immemorial by all sagacious persons, and even by some who are not very sagacious. But there are exceptions to all rules, and our man had neglected this caution; consequently, the line, being all run out, vanished at once through the rings of the rod, and streamed fair and ample below the surface of the water. The mermaid may, but that line shall no terrestrial ever see again.

"Demnition hard that, sir. What an extraordinary incident! Fish well managed, dexterously, artistically. Very odd indeed, sir: beautifully played;—fine rod, fine hand. Demnition hard, I must say. Now how far must I go to get a line?"

"If you mean to get the same, probably to the middle of the Irish Channel, or the mouth of the Shannon; but if you seek a new one, which I think would be the most prudent course, walk up to the road, and you will see a mile-stone, which says, 'To Inverness 120 miles'—exactly a mile for every yard of line you have lost, and I am sorry for it."

William Scrope,
Days and Nights of Salmon-Fishing, 1843.

HINTS TO ANGLERS ABOUT NORWAY

As a great many English anglers are going to Norway in search of sport, a few hints as to tackle and angling in Norwegian waters should be welcome to sportsmen not previously acquainted with the rivers and lochs of that country.

HOW TO GET FISHING IN NORWAY

All the principle salmon rivers are held by Englishmen, on long

The 20-foot cane-built steel centre you made for Mr. Wilfrid Kennedy has proved itself a grand rod, and has killed no end of big fish, the largest, 68 pounds, took some fearful pulling, as you may imagine.
Letter from Norway quoted in Hardy Brothers Catalogue, *1907.*

leases, and seldom come into the market. A vacancy for a rod or two is sometimes advertised in the papers, but good free salmon-fishing is much more difficult to get in Norway than in Scotland, where the hotel-waters afford opportunities for a good day's sport.

Many small rivers on the long coast of Norway are still unlet, but they are uncertain and heavily poached by the natives, and deserve more the name of sea-trout than salmon rivers.

Trout-fishing is to be had almost everywhere both in river and loch, but the angler ought always to ask for permission, which is seldom denied, if he sticks to fair rod-fishing. If the angler is going in for loch-fishing it is best to ask before-hand if the lake in question is much fished by "otters", by which means many of the best lochs in the country have been ruined.

One common error Englishmen make now-a-days is, to think that they can combine a travelling and fishing trip, going from place to place on the beaten tourist tracks; all waters situated along the most frequented routes are whipped to death, and are not worth wetting a line in. The best fishing is to be had in the mountains, the angler having to take up his quarters at a small farm or "saeter" hut (small chalet for the shepherds), which only can be reached by mountain tracks (paths); the luggage has to be brought forward in carts, or by pack horses.

A few tinned provisions, biscuits, tea, and drinkables, must be brought; also blankets, an air pillow, and a small canteen, with cooking and dining things.

The last week in July and August is the best time for that sort of fishing, and in the latter half of August such a trip can be combined with shooting.

HOW TO FISH

The rivers and lochs of Norway are somewhat similar to the Highland waters, both in character and in the way of working the tackle. The capital angling hints in Stewart's *Practical Angler*, hold good in Norway everywhere. The wet fly is generally used either up- or down-stream, according to the rapidity of the current; the dry fly only comes in occasionally on the large still flats in some not too rapid rivers, when a peculiar rise of fly is going on, or as an occasional substitute for the wet fly, just as in Great Britain.

DRESS

The best fishing-dress is a rather thick tweed knicker-bocker suit, thick nailed boots and leggings, with flannel underclothing; a good waterproof coat and cap are indispensible.

The angler's great nuisance on most rivers in Norway in summer time are the mosquitoes. A good veil, gauntlet-gloves, a flat pocket-phial with "angler's defence" and some strong carbolic acid or ammonia, are well to bring out.

RODS

Regular salmon rods with spare tops, 16 to 18 feet, suitable for the Scotch and Irish rivers, will do as well in Norway; the best harling-rod for the large rivers in the north is a strong built rod, 16 feet long with snake rings, same as used for harling in Loch Tay.

For trout-fishing three rods ought to be taken out: an 11 or 12 foot single fly-rod for river-work, a double-handed 14 foot fly-rod, with a short stiff trolling top, besides the two fly tops for sea-trout-angling and loch fishing; lastly, a spinning rod with upright snake-rings. This rod and the double-handed fly-rod furnished with the short top are excellent for trailing spinning baits in lakes for big trout.

REELS

Trout-reels capable of holding from 40 to 60 yards waterproof dressed silk-lines to match the balance of the rods, and salmon-reels holding from 100 to 200 yards similar line, are the best.

LANDING NETS

A landing net is indispensable, either a Y shaped or collapsing ring, which can be strapped to the rods; the ring ought not to be too small in the diameter if the net is to be used both as a river net carried by the angler himself and also for loch-fishing, where a large net on a long handle is most practical; if the trout run large, a gaff-hook fitting the same handle often comes in handy.

FISH-BAG

For knocking about in Norway, a fish-bag which you can pack up amongst the luggage is more handy than a creel, which is apt to get smashed when rough travelling with pack-horses in the mountains.

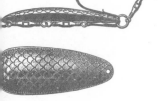

GUT

Fine and medium gut is all that is necessary for the Norwegian trout, which are not by far so highly-educated as the English, wanting drawn gut and gossamer-lines. For the salmon, single and treble gut lines are necessary. Besides fly-casting lines—swivel traces for spinning must not be omitted, with or without leads.

The "Norwegian" scaled Spoon (1912).

BAITS

Although minnows are found in most parts of Norway, they are difficult to get when just wanted, so the angler fond of using the natural bait had better bring his own salted minnows or small herrings suiting Hardy's "Crocodile" Tackle. Of artificial minnows, phantoms are the best. For salmon, blue back, with silver belly, Nos. 5, 6 and 7. For trout, brown back, gold belly, Nos. 2, 3, and 4.

Devons and spoons are also good killers; the spoons for salmon are best armed with an upper triangle besides the tail triangle.

For minnow-spinning in trout rivers, an "Amber" minnow or "Halcyon" spinner, which can be thrown with the fly-rod is often good.

A few Stewart's three-hook worm-tackles, and some prawn-tackles for salmon for ensuring sport on days when the fly or minnow do not kill, complete the list.

FLIES

The following is a good general list of salmon-flies for Norway:—

Jock Scott.	Stephenson.
Silver Doctor.	Snow-fly.
Blue Doctor.	Durham Ranger.
Dusty Miller.	Red Ranger.
Butcher.	Black Ranger.

1907

Black Dose.	Popham.
Sir Francis Sykes.	Black Prince.
Namsen.	Shrimp.

The hooks varying from No. 2/0 to 7/0 Dublin—Limerick numbering. A list of killing trout flies:—

Coachman.	Red Spider.	Stewart's pattern.
Governor.	Dun Spider.	
Hare-lug.	Gravel-bed.	
March-brown.	Evening-dun.	
Small Alexandra.	Hardy's Favourite.	
Green Drake.	Coch-y-bondhu.	
Blue-dun.	Black Gnat.	
Yellow-dun.	Hen Pheasant Hackle.	
Iron-blue.	Dark Snipe.	
Broughton point.	Woodcock Brown.	
Black Spider—Stewart's pattern.		

The hooks varying in size from No. 12 to 15 (old numbers) Pennell-Limerick down-turned eyed. Most Scotch loch-flies will kill in Norway. Some approved patterns are the following:—

Claret and Mallard.	Hare-lug.
Green and Mallard.	Heather-moth.
Zulu.	Blue Jay (also good in rivers).
White-tip.	Greenwell's Glory (used large).
Black Palmer.	Professor.
March-brown.	Orange and Bustard.
Red Palmer.	Alexandras.
Heckum Peckum.	Teal wings. bodies
Hardy's Favourite.	Woodcock Wings. varied.

The Aöra salmon fly, wi
spinning head (1898)

All dressed on Pennell-Limerick hooks No. 5 to 9 (old numbers). By addition of a few sea-trout flies of the most approved Scotch patterns, with mallard, teal, and blue jay wings, and different bodies the fly-lists are complete.

WADING

Wading-gear is sometimes useful; for deep wading in some of the salmon-rivers trousers are best, but for ordinary trout-fishing wading stockings and brogues will do.

Hardy Brothers Catalogue, 1894.

In 1905, I was on a trip to London, where I went to Messrs. Hardy Brothers and bought a trout rod, 10 feet long, made of Greenheart. The price was then £2 10s. 0d. That rod has been my friend for more than 25 years, but now old age has claimed it.

In 1915 I got in one forenoon 120 pounds seatrout with it, the three biggest 22, 18, and 17 pounds. It was in the Ardal river in Sogn. But the biggest masterpiece done by me or the rod was the 28th May, 1928, when I with this rod, trout line and 1¾-inch Devon bait got a salmon in the Arø river in Sogndal in Sogn.

The weight of the salmon was 48 pounds, and I used 3 hours to land it, and you can bet it was some kind of strain on the rod, but it was just as good after I landed the fish as it was when I started fishing.

Letter from Norway quoted in Hardy Brothers Catalogue, *1937.*

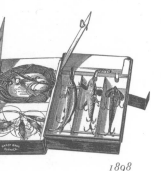

1898

NORWAY, A NOTE

One of the partners of Jos Dixon & Son, Sheffield, Mr. Fawcett says: We fished the upper length of Vefsoen belonging to the North of Europe Land Co. whose headquarters are in London, but found it too cold and Salmon had not got up—however we went over to a lake called Feflingsland and had grand sport with the Trout catching 350–400 pounds in 7½ days. The spoon bait and Devon proved the most killing baits. The weather was too cold for fly fishing. Average weight of Trout 2 pounds—the smallest being 1¼ pounds and the largest 4½ pounds.

Handwritten note in *Hardy Brothers Catalogue, 1894.*

NORWAY: THE AARO RIVER

As we had only been fishing with the fly, I thought there was a chance of trying spinning before luncheon. The tide was beginning to go out. It was noon. I went to the second platform to get as close as possible to the opposite bank where there was some good, deep water. I might perhaps find a good fish! I sent my ·353 ounces Carrère, weighted under the swivel, across the river and brought it slowly back so that it should work along the bottom. After several casts without result, I left the platform and waded out into the current which soon stopped me. My lure went out and sank 2 yards from the opposite bank, and I saw a monster leap out of the water and fall back with an enormous splash! Nicolas shouted: "Charles! A huge sea trout!"

I had but one idea: to cast again at once and try and place my spoon over the fish. I started reeling in quickly, but a powerful tug bent my rod in two. Good God, I had it on! I was certain that it was a salmon, it was too big for a sea trout. What was I to do? My line was running out at full speed. Everything would break! And I remembered all my misfortunes in July! Another jump! On ·010 inches! I had merely to resign myself to waiting for the end! This was it! I was broken! I turned the reel and the line came in. How very strong the current must have been! For I felt much more than the normal pull. Incredible! I still had my fish and he was coming slowly but surely in! I regained courage. After all, I was quite close to the fjord and in a position to follow my fish wherever he might go, particularly since the boat was not far away. I called to Anton: "Be prepared! Bring the boat over!"

I was terrified. I had had the most extraordinary luck at the two first jumps, the fish's tail had not touched my line. If it did so, I should see it no more! Then, I raised my little 7-foot rod above my head, having put on my brake practically to its utmost extent, so as only to work on the reel. The salmon was still coming toward me. It was incredible! It was going down the current towards the fjord. I understood. It did not know what had happened to it. It could feel neither my rod nor my reel and was allowing itself to go with the current! I would try Nicolas' trick. I began going slowly backwards downstream, regulating my speed in accordance with the fish, in such a way as to maintain only a light and uniform tension and let it fight only against the spoon of which it was trying to rid itself. I tried not to let it feel that it was held on a lead. Backwards! Forwards! Stop! Then it began all over again and, incredulously, I began to realize that the fish had completely lost its head and was still going down the current, from time to time making a momentary halt, followed by a move towards the centre, each time with less decision. It was now just below the surface. Its dangerous tail was close to my line; I was trying to hold the line so that it was not in alignment with the fish's body when it came to the surface. What a dance! It went right, left, backwards and forwards; and I kept a smooth, uniform tension, increasing it almost imperceptibly when

Feathered spoons (1894)

I felt that the fish was beginning to slow down. This manœuvre seemed to be succeeding, for we were approaching the end of the current and entering the fjord. But I was in the water up to the top of my boots. Luckily Anton had come up, and I got into the boat in order to reach the gravel bank from which I could get to the little false arm beside the boat house, the perfect place for the finish, if my great had come! Anton manœuvred the boat perfectly and the salmon was still following! I felt I was going to bring it to the gaff. And now we had reached the gravel bank. I disembarked just in time, for a new rush obliged me to hurry to the centre. But it was only a short alarm. The fish stopped once more; and then the performance began all over again. It was continuously coming towards me; my reel was almost full. Then it came to the surface again! I could see it! Over twenty pounds! It shook its head and jumped out of the water but I was just behind it, watching out for my line. I moved quickly to the right and avoided the danger. Finally the fish stopped and remained motionless, letting itself be led on like a dog on a lead! I went back, and then back again, 10, 20, 30 yards, and drew near to the boathouse. I was now on the great expanse of smooth water with a depth of 2 feet at the most. I went backwards again. There was now no more than about 20 inches of water and my fish, realizing the trap into which it had fallen, became desperate and tried to escape, but it no longer could. It no longer had the strength to make a rush and only succeeded in floundering on the surface, almost touching my line, which I managed to keep out of its way by raising my arms as high as I could, though they were already tired from holding this position, for which I had not taken the precaution of training myself!

It was over! Here was the fish belly upwards. It was unbelievable! Nicolas, who was with me, gave me a last piece of advice: "Charles, go to the narrow end of the current and bring him on to the stones, but only when you have got him completely exhausted."

I asked him to get the gaff ready, but we only had the little stick with the cod hook, which Antoine used for sea trout! This was the climax! I went backwards and dragged my fish till it touched the bank. Nicolas gaffed it and pulled it towards him. The stick broke, but Anton was there and, lifting the fish on to the bank with a kick, fell on it and managed to hold it. For the first time, I heard: "Bravo, Charles!"

We had no need to be concerned. The fish was completely exhausted and was not even flapping its tail. It was a splendid female still in perfect condition, its belly full of eggs.

I shall not try to say what I felt at that moment. I turned to Nicolas and saw his expression. It was certainly one of the most splendid moments of my life as a fisherman. My stop-watch showed 55 minutes; and on the scales my fish marked 25 pounds! Two days later, at the same time and place, I got another salmon with my first cast, and though exactly the same procedure followed, I was really able this time to savour each moment of the wonderful fight against an adversary which defended itself with the fury of a wild beast to preserve its liberty. Forty-five minutes later, a 27 pounder received in its flank the little hook which had been mounted on a new stick. We had never imagined that the same thing could happen twice.

Charles Ritz,
A Fly-Fisher's Life, 1959.

SWEDEN; THE EM

We all dream of taking a very big trout with a small rod. We insist that our tackle dealer should give us a reel big enough to contain safe backing. During the whole of our fishing lives, we are continually in search of this marvellous experience and the Paradise in which one may secure it. Any one of us who succeeds in doing it is envied by the rest; he becomes a hero, he is spoken of for years. The monster's photograph never leaves his pocket book, it becomes dirty and its edges torn. He is always on the look-out for an opportunity of showing it. He'll even pay for a round of drinks in order to be able to tell the story of the great fight for the hundredth time. The locality in which he caught it becomes legendary, almost a place of interest to tourists! In the days of our grandfathers, more big trout were caught and they were less talked about! Today, we content ourselves for the most part with thinking about the giant rainbow trout in New Zealand, South America or Alaska, the steel-heads of Oregon and British Columbia, and the famous marble trout of Yugoslavia.

But the great Paradise still exists today. Its secret is jealously guarded by the few people privileged to enter it. I tried for more than ten years, but in vain, to gain access to it. At last, in May 1952, thanks to my good friends in Goteborg, I received a letter telling me that I would have the right to fish there from the 12th–24th September. At last! I could test myself against the giant sea trout of the Em, which is the most extraordinary river of big trout in the world.

On the appointed day, I arrived at eleven o'clock in front of a big white house. I had hardly opened the door of the car when two pretty young Swedish women in pale blue dresses, aprons and white caps, seized hold of all my paraphernalia and hurried off with it! Then my host appeared. A tall man who looked completely English: the Chevalier Ulfsparre, followed by a splendid looking woman with all the air of a great lady of the court of Louis XIV. She will always be for me the queen of hostesses. I was then presented to H.R.H. Prince Wilhelm of Sweden, to M. Gabrielson, the maker of Volvo cars, to M. Magnus, a client of the Ritz, and several other men among whom I had the pleasure of recognizing my friend Arvid Carlander, the champion tunny fisher. They were all accustomed to fishing the Em.

The fishing is some seven kilometres in extent, but it is in the last 1,000 yards in particular, as well as in the river mouth on the Baltic, that most fish are caught. The upper reaches are encumbered with weed and the banks too difficult of access. Wading is risky, and the pools are few and far between.

The Em resembles a Normandy chalkstream, but with numerous rocks and more rapid currents. There are also slow currents and smooth water. As for the fish, they are to be found practically everywhere. Wading is difficult. One needs a third leg owing to the big stones on the bottom and the poor visibility. The water is transparent, but dark, as in many Northern rivers. The Em is fished in April and in September. It contains 90 per cent sea trout (fish of less than 5 pounds are rare) and 10 per cent salmon. There are also pike which will sometimes take a fly and whitefish, like pollan, which make excellent eating, as well as chub.

After luncheon, I went to the fishing-room and saw on the rack big two-handed rods of 13 and 14 feet. I decided nevertheless to fish with my 9½-foot rod.

On the 12th, 13th, 14th, and 15th September, I caught nothing, merely losing three fish of which two were big ones. I fished in the mornings before breakfast, then from 10 to 12.30 and in the afternoon from 5 to 7. At last, on the 17th September, the fish became more active, and, in the morning, before breakfast, I took my first trout in Lawson's Pool. Then, in the Sea Pool (at the mouth), at my second cast, my reel began emptying at full speed and I had the impression of having on the end of my line the fish one can only find in Paradise! I was all alone and was wondering where and how I would take my fish with my pocket gaff. At 9 o'clock I went back to the house, painfully carrying my two fish which weighed $13\frac{1}{2}$ and 20 pounds on the scales!

During the following days, I took another six trout, making eight in all, on my Parabolic with nylon tapered to ·014 inches: they weighed 9, 10, $13\frac{1}{2}$, 17, $17\frac{1}{2}$, 17, 18 and 20 pounds. Average 15 pounds.

Here are a few words on the technique of fishing the Em.

Rapids. Moderate currents. Deep water. You fish with a wet fly as for salmon. The artificial fly should as far as possible drift down the current well ahead of the leader and without drag. Whenever the current forms a loop or pocket in the line, you must mend the line by moving the rod tip in the opposite direction, which raises the line, replaces it upstream and straightens it out. You also play fast and loose (the raising of the rod followed by lowering it again) to straighten the end of the line and the leader, particularly at the end of the drift. The depth at which the fly drifts depends on the size of the hook.

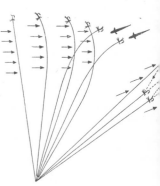

Mending the line by moving the rod tip

Low water. Calms. Shallows. In these you fish with a greased line. The fly should drift at about a foot beneath the surface. The line should be greased to within 2 or 3 yards of its point and it is this ungreased part, the whole of the leader and the fly which must always be submerged. The fly sometimes has a tendency to come to the surface, but a horizontal, rapid and abrupt movement of the point of the rod will make it sink again. This method of fishing is very exciting from the fact that it resembles dry fly fishing and that one can see the fish take.

Flies. All the principal patterns for salmon or sea trout from 8 to 3/0. The smaller ones for the greased line. Colour: clear light, pale coloured flies; bad light, dark coloured flies. I have a weakness for the prawn fly whose supple hackle round the body often gives a semblance of life and on which I have caught all my fish with hooks No. 2 (General Practitioner).

The sea trout of the Em systematically refuse the floating fly while, on the Laerdal in Norway, it is accepted when conditions are favourable.

Charles Ritz,
A Fly-Fisher's Life, 1959.

FISHING IN FINLAND

FINLAND is called the land of a 1,000 lakes, but actually there are 36,000, not to mention the small rivers and streams.

The Finnish coast has the total length of 16,000 Km. The country in the south and west is bounded by two inland seas, the Gulf of Finland and the Bothnian Gulf, and in the north by the Arctic Ocean. It is therefore no wonder that Finland offers anglers the most wonderful fishing.

Of all the fishing to be had in Finland the Salmon (*Salmo salar*), trout (*Salmo fario*), grayling (*Thymollus vulgaris*) and pike (*Esox Lucius*) are the best. The salmon run up to 70 pounds, the best fish in 1935 on rod and line was 52·2 pounds, the trout run up to 25 pounds, the best fish in 1935 18 pounds. The grayling weigh up to 5 pounds and the pike very seldom exceed 30 pounds.

Salmon Fishing: The season opens on the 1st May and closes on the 15th September, both days included, with the exception of the Petsamo-river where the season closes on the 1st of September.

Of the rivers running into the Bothnian Gulf, Oulujoki and Kemijoki are the best, particularly suited for sport fishing; the method used in these two rivers with the greatest success is harling, on account of the great width of these rivers. The fishing rights are let on lease direct from the landowners.

TACKLE FOR OULUJOKI

The flies such as Black Doctor, Jock Scott, Mar Lodge, and the Finnish fly Wasastjerna have had the most success. Sizes 3/0–1/0.

At Kemijoki fly fishing has never been successful, but spoons made by the local farmers of their own design have been very good.

Of greater interest to the salmon fisher are the rivers running into the Arctic Ocean, the Paatsjoki and Petsamojoki. The latter offers the angler who prefers wading about 10 Km. of wonderful sport; in Paatsjoki the fishing is only practised from a boat. The salmon here are much larger than those which run in the Petsamojoki, which is a much smaller river. The total weight of salmon caught by anglers at Paatsjoki between 21st June and 27th July, 1935, was 823 pounds, giving an average weight of 25 pounds per fish.

TACKLE FOR KOLTTAKÖNGÖS, PAATSJOKI

Hardy's Bergen Spoon, Silver Pennell and Pioneer Devon 3 inches. **Flies:** Silver Doctor, Silver Scott, Dusty Miller, Murdoch, Silver Rower, Black Prince, sizes 6/0–4/0, and also the same flies, but with double hooks, type Hardy's Short Point.

A fee of four shillings a day is charged for the licence to fish with the addition of one shilling an hour for the hire of boat and boatman.

At Petsamojoki the writer caught 515 pounds of salmon from 1st July to 1st September. On this river the fly is the principal lure, spinning also gives good sport, but only at the end of June and the first week in July.

Tackle: $2\frac{1}{2}$–3 inch Pioneer Devon Silver, Bergen Spoon.
Flies: Silver Doctor, Dusty Miller, Silver Rower, Silver Scott, Mar Lodge, Red Drummond, Black Dose, Sweep. Sizes 5/0–3/0.

It is noted that there are in the Petsamojoki, a great many rapids and the bottom is very stony, therefore only the strongest casts such as Crown or Hardy's twisted for Heavy Norwegian Angling should be used.

The government charges a fee of 50 shillings for the whole season's fishing. Trout fishing is allowed by law from 1st December till 15th September, but Private Clubs and the Angler's Society in Finland do not allow fishing in their waters before the 1st May.

In most parts of South and Central Finland the trout rivers are let to clubs and the Angler's Society.

But foreigners can join the Angler's Society or be invited to fish in these rivers by members of the clubs; some of the rivers are still owned by farmers and may be rented at very moderate prices. In the waters belonging to the Angler's Society the trout run to between 20–25 pounds. Here are a few names of places belonging to the Society, with the weight of fish taken in one season:

Name of Place				Number	Total weight.
Imatra in Wuoksen	–	–	–	180	360 pounds
Hilmo- & Potmo rapids	–	–		109	260 ,,
Mankala rapids –	–	–	–	128	230 ,,
Vuolenkoski rapids	–	–	–	267	310 ,,

Natural baits are as a rule the best to use. For example Hardy's Salmon Minnow, and if one uses flies, the same flies as used in England, but with a larger size in hooks. Salmon flies can also be used in sizes 1–9.

Petsamo and Lapland, far up in the North of Finland where the sun shines for 24 hours, is the fisherman's Eldorado; here one will find rivers so far completely unfished.

Amongst the trout waters I specially wish to mention Virtaniemi, situated on the upper reaches of the Paatsjoki, which offers exceptionally good sport to the angler. In 1934, 2,173 trout and 144 grayling were taken in Virtaniemi, the total weight being 2,400 pounds. The fee charged by the Government is 20 Fmks per day.

The whole of Lapland is traversed by small rivers full of trout and grayling; with the exception of the rivers belonging to the Angler's Society, the rest of the fishing is free. The fish in these small rivers run from 1 to 5 pounds, depending on the water.

The tackle used is practically the same as in England.

Pike fishing along the coast of Finland is generally done by spinning, but in the lakes trolling from a boat gives better results than spinning.

Hardy Brothers Catalogue, 1937.

I have during the fishing months July and August, 1936, caught ninety-eight trout, and eight pike all with your fishing tackles and it has been a pleasure.

Letter from Denmark quoted in Hardy Brothers Catalogue, *1937*

1924

THE LADY OR THE SALMON?

[*The* Apologia pro morte et vita sua *of the Hon. Houghton Grannom, found drowned in the Tweed clutching his salmon rod with all the line run out and a salmon fast at the other end. (Verdict: accidental death.)*]

Dear Smith, Before you read this—long before, I hope—I shall have solved the great mystery—if, indeed, we solve it. If the water runs down to-morrow, and there is every prospect that it will do so, I must have the opportunity of making such an end as even malignity cannot suspect of being voluntary. There are plenty of fish in the water; if I hook one in "The Trows", I shall let myself go whither the current takes me. Life has for weeks been odious to me; for what is life without honour, without love, and coupled with shame and remorse? Repentance I cannot call the emotion which gnaws me at the heart, for in similar circumstances (unlikely as these are to occur) I feel that I would do the same thing again.

Are we but automata, worked by springs, moved by the stronger impulse, and unable to choose for ourselves which impulse that shall be? Even now, in decreeing my own destruction, do I exercise free-will, or am I the sport of hereditary tendencies, of mistaken views of honour, of a seeming self-sacrifice, which, perhaps, is but selfishness in disguise? I blight my unfortunate father's old age; I destroy the last of an ancient house; but I remove from the path of Olive Dunne the shadow that must rest upon the sunshine of what will eventually,

I trust, be a happy life, unvexed by memories of one who loved her passionately. Dear Olive! how pure, how ardent was my devotion to her none knows better than you. But Olive had, I will not say a fault, though I suffer from it, but a quality, or rather two qualities, which have completed my misery. Lightly as she floats on the stream of society, the most casual observer, and even the enamoured beholder, can see that Olive Dunne has great pride, and no sense of humour. Her dignity is her idol. What makes her, even for a moment, the possible theme of ridicule is in her eyes an unpardonable sin. This sin, I must with penitence confess, I did indeed commit. Another woman might have forgiven me. I know not how that may be; I throw myself on the mercy of the court. But, if another could pity and pardon, to Olive this was impossible. I have never seen her since that fatal moment when, paler than her orange blossoms, she swept through the porch of the church, while I, dishevelled, mud-stained, half-drowned—ah! that memory will torture me if memory at all remains. And yet, fool, maniac, that I was, I could not resist the wild, mad impulse to laugh which shook the rustic spectators, and which in my case was due, I trust, to hysterical but *not* unmanly emotion. If any woman, any bride, could forgive such an apparent but most unintentional insult, Olive Dunne, I knew, was not that woman. My abject letters of explanation, my appeals for mercy, were returned unopened. Her parents pitied me, perhaps had reasons for being on my side, but Olive was of marble. It is not only myself that she cannot pardon, she will never, I know, forgive herself while my existence reminds her of what she had to endure. When she receives the intelligence of my demise, no suspicion will occur to her; she will not say "He is fitly punished"; but her peace of mind will gradually return.

It is for this, mainly, that I sacrifice myself, but also because I cannot endure the dishonour of a laggard in love and a recreant bridegroom.

So much for my motives: now to my tale.

The day before our wedding-day had been the happiest in my life. Never had I felt so certain of Olive's affections, never so fortunate in my own. We parted in the soft moonlight; she, no doubt, to finish her nuptial preparations; I, to seek my couch in the little rural inn above the roaring water of the Budon.*

---

* From motives of delicacy I suppress the true name of the river.

> Move eastward, happy earth, and leave
>> Yon orange sunset fading slow;
> From fringes of the faded eve
>> Oh, happy planet, eastward go,

I murmured, though the atmospheric conditions were not really those described by the poet.

> Ah, bear me with thee, smoothly borne,
>> Dip forward under starry light,
> And move me to my marriage morn,
>> And round again to——

"River in grand order, sir," said the voice of Robins, the keeper, who recognized me in the moonlight. "There's a regular monster in the Ashweil," he added, naming a favourite cast; "never saw nor heard of such a fish in the water before."

"Mr. Dick must catch him, Robins," I answered; "no fishing for me to-morrow."

"No, sir," said Robins, affably. "Wish you joy, sir, and Miss Olive, too. It's a pity, though! Master Dick, he throws a fine fly, but he gets flurried with a big fish, being young. And this one is a topper."

With that he gave me good-night, and I went to bed, but not to sleep. I was fevered with happiness; the past and future reeled before my wakeful vision. I heard every clock strike; the sounds of morning were astir, and still I could not sleep. The ceremony, for reasons connected with our long journey to my father's place in Hampshire, was to be early—half-past ten was the hour. I looked at my watch; it was seven of the clock, and then I looked out of the window: it was a fine, soft, grey morning, with a south wind tossing the yellowing boughs. I got up, dressed in a hasty way, and thought I would just take a look at the river. It was, indeed, in glorious order, lapping over the top of the sharp stone which we regarded as a measure of the due size of water.

The morning was young, sleep was out of the question; I could not settle my mind to read. Why should I not take a farewell cast, alone, of course? I always disliked the attendance of a gillie. I took my salmon rod out of its case, rigged it up, and started for the stream, which flowed within a couple of hundred yards of my quarters.

There it raced under the ash tree, a pale delicate brown, perhaps a little thing too coloured. I therefore put on a large Silver Doctor, and began steadily fishing down the ash-tree cast. What if I should wipe Dick's eye, I thought, when, just where the rough and smooth water meet, there boiled up a head and shoulders such as I had never seen on any fish. My heart leaped and stood still, but there came no sensation from the rod, and I finished the cast, my knees actually trembling beneath me. Then I gently lifted the line, and very elaborately tested every link of the powerful casting-line. Then I gave him 10 minutes by my watch; next, with unspeakable emotion, I stepped into the stream and repeated the cast. Just at the same spot he came up again; the huge rod bent like a switch, and the salmon rushed straight down the pool, as if he meant to make for the sea. I staggered on to dry land to follow him the easier, and dragged at my watch to time the fish; a quarter to eight. But the slim chain had broken, and the watch, as I hastily thrust it back, missed my pocket and fell into the water. There was no time to stoop for it; the fish started afresh, tore up the pool as fast as he had gone down it, and, rushing behind the torrent, into the eddy at the top, leaped clean out of the water. He was 70 pounds if he was an ounce. Here he slackened a little, dropping back, and I got in some line. Now he sulked so intensely that I thought he had got the line round a rock. It might be broken, might be holding fast to a sunken stone, for aught that I could tell; and the time was passing, I knew not how rapidly. I tried all known methods, tugging at him, tapping the butt, and slackening line on him. At last the top of the rod was slightly agitated, and then, back flew the long line in my face. Gone! I reeled up with a sigh, but the line tightened again. He had made a sudden rush under my bank, but there he lay again like a stone. How long? Ah! I cannot tell how long! I heard the church clock strike, but missed the number of the strokes. Soon he started again down-stream into the shallows, leaping at the end of his rush—the monster. Then he came slowly up, and "jiggered" savagely at the line. It seemed impossible that any tackle could stand these short violent jerks. Soon he showed signs of weakening. Once his huge silver side appeared for a moment near the surface, but he retreated to his old fastness. I was in a tremor of delight and despair. I should have thrown down my rod, and flown on the wings of love to Olive and the altar. But I hoped that there was time still—that it was not so very late! At length he was failing. I heard 10 o'clock strike. He came up and lumbered on the surface

of the pool. Gradually I drew him, plunging ponderously, to the gravelled beach, where I meant to "tail" him. He yielded to the strain, he was in the shallows, the line was shortened. I stooped to seize him. The frayed and overworn gut broke at a knot, and with a loose roll he dropped back towards the deep. I sprang at him, stumbled, fell on him, struggled with him, but he slipped from my arms. In that moment I knew more than the anguish of Orpheus. Orpheus! Had I, too, lost my Eurydice? I rushed from the stream, up the steep bank, along to my rooms. I passed the church door. Olive, pale as her orange-blossoms, was issuing from the porch. The clock pointed to 10.45. I was ruined, I knew it, and I laughed. I laughed like a lost spirit. She swept past me, and amidst the amazement of the gentle and simple, I sped wildly away. Ask me no more. The rest is silence.

Andrew Lang,
Angling Sketches, 1891.

GILLIES

Gillies, it does not take you long to discover, need diplomatic *but firm handling*. The local man always knows more than you do. Also, although he may be clever enough to conceal it, he resents your presence: this "foreigner" he is taking around. This, despite the fact that most of them could not throw a straight line themselves, that they would use line thick as a rope, anyway; and that there is no more suppleness in their thick wrists than if they were casting a clothes pole. I do not succumb to the philosophy of the local man.

This youngish gillie I had at Scourie broke the tip of one of my rods (a fine two-piece Hardy) by trying to cast a Devon with it when I was far off, fishing from the opposite bank. In a rocky pool not much larger than the average bathroom, in which we watched four large salmon making up their minds whether they were going to run up or not—he wanted to gaff one. With white bumps being raised on me all over by the klegs my temper was never very sweet. I had noticed that every time we came to a small stone bridge on the way home he always asked me to stop the car, while he went off to look at something under the arch of bridge. One night, when he jumped out of the car, I saw that he had my collapsible gaff in his hand. He ran to the bridge. Before I could stop him I heard a thrashing of water —and a fine 10 pound salmon lay on the grass.

"I've been watchin' him for days!" he said.

"Now what are you going to do with him?" I asked. "You can't put him back, you've gaffed him through the stomach."

"For you," he said.

"Not me."

"Well . . . Sir . . ."

"He's your fish," I said.

Now he was in a pickle, and I enjoyed it. The ex-gamekeeper who ran the inn knew pretty well if one of "his men", as he called them, got an illicit salmon or not. Gossip travels fast in those parts. "You can't throw that fish back; you have ruined it," I insisted. "You must take him home. You killed it."

The gillie glared at me angrily. "I'll get into trouble," he growled. I told him he could get into it. "But I'll tell you what I'll do," I said. "You needn't come with me to the hotel. I'll drop you on the way, and you can cut across the hills for home. I'd put that salmon under my shirt."

The next day he was a subdued gillie—until almost lunch time.

Then there was old Tom, on the Lakes of Killarney. I was living at Flesk Castle with one of the Macgillicuddys whose mountains, the Reeks, are named after this ancient Irish family. Tom was lazy. When I wanted to fish the mouth of the Flesk River he always said it was too early for "throut" there. Finally, I told the hotel, I would go out without Tom. Next day, when I got down there, I found the boat—but no oars. The hotel said that old Tom owned the oars. I got oars. That afternoon I found the boat—but it had no thole-pins. Tom had heard about me getting the oars. So I cut thole-pins from a stick of green sapling. Of course, the wind *would* rise and my green thole-pins bent. I slithered all over the lake like this. Then I made Tom take me to the mouth of the Flesk; I brow-beat him into it verbally.

There I got eleven fine trout, all with almost salmon-red flesh from feeding on the plentiful crayfish. Even Tom was enthused.

"Now," I said; "what about it being too early in the year? How do you account for these, Tom?"

"Ah . . . shure . . . I've killed throut here meself . . . before St.

Patrick's Day!"

And when I said to him one day, looking around the almost unearthly beauty of the Lakes: "You're lucky, Tom, to live in such a place as this!" he merely sniffed and replied: "Ah, sur—I see it every day."

Negley Farson,
Going Fishing, 1942.

AUSTRIA: AN INCIDENT AT ISCHL

On our first day we got more trout than our attendant's barrel would accommodate,* so, on the second, two of them went with us. They showed us some of their flies, tied on stuff more of the nature of a barge-rope than of ordinary English gut casting lines, and also bait tackle of the same rough character, the sinker being a rifle bullet with a hole drilled through it. As the river was quite clear, they were unable to do any good with such primitive tackle; they also used nets set round the pools, and then tried to drive the trout (the bottom of the river was of such a nature as to preclude the use of a seine), but these set nets, being made of coarse twine, the trout naturally declined to go into them. Except the char, then, they were very short of fish to sell. Trout and grayling were to be caught from the town upwards (even fishing from the banks of that part of the river actually in the town itself), the best streams and pools being near Halstadt, some 10 miles distant. At this last-named place was a small inn, at which we stayed for a day or two. The spot was beautiful, immediately below a mountain, at the foot of which lay a large lake out of which flowed the Traun. At this point were sluice-gates, one of which only was kept open; below the open sluice was a long gliding piece of water, down which one afternoon were floating, in a half-drowned state, quantities of flies on which the fish were greedily

---

* The author had been given permission to fish subject to the customary proviso that his catch was to be kept alive in a barrel of water: at the end of the day it would be handed to the local fishmonger, who had the rights in the fishing.

feeding. There, casting from the bank, trout and grayling were taken literally at every throw. Never do I remember landing fish so quickly or in such number; they were not of any remarkable weight, running from ¾ pound to 1½ pounds, but strong for their size and well-shaped. Whilst engrossed in the sport a smart Austrian gentleman, accompanied by a Skye terrier, approached and asked me to sell him some of my catch to take home to Ischl, whence he had driven a four-in-hand, with a picnic party. I replied that it was not my habit to sell fish, but that he was welcome to as many as he pleased. After a profusion of apologies, he accepted seven or eight and remained a few minutes watching my performance. During that time the terrier from Skye amused itself with barking at the fish when landed, and jumping round them, with the result that in one of his jumps the drop-fly (for I was using two flies) got fast in his fore-leg. His master was in distress at the accident, so, telling him to hold the dog fast, I got out my knife to cut the little bit of skin which held the hook. The Austrian, however, not keeping a firm hold, his dog fastened on my arm, and the act of shaking him off broke the gut close to the hook, which he had consequently to carry back to Ischl, and I continued my fishing with one fly. (Here it may be as well to remark that, not long after this incident, I discarded the use of a second fly, partly on account of the extra risk of losing fish in weedy or rocky streams.) At Ischl I remained for some three weeks much enjoying myself, the sport being generally good, at times very good, the scenery and the weather both delightful. Possibly I might have remained a few days longer, but my departure was hastened by an incident which, as showing the risk incurred by setting the law at defiance, especially abroad, may as well be mentioned. Having desired the two men with their barrels to meet me, I waited at the spot appointed for nearly an hour, when, as they had not put in an appearance, and the day was slipping away, I walked off without them to some streams about 5 miles off. After a bad day, resulting in the take of a few small trout, which were returned to the water, and half a dozen grayling, it came on to rain, so taking down the rod, I made the best of my way home. On the road, however, having no desire to be burdened with the grayling, I handed them over to some peasants who were just leaving the fields, where they had been at work. As the town of Ischl was reached the two men who ought to have been with me sprang so suddenly out, from round a corner, that they had me by the collar in a moment, one of them roughly opening the fishing basket to see what it contained. My indignation at this treatment was extreme, heightened, too, by the fact that they knew well enough where to find me, and that their violence was therefore unnecessary. Moreover, besides an occasional tip, they had frequently consumed beer and tobacco at my expense. Without considering the possible consequences, a dig in the ribs with the elbow freed me from one of my assailants, whilst I shook myself, somewhat roughly, free from the grasp of the other. Then, turning, I felt able to withstand offensive measures with the butt of the rod; the men, however, showed no sign of further hostility, but followed at a respectful distance to my inn. Whilst finishing a bottle of "Vorslauer" after dinner, my landlord came to my table to speak to me. He said I had been guilty of an assault on these two river-keepers in the execution of their duty, and that they would certainly lay an information against me the next morning; that the consequences would be most unpleasant, involving probably some days in prison besides a fine. I pointed out that had these men addressed me civilly I should have been ready to go with them before a magistrate, and that, besides, they could not prove that I had broken my agreement with the fishmonger, whose servants they were; they had not seen me fish, and had found nothing in the basket. The landlord replied that the magistrate would certainly not consider my defence as justifying violence on my part, and that, though sorry to lose a guest for whom he had the greatest esteem, his advice to me was to take the early coach for Dresden at 5 A.M., and depart before a warrant for my arrest could be made out.

C. S. Barrington,
Seventy Years Fishing, 1902.

AN OLD ETONIAN TRAMP

When the Hispana crossed the Bridge of Larrig His Majesty's late Attorney-General was modestly concealed in a bush of broom on the Crask side, from which he could watch the sullen stretches of the

Lang Whang. He was carefully dressed for the part in a pair of Wattie Lithgow's old trousers much too short for him, a waistcoat and jacket which belonged to Sime the butler and which had been made about the year, 1890, and a vulgar flannel shirt borrowed from Shapp. He was innocent of a collar, he had not shaved for two days, and as he had forgotten to have his hair cut before leaving London his locks were of a disreputable length. Last, he had a shocking old hat of Sir Archie's from which the lining had long since gone. His hands were sun-burned and grubby, and he had removed his signet-ring. A light ten-foot greenheart rod lay beside him, already put up, and to the tapered line was fixed a tapered cast ending in a strange little cocked fly. As he waited he was busy oiling fly and line.

His glass showed him an empty haugh, save for the figure of Jimsie at the far end close to the Wood of Larrigmore. The sun-warmed waters of the river drowsed in the long dead stretches, curled at rare intervals by the faintest western breeze. The banks were crisp green turf, scarcely broken by a boulder, but five yards from them the moss began—a wilderness of hags and tussocks. Somewhere in its depths he knew that Benjie lay coiled like an adder, waiting on events.

Leithen's plan, like all great strategy, was simple. Everything depended on having Jimsie out of sight of the Lang Whang for half an hour. Given that, he believed he might kill a salmon. He had marked out a pool where in the evening fish were usually stirring, one of those irrational haunts which no piscatorial psychologist has ever explained. If he could fish fine and far, he might cover it from a spot below a high bank where only the top of his rod would be visible to watchers at a distance. Unfortunately, that spot was on the other side of the stream. With such tackle, landing a salmon would be a critical business, but there was one chance in ten that it might be accomplished; Benjie would be at hand to conceal the fish, and he himself would disappear silently into the Crask thickets. But every step bristled with horrid dangers. Jimsie might be faithful to his post—in which case it was hopeless; he might find the salmon dour, or a fish might break him in the landing, or Jimsie might return to find him brazenly tethered to forbidden game. It was no good thinking about it. On one thing he was decided: if he were caught, he would not try to escape. That would mean retreat in the direction of Crask, and an exploration of the Crask covers would assuredly reveal what must at all costs be concealed. No. He would go quietly into captivity, and trust to his base appearance to be let off with a drubbing.

As he waited, watching the pools turn from gold to bronze, as the sun sank behind the Glenraden peaks, he suffered the inevitable reaction. The absurdities seemed huge as mountains, the difficulties innumerable as the waves of the sea. There remained less than an hour in which there would be sufficient light to fish—Jimsie was immovable (he had just lit his pipe and was sitting in meditation on a big stone)—every moment the Larrig waters were cooling with the chill of evening. Leithen consulted his watch, and found it half-past eight. He had lost his wrist-watch, and had brought his hunter, attached to a thin gold chain. That was foolish, so he slipped the chain from his buttonhole and drew it through the arm-hole of his waistcoat.

Suddenly he rose to his feet, for things were happening at the far end of the haugh. Jimsie stood in an attitude of expectation—he seemed to be hearing something far up-stream. Leithen heard it too, the cry of excited men. . . . Jimsie stood on one foot for a moment in doubt; then he turned and doubled towards the Wood of Larrigmore . . . The gallant Crossby had got to business and was playing hare to the hounds inside the park wall. If human nature had not changed, Leithen thought, the whole force would presently join in the chase— Angus and Lennox and Jimsie and Davie and doubtless many volunteers. Heaven send fleetness and wind to the South London Harrier, for it was his duty to occupy the interest of every male in Strathlarrig till such time as he subsided with angry expostulation into captivity.

The road was empty, the valley was deserted, when Leithen raced across the bridge and up the south side of the river. It was not two hundred yards to his chosen stand, a spit of gravel below a high bank at the tail of a long pool. Close to the other bank, nearly thirty yards off, was the shelf where fish lay of an evening. He tested the water with his hand, and its temperature was at least 60°. His theory, which he had learned long ago from the aged Bostonian, was that under such conditions some subconscious memory revived in salmon of their early days as parr when they fed on surface insects, and that they could be made to take a dry fly.

He got out his line to the required length with half a dozen casts in the air, and then put his fly three feet above the spot where a salmon was wont to lie. It was a curious type of cast, which he had been practising lately in the early morning, for by an adroit check he made the fly alight in a curl, so that it floated for a second or two with the leader in a straight line away from it. In this way he believed that the most suspicious fish would see nothing to alarm him, nothing but a hapless insect derelict on the water.

Sir Archie had spoken truth in describing Leithen to Wattie Lithgow as an artist. His long, straight, delicate casts were art indeed. Like thistledown the fly dropped, like thistledown it floated over the head of the salmon, but like thistledown it was disregarded. There was indeed a faint stirring of curiosity. From where he stood Leithen could see that slight ruffling of the surface which means an observant fish . . .

Already ten minutes had been spent in this barren art. The crisis craved other measures.

His new policy meant a short line, so with infinite stealth and care Leithen waded up the side of the water, sometimes treading precarious ledges of peat, sometimes waist deep in mud and pond-weed, till he was within twenty feet of the fishing-ground. Here he had not the high bank for a shelter, and would have been sadly conspicuous to Jimsie, had that sentinel remained at his post. He crouched low and cast as before with the same curl just ahead of the chosen spot.

But now his tactics were different. So soon as the fly had floated past where he believed the fish to be, he sank it by a dexterous twist of the rod-point, possible only with a short line. The fly was no longer a winged thing; drawn away under water it roused in the salmon early memories of succulent nymphs . . . At the first cast there was a slight swirl, which meant that a fish near the surface had turned to follow the lure. The second cast the line straightened and moved swiftly up-stream.

Leithen had killed in his day many hundreds of salmon—once in Norway a notable beast of fifty-five pounds. But no salmon he had ever hooked had stirred in his breast such excitement as this modest fellow of eight pounds. " ''Tis not so wide as a church-door,' " he reflected with Mercutio, " 'but 'twill suffice'—If I can only land him." But a dry-fly cast and a ten-foot rod are a frail wherewithal for killing a fish against time. With his ordinary fifteen-footer and gut of moderate strength he could have brought the little salmon to grass in five minutes, but now there was immense risk of a break, and a break would mean that the whole enterprise had failed. He dared not exert pressure; on the other hand, he could not follow the fish except by making himself conspicuous on the greensward. Worst of all, he had at the best ten minutes for the job.

Thirty yards off an otter slid into the water. Leithen wished he was King of the Otters, as in the Highland tale, to summon the brute to his aid.

The ten minutes had lengthened to fifteen—nine hundred seconds of heart-disease—when, wet to the waist, he got his pocket-gaff into the salmon's side and drew it on to the spit of gravel where he had started fishing. A dozen times he thought he had lost, and once when the fish ran straight up the pool his line was carried out to its last yard of backing. He gave thanks to high Heaven, when, as he landed it, he observed that the fly had all but lost its hold and in another minute would have been free. By such narrow margins are great deeds accomplished.

He snapped the cast from the line and buried it in mud. Then cautiously he raised his head above the bank. The gloaming was gathering fast, and so far as he could see the haugh was still empty. Pushing his rod along the ground, he scrambled on to the turf.

Then he had a grievous shock. Jimsie had reappeared, and he was in full view of him. Moreover, there were two men on bicycles coming up the road, who, with the deplorable instinct of human nature, would be certain to join in any pursuit. He was on turf as short as a lawn, cumbered with a tell-tale rod and a poached salmon. The friendly hags were a dozen yards off, and before he could reach them his damning baggage would be noted.

At this supreme moment he had an inspiration, derived from the memory of the otter. To get out his knife, cut a ragged wedge from the fish, and roll it in his handkerchief was the work of five seconds. To tilt the rod over the bank so that it lay in the deep shadow was the work of three more . . . Jimsie had seen him, for a wild cry came down the stream, a cry which brought the cyclists off their machines and set them staring in his direction. Leithen dropped his gaff after the rod, and began running towards the Larrig bridge—slowly, limpingly, like a frightened man with no resolute purpose of escape. And as he ran he prayed that Benjie from the deeps of the moss had seen what had been done and drawn the proper inference.

It was a bold bluff, for he had decided to make the salmon evidence for, not against him. He hobbled down the bank, looking over his shoulder often as if in terror, and almost ran into the arms of the cyclists, who, warned by Jimsie's yells, were waiting to intercept him. He dodged them, however, and cut across to the road, for he had seen that Jimsie had paused and had noted the salmon lying blatantly on the sward, a silver splash in the twilight. Leithen doubled up the road as if going towards Strathlarrig, and Jimsie, the fleet of foot, did not catch up with him till almost on the edge of the Wood of Larrigmore. The cyclists, who had remounted, arrived at the same moment to find a wretched muddy tramp in the grip of a stalwart but breathless gillie.

"I tell ye I was daein' nae harm," the tramp whined. "I was walkin' up the water-side—there's nae law to keep a body frae walkin' up a water-side when there's nae fence—and I seen an auld otter killin' a saumon. The fish is there still to prove I'm no leein'."

"There is a fush, but you wass thinkin' to steal the fush, and you would have it had it in your breeks if I hadna seen you. That is poachin', ma man, and you will come up to Strathlarrig. The master said that anyone goin' near the watter was to be lockit up, and you will be lockit up. You can tell all the lees you like in the mornin'."

Then a thought struck Jimsie. He wanted the salmon, for the subject of otters in the Larrig had been a matter of dispute between him and Angus, and here was evidence for his own view.

"Would you two gentlemen oblige me by watchin' this man while I rin back and get the fush? Bash him on the head if he offers to rin."

The cyclists, who were journalists out to enjoy the evening air, willingly agreed, but Leithen showed no wish to escape. He begged a fag in a beggar's whine, and, since he seemed peaceable, the two kept a good distance for fear of infection. He stood making damp streaks in the dusty road, a pitiable specimen of humanity, for his original get-up was not improved by the liquefaction of his clothes and a generous legacy of slimy peat. He seemed to be nervous, which indeed he was, for if Benjie had not seized his chance he was utterly done, and if Jimsie should light upon his rod he was gravely compromised.

But when Jimsie returned in a matter of ten minutes he was empty-handed.

"I never kenned the like," he proclaimed. "That otter has come back and gotten the fush. Ach, the maleecious brute!"

John Buchan,
John MacNab, 1925.

HINTS ABOUT NEW ZEALAND

I have just had a fortnight among the mountain streams of the interior in company with R. C. and E. B., both of this city, and a right good time we have had. We took two tents and provisions, and camped on the banks of a large stream, called the Waikaia. This stream has a gravelly bottom, with banks of clay and mould 6 to 8 feet high, with plenty of rapid runs into large deep pools. I have one of your 11-foot steel-centre cane rods, and I was glad I brought it with me. I was very nearly persuaded to leave it at home, as a gentleman who had visited this stream told me that the fish were all large, and I would never be able to check them with such light gear; but I

I have been fishing last year on the frontier of upper Hungaria during 6 weeks, I had to deal with very heavy fishes in an uncommon fast running water between abrupt rocks where a landing net was not always possible to use. The average was twenty-five to forty trout a day.

Letter quoted in Hardy Brothers Catalogue, *1907*.

found out from experience that such a rod is not to be beaten for these very active large fish, the extraordinary elasticity, combined with the great strength of the cane, we found was just the thing, for whenever the fish made a strong rush out into heavy water, we could put on any amount of strain knowing that the rod would not fail us, and how easy it was to strike the hook home when a fish rose; the great elasticity of the rod never allowed you to bring up the slack with a jerk, and thus have a chance of breaking the casting line, but the strain being so equal from butt to point it was almost a dead certainty that you hooked your fish. All the settlers (called cockatoos out here) were daily enchanted with the rods, and looked on in amazement to see us landing such big fish—and strong fish—with such light tackle; they were used to heavy minnow rods, and fished with minnow only; they had never seen fly-fishing like this. Our camp was quite the talk of the district, we being the first lot of Dunedin anglers who had had a successful time of it on this stream. A Runholder in the vicinity of our camp remarked to the farmer, who was kind enough to write to me and advised me to try this stream: "What on earth induced you to tell them to come out here; why, they'll clean out the river in no time." If we had caught all the fish I saw in one pool, we should have had a bag the weight of which would have astonished the anglers of New Zealand. Why, the river was fairly alive with big fish, from 10 pounds to 1 pound in weight; so that the Runholder need have had no fear of our clearing out the river. I only wish some of your expert men were out here for the January and February fishing in these streams; they would be astonished at the bags they would make. Bye-the-bye, I must say a word in praise of those tapered casts of yours. R.C. fished for 5 days with one cast, and never lost a fish by breakage. I will give you a sample of his sport, fishing only for 3 hours in the morning—1st day, five fish, 14 pounds; 2nd day, four fish, 12 pounds; 3rd day, four fish, 10 pounds; 4th day, six fish, 20 pounds; 5th day, eight fish, 21 pounds; in Waikaia River. In the Pomahaka—Wednesday, five fish, 18 pounds; Thursday, eight fish, 23 pounds; Friday, five fish, 19 pounds. Myself—Wednesday, six fish, 22 pounds; Thursday, four fish, $18\frac{1}{2}$ pounds; Friday, nine fish, 42 pounds; Saturday, in 1 hour, three fish. E. B.—On Wednesday, twelve fish, 52 pounds. E. B. left for home on Thursday, and R. C. and myself stayed on until Saturday morning. On this day, Mr. B., manager of the Clinton Hatcheries, came over with a buggy to take us back to catch the train home. Having a couple of hours to spare, he took Mr. C.'s rod and went up the stream for about 2 miles, in that time killed four splendid fish, weighing $15\frac{3}{4}$ pounds. I went down-stream, but having an old hickory minnow rod with me, I unfortunately broke it at the second joint, by striking a fish rather too hard; after splicing this break with flax and got fairly at it again, another big fish rose, and away went the top joint this time. I then gave up in disgust, vowing that I should not go out another year without a "Hardy Steel-Centre Minnow Rod". Mr. C. had one and he could always kill his fish in half the time that I could with my hickory and greenheart rod. The fly rods of your make were too slender for using with heavy minnows, and, besides, the reel would not carry enough line for such large fish in such heavy water. That is another thing I must have—a good light reel, easy running. I lost a big 6 pound fish on Friday, the day I got nine, through the reel not letting the line off fast enough he broke me, taking cast and minnow with him. In the same pool our party killed seven big fish from $5\frac{1}{2}$ pounds (which I caught) to $3\frac{3}{4}$ pounds each. In one run Mr. B. and I killed four big fish; as soon as he hooked one, I went and had a cast, and also hooked one, taking care to work it down quickly into the pool, in this way we caught four fish in the run, all large. The river is one series of cascades and pools, running alternately through gorges and open plains with nothing on the edges to stop casting as long a line as you like. Two can fish the stream, one on each side, facing each other, as it is so wide, and the stream cut up into runs through rocks, it is a perfect picture of a trout stream, and is just as full of fish as a plum pudding is full of plums. Angling people come from all parts of New Zealand to fish this stream. It is at its best in January, February, and the half of March, sometimes it is good right up to the end of March, then ducks are plentiful, and large herds of red deer are in the forests through which it runs; the season for shooting these begins when the fishing ends. The fee for fishing is £1, available for the whole colony, and the licence to kill deer is £2 for two months. The land is the property of the Crown, and is free to all licence holders. Trout streams have a chain reserve on each bank. Some of the small streams were sold out and out before the Act came into force, but all the best and largest rivers have the reserve for the public.

Our best Otago rivers are the Waipahi, the Waikaka, the Mataura, the Waikaia, the Pomahaka, the Shag, and the Molyneux, a very large and deep river flowing out of Lakes Wanaka, Hawea, and Wakatipu. This river is full of big fish that take the minnow readily; perch are also very plentiful in it. In two lakes which drain into it, namely, Tuakitoto and Kaitangata, the perch are so numerous that an expert minnow fisher can catch 50 or 60 pounds weight in a morning, wading out about 10 yards and casting all around him. You need never shift if you strike a shoal. I killed, in a little creek that flows into the first-mentioned lake, forty fish in 4 hours, from $\frac{3}{4}$ pound to $2\frac{1}{4}$ pounds, and returned twenty more as I had no room in my basket for them.

The Waitaki, the large river that drains the best part of the Southern Alps, Mount Cook included, has afforded splendid sport this year; bags of 70 and 80 pound for one day's angling were not uncommon in October and November. This is an early river—the snow begins to melt in December, and then it is not much use fishing until March, when the snow is all melted. At that date, however, the stream is full of whitebait, but they do not take the artificial then so readily as they would in October and November; as this river goes off, our Southern streams come into form, and thus you will see that we have capital fishing the whole six-and-a-half months, ending with unlimited duck, pigeon, kaka, pukaki, wild black swans, and deer shooting. Wild goats are also very plentiful in the interior among the mountains, which are quite easy to get to from this city.

The rod most suited for our rivers is one about 15 feet long, with one top pretty stiff for minnow, and one top fairly fine that would do for cricket and fly-fishing on the larger streams. The 11 and 12-foot fly-rods are right for the ordinary streams, only the spare top should be heavier than the fly top, so that, if necessary, the heavier top could be used for the minnow. An angler with two rods as above would be set up for any of our rivers. If you are fitting up any one for New Zealand rivers, give them a good stock of tapered casts from stout lake to very fine-drawn 3 yards, also 1 or 2 dozen Soleskin Phantom Minnows, only the belly to be silvered, and all the rest a parchment color, with no paint on—the color parchment has when it is wet; I killed 1 hundredweight with minnows like this. A gaff is better than a landing net for the big streams, and it has to have a fine point or it will not go into the thick skin of our trout.

If at any time you are recommending anyone to come out here for angling, shooting, &c., you are quite at liberty to give them letters of introduction to me, and I shall on my part be only too happy to give them the most authentic and latest news of rivers, how to get to them, and, in fact, everything relative to our sport.

I remain, yours truly, G.M.M.

Hardy Brothers Catalogue, 1894.

Fly minnows (1894).

THE WANNACALILE RIVER

I was fishing one of our big rivers called the "Wannacalile" near Christchurch, using what is called here a "White Bait" Minnow or Phantom, and walking along a high bank say 17 or 18 feet over the river, all along the bank large blocks of solid earth had fallen out of it, and into the river, of course making the water very rough all along the banks. A friend who was with me and walking along this bank stopped suddenly and said to me—

"I saw a large fish rise just now, right under me, suppose you try for him."

I told him it would be utter madness, as no *rod* in the world could hold a fish in such waters, with rock at the bottom of the river, all covered with broken banks. "No thank you," said I, "I would only loose my minnow (which was a good one) and perhaps break my favourite rod." He immediately said "If you lose your minnow, I will give you another, and if you break your rod, I will send it home to Hardy's for you, and get it put right. I know you are a good hand, and want to see how you shape in a difficulty, and how that rod you *think so much of* will show up." (He was fishing with a rod of mine, an Irish made one, of which more hereafter.) "All right," I said, "on these terms I am on, where did you see the big fish rise?" he pointed out the spot. It was blowing half a gale of wind against me. I let out about 15 yards of line, which I held in a coil in my left hand, till I made a cast with my right, and sent the minnow flying out *against* the wind into the stream, and brought it in a curve under the bank, and over the fish he saw rise; when at it the fish came with a dash, and I was fast at once (I must tell you I was fishing with a *steel trace*, and the minnow hooks on treble gut, nothing else will stand these big fish), the fish appeared to be 10 to 12 pounds, perhaps larger, and I had to simply hold him—fancy a fish say 12 pounds, shaped like a roach, and you trying to hold him in a heavy stream, with broken banks at the bottom; it was no use, he broke away, but only the hold, and kindly left me my bait, the rod was all right. My friend said "try again". I said "you have a try". "Oh! no," said he, "this is not my rod, but yours" (speaking of the rod I lent him). I said, "I will hold *you* harmless as far as the rod is concerned, but you risk your own minnow." "All right," said he, "here goes," and in bringing it round under the banks, he got fast to a fish about 10 pounds, which, as he had to hold him all he knew, broke the *rod* right off at the ferrule of the butt piece, and he was done for the day. You should have seen his face, it made me laugh—not at his misfortune, oh! no; but at his ludicrous expression. The rod he had was an Irish 16-foot rod, but it could no more stand the strain than a 9-foot split-cane rod, not as well, I believe.

After this, of course, he could fish no more, and was very anxious to see how my split-cane would show up on a similar test, and persuaded me to try the same place again, which I did in fear and trembling after his experience; to make a long story short, I went to work with the result that I ran eight large fish, and only hooked three of them, the first one I hooked with fully 15 yards of line out. I held, and such a job I never had (the fish, on weighing afterwards, turned the scale at 9 pounds), it had to be absolutely dragged over these sunken pieces of bank; if he or rather she (for it was a fine female fish in splendid condition) had once got down 3 feet to the sunken banks, it would have been all up, but your splendid rod stood the strain, and I got her away into clear water, about 20 yards from the danger, into a back water, about 40 or 50 yards wide, without broken banks, so I eased off a bit, and immediately the great strain was released, the fish was off with at least 30 yards of line, and made direct for the broken banks again, and I had a heavy job to stop her when she once got under way, but I did it, and brought her back as before, and kept her in the back-water for about 20 minutes till she gave in, and my friend got a chance with the gaff and landed her, greatly to my relief. My minnow, although new, was quite destroyed; but the rod was as good as ever, not a bend or warp in it, at which my friend was amazed.

The next fish was as near as we could guess about 12 pounds, but I could not hold him and he broke away; the third fish, after a similar performance as the first, landed; we grassed a fine male fish weighing a little over 8 pounds, and still the rod was as straight as an arrow in spite of the terribly severe strain it had gone through. So I must say that your rods are, without exception, the finest rods in the world; for combined with lightness and durability they have immense strength, and at the same time, what is most valuable in a good rod, inflexibility. I would not take twice its price for it after these years.

Hardy Brothers Catalogue, 1894.

PARADISE

1888

Among the mountains in the south of the South Island of New Zealand lies Lake Te Anau—a narrow lake 30 miles long, of great depth, a cold lake: it is fed by numerous snow rivers, southernmost of all the Clinton River. The water of the Clinton River is crystal clear; the bottom of its deepest pools, 30–40 feet deep, is not obscured, only blued by it: high above, 4–5,000 feet above, on either side, can be seen its source, ice and snow. Its bed is of clean white gravel and sand, except where dark green moss covers the stones. Its banks are covered with a thick forest and undergrowth of tree and many other kinds of ferns, very damp, very beautiful, very luxuriant, almost impenetrable. The river is 60 yards wide, on an average 10 feet deep, but long shallows are by no means rare, as are also deep pools; the current is swift. Great forest trees everywhere overhang the water, and dying fall into the river, and stretch out gaunt arms under water, or, carried by some flood, lie stranded on the shallows, dark brown against the white bed. Great brown trout live in the lake—these ascend the river to spawn, and finding pleasant quarters here sheltering under the submerged trees, feeding on the insects which drop from the foliage above and on the quantities of ephemeridæ which live amongst the stones and moss of the river-bed, these fish, instead of returning to the lake, settle down to spend the summer in the river. They have been wooed with many kinds of flies and baits, but only by the net have they been brought to bank. Nevertheless, it is impossible to persuade the angler not to fish if he has once seen these grand fish in the crystal water.

On 11th February I forced my way through the bush, and, choosing a place where the water was not too deep, entered the river. Wading cautiously up-stream, I soon spotted a fish lying close under my bank beside a sunken tree. I cast many flies over his nose, both wet and dry, large and small: he was asleep. At last I awoke him: he sailed slowly to the other side of the river. Wading up I, in like manner, disturbed two more. No. 3 calmly gazed on an imitation beetle for a little while; that was all. It was now about 11 o'clock; I was seated on a boulder, sadly thinking—thinking about these fish. Did they ever feed? if so, when, and on what? It was then that I first saw a dun on the water; quickly others appeared, and very soon I saw a great neb break the surface on the far side of the water—my questions were soon answered. *Delealidium Lillii*, I afterwards found, was the dun's name; $\frac{3}{4}$-inch across the wings; body, a very dark olive, almost black; wings, very long, and of an even dark smoky colour; three setæ; a brother of our blue-winged olive, so I called him the black-winged black. At once I got out my fly-tying book, and soon had three fair imitations made. (A water-side fly-tying outfit is valuable at home, but in a strange country an absolute necessity.) Entering the water, I soon found a rising fish above me; placing the fly in front of him he at once took it; deliberately tightening on him, I got a firm hold; he ran 10 yards, no more, up-stream, disappeared under a log by the riverside, and was seen no more. A new fly placed over a new fish resulted similarly, except that the tree was in mid stream, and opposite me. I was fishing with the finest undrawn gut, a May-fly cast; however, salmon gut would not have saved them. I now decided to choose a less snaggy part of the river, and soon found a place at the head of a long pool almost devoid of submerged obstructions.

I purchased one of your Rods from Tisdall, Wellington, N.Z., last year, which enabled me to make a record catch of rainbow trout in the Waimakiri river, numbering twenty-six, with fly.
Letter quoted in Hardy Brothers Catalogue, *1907.*

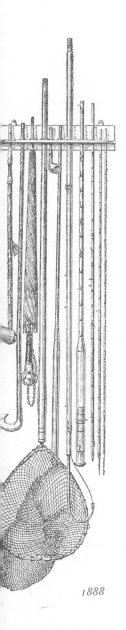

1888

Here I saw a fish rising about one third of the way across the river, which, by wading out, I could easily reach. The second time over him out came his nose and down went my fly. Tightening, I pulled the hook well in: at once he rushed up-stream keeping to the middle of the river. I checked him all I dared. At about 40 yards he jumped; then I steadied him and brought him down. He next ran across towards a timber tree on the far side, but I was able to stop him with plenty of room to spare. After that I had him well in hand, and although he bored down a good way I soon had him beached— 5 pounds he weighed.

Another kind of dun now began to hatch out: I called it the large pepper winged olive—the entomologists *Coloburiscus humeralis*—best described as like a small May-fly, 1-inch across the wings. However, I took no notice of this, but kept on with the black-winged black dun.

The next fish was a 4½-pounder, followed quickly by a 5-pounder, then I had another break in this way:—A fish was hooked close under my bank, dashed across and then up-stream. Before I could lift the line clear it was round a rock in mid-stream. I could feel the fish around the corner, but the water was too deep to wade out, so I couldn't clear the line. Very soon I felt that sickening slackness in the rod top—another fly gone. Having now lost all the flies I had tied; I had to sit down and tie some more. However, I saved some time by eating my lunch at the same time.

Passing further up-stream, far easier written than done, for it means fighting through the bush in those places where wading is impossible—a frequent occurrence—I came to a great pool, very deep, and bordered on my side by a cliff: at the head I saw a great fish, 12 pounds at least, rising, taking duns, a wonderful sight: how gracefully he moved his great bulk from side to side and up and down: in order to cast to him I had to get down the cliff, and whilst doing so I loosened a good piece of ground, which came tumbling down with me, splash into the water, fortunately shallow at this spot—the fish was gone.

I have killed 1,300 pounds of trout, averaging 3 pounds, on the little split cane steel centre rod you supplied me with in 31 days, fishing in Rotoiti Lake with the fly, and it is as good as new.
Letter quoted in Hardy Brothers Catalogue, *1912.*

A little above this pool's head, at the tail of the pool above, and in front of a submerged tree, I found a good fish rising—to get within casting distance I found it necessary to walk out into the water on the tree, for all around it was too deep for wading. Standing thus, I put the fly over the fish, slowly and unsuspectingly he sucked it in: I was afraid he would take cover under my feet, so when I tightened on him I at the same time stood up and waved my free arm. This had the desired effect, he fled up-stream, where I knew all was clear, so I let him go—at about 50 yards he stopped, and I began to pull him down. It now became apparent that I could not land him where I was, standing on a snag. I must get up to the fish—there was only one way; by stepping down from my perch. It is very hard to judge the depth of clear water. I stepped; down I went to half-way up my chest. I struggled up-stream, holding the little 8-foot rod high in the air. I was pleased to find the water getting shallower, here I found the fish still on, and after several heavy rushes and a couple of jumps, or rather plunges, I had him beat, all except for the final tiring out, which took a minute or two, and then he came to gaff 6 pounds.

Chilled by the icy water, having caught as many fish as I could drag through the bush (four fish weighing $20\frac{1}{2}$ pounds), the batch of fly now beginning to lessen, a thirst for some hot tea overtaking me, having drained my waders by sitting down with my feet cocked up against a tree, I decided to collect the dead and make for home, and thus finish a perfect day's dry-fly fishing.

With one of your 13-foot Steel Centre "Palakona" Split-Cane Fly Rods, and a 14-foot Spinning Rod, with tackle supplied to me by you, I caught for the past season 1,591 rainbow and brown trout, weighing 10,615 pounds, or 4 tons, 14 hundredweights, 87 pounds. The largest fish being 18 pounds, and my best day's catch, thirty fish, weighing 273 pounds, all of these being rainbow.
Letter from New Zealand quoted in Hardy Brothers Catalogue, *1912.*

The next day between 11 and 1 p.m. I had two fish, $6\frac{3}{4}$ and $8\frac{1}{4}$ pounds, and one break by a fish of about 4 pounds—the latter fish was bulging, and would not take a dry fly. Instead of troubling to tie a nymph, I cut down a small March brown I had in my fly box; quite a good nymph can be made this way—cut the wings down until only the stumps remain, cut off all the hackle as short as possible,

reduce the whisks by two-thirds. The third or fourth time over the
the fish followed down and took it; as he turned I tightened up—
down went the fish past me, making the line whiz on the water,
down, down and across. I could see his home now—below me, and
on the far side, a group of sunken trees. I put all the drag on I dared,
and managed to hold him a few yards from home. In this way we
remained for quite 10 seconds, the fish swimming for all he was
worth, and at the other end I holding on. At last the fish turned and
come towards me; I gathered in some line, and was glad of a
breather. Suddenly, round went the fish, and, taking me quite by
surprise, got home before I could stop him; the line came back minus
the fly. I never felt less sorry at losing a fish. Then the rain began, so
I made an end.

Jim Jam,
Journal of the Flyfishers' Club, 1911

Under separate cover I am posting a copy of our local paper, which I thought might be of interest to you,
giving an account of my landing an 18 pound Brown Trout with one of your 10-foot Hardy Rods, which
on measuring I find to be 11 feet.
Letter from New Zealand quoted in Hardy Brothers Catalogue, *1937.*

TROUT AT TAUPO

My tent was pitched over a wooden floor in the Lodge camping
ground. It was well equipped within for all the needs of a solitary
fishing holiday. Routine was established, and Taupo routine, camping or otherwise, is generally to rise about 4.30 in the morning for
fishing at the earliest permitted hour of 5 o'clock.

On this particular morning the kettle was boiling on the primus
stove, again as a matter of routine, while I pulled on slacks, shirt
and sweaters. A cup of tea and a slice of toast, and then into waders
and down through the cool of the early morning to the mouth of the
river where it spills across the lake shore, only a couple of hundred
yards away from my tent. The muted music of the rip had been in
my ears from the moment of waking.

From different paths through the lupin bushes, four or five other
anglers converged upon the beach. Torches flashed intermittently

in the darkness of the hour before dawn. Someone looked at a wrist-watch and called out "Five o'clock", and we all entered the water together, moving slowly and quietly from the shore and casting into the patch of broken water, vaguely visible, where the pressure of the lake restrains the urgent river current and creates a steep lip, perhaps 10 feet or more in depth.

Here the technique is to cast a fairly long line across the current and allow the fly to swing round in an arc until the line straightens; then, with the fly deep sunk, a slow retrieve up to and over the lip.

It is not just "chuck-and-chance-it" fishing. The trout congregate at the river mouths to feed voraciously on small native fish and build up their condition for their ultimate spawning run. Much can be achieved by an acquired knowledge of the currents and what they do with line and fly. The trout often take on the swing of the fly before the line straightens; or again, during the first few gathers of the retrieve; or, quite possibly, just as the fly comes up over the lip and you find yourself with a handful of line which has to be freed before you can get your fish on the reel.

At the first cast on this late summer's morning I hit a fish. Two of my fellow-fishermen did the same. Three reels shrilled in different pitches of sound. Out in the darkness three fish splashed noisily as they ended their first desperate runs and came angrily to the surface. All three of us moved down-current to our right and then diagonally backward to the beach, allowing sufficient space between one another for the handling of the fish. We gradually worked them out of the current and into slack water, and the three separate battles were fought out simultaneously from the beach until, within minutes of one another, three rainbows were eased gently up on to the pumice sand.

Torches shone as we killed our fish, regained our flies and, each at his own marked spot, buried the trout in wet sand. By the time we were back in the water two more fishermen were moving shoreward in the darkness in the same happy, absorbing ritual.

With the fish disturbed, the first exhilarating flurry of early morning ended. But the trout were still there and, as the light seeped into the eastern sky, a tug or an occasional strike would prove that the fish were moving in and out of the current.

The dawn came splendidly, as it does at Taupo. Soon the whole westward expanse of the lake lay before us, with sky and water merging opalescent in a setting of distant purple hills. The stilted plovers awoke to life, wheeling over our heads and uttering their fretful cries. And then the sun rose behind us, warming our backs, obliterating the pastel dawn tints and splashing the whole scene with strong colour. Half a mile out in the bay a couple of boats with outboard motors chugged away quietly while their occupants trolled for trout.

I fished that morning until just after 7 o'clock and left the beach carrying three fine trout on the cord with the wooden grip, specially rigged for the purpose. Those three fish weighed all told just over 17 pounds. It had been a grand morning, though not exceptional. A glance back at my fishing diary shows that in just over 2 hours a maximum of seven rods took between them twenty-two trout. Old Awhi Northcroft, one of my Maori friends, topped the list with five. . . .

There followed 4 hours of river fishing at its very peak. It was a day for high spirits in both fishermen and fish. Wall's Pool, where the river used to deepen under a high bank before pouring away in a sharp left-hand bend, yielded me two fish, with two more lost and several hearty tugs. I could have fished on there, I suppose, indefinitely, for it was always a holding pool in which the fish came freely at the fly. (The pool, alas, is no more. A few years after this expedition of mine, the Maoris cut the bank and diverted the river in a search for the body of a small child who had been drowned farther upstream. The current carved a new course, by-passing the pool entirely, and no one yet has tackled the job of restoration.)

It is not fishing to take a sort of Glasgow lease over one piece of water. A move on to the Cliff Pool allowed me to hook into one of its massive fish which ran down into the white water at the tail of the pool and comprehensively broke me. Poi Pool made amends with a spanking 7-pounder which seemed to fight as much in the air as in the water. The Lady's Pool, immediately below, provided another of only slightly less splendid proportions. In the Fence Pool I played for at least five minutes what was probably a heavy jack. It did not once break water and finally wrapped the cast round a submerged manuka snag, with the inevitable result.

This was indeed a day of days. The whole river was holding fish, and they were taking the fly with a rare, unsophisticated enthusiasm. You felt confidence in moving on and exploring new water, rather than lingering over a pool, resting it and fishing it again. Lane's Reach was next on the downstream course, a clean 100 yards or more of swift water, deepening under the far bank, with a long diagonal flow in the current. I had fished it about a third of the way down when a trout took the fly with a smack and careered madly down the river on its tail.

Fortunately the left bank of the reach is reasonably clear and you can follow your fish as he runs. It was just as well, because the spot where I finally stopped this fellow and managed to coax him into relatively quiet water was at least a 150 yards below where he struck. Time ceases to have any meaning on a trout stream, but that trout must have taken a full quarter of an hour to land. There were moments when I was devoutly thankful that my reel carried 100 yards of backing in addition to its 40 yards of dressed line.

In a series of vigorous rushes, with intervals of spectacular leaping and fierce tugging, the trout, on his downstream dash, tore through three good lies in the reach itself and through two potentially fruitful pools below it. He weakened, and the rod took charge of him, just before he disturbed a third pool where the water shallows at the left bank, preparatory to taking an abrupt left-hand turn, Thankfully I played him out in the shallow water where he could no longer use the current, beached him safely, and sat down to gaze upon the admirable symmetry of a 6-pound rainbow in superb fighting condition.

Such a struggle with such a fish can produce for a time a sense of utter emotional exhaustion, so complete as to be satisfying in itself. It had been the same earlier with the fish that fought so bravely in Poi Pool—fought in a series of short, explosive rushes and leaps all within the reasonably wide confines of the pool itself. It was even more so after this hurried scramble to the bank and this anxious dash down-stream, intent on keeping a tight line on the trout and at the same time sparing a thought and an eye at intervals for the local hazards—manuka stump or pothole—which might have sent me sprawling. Twice in that breathless pursuit I had to hold my rod high, with line taut, to clear tall manuka bushes right at the water's edge.

During a fight like this you take in the extra hazards more or less subconsciously and react to them through reflexes. You are concentrating so fiercely on narrowing the gap between yourself and the fish that everything else has to be done almost automatically. You know that for the time being the fish is in charge and that the best you can do is to keep a tight line and pray that the hook holds.

It is only when the trout weakens and you take the battle to him, and you fight it out to a finish and sit down with nerves tingling, that you realize all the disastrous things that might have happened, how much luck was on your side, and how, for a blissfully agonizing period, you attained complete singleness of purpose, utterly oblivious of everything but the task in hand.

So, on this golden day which had slipped unobtrusively past its high noon, I sat on the river bank and smoked myself back into a state of mind capable of grasping once more my own surroundings. I could still pin-point the spot where I sprawled on some dead manuka branches, watching the river sweep past in the curve of its course. How magically and how gently the music of a running river calms the senses!

Slowly I got to my feet, strung the latest fish on my carrying cord and moved off downstream to the pools which lay ahead. I was tempted to go back and fish the water through which my fine trout had charged so madly, but the lies had been thoroughly disturbed. Apart from that I was beginning to feel distinctly hungry—and thirsty. Breakfast had been a full six hours ago, and back at the camp there was beer cooled to perfection in the creek. The trout, too, were proving a fair weight to carry, although not for a moment did I resent that fact. And it was not as if there were no more fishable water; I could still cast my way home.

Other fishermen started to appear on the river. Earlier in the day, in the vicinity of Poi Pool, I had encountered two other rods; two more, walking upstream, had passed me as I was starting to fish Lane's Reach. Now I was approaching water within easy distance of the main road, and several pools were occupied. But it was still a calm, fine day, holding the devotees of the mouth at the mouth, and the river was not overcrowded. A fresh westerly might have thrust twenty or more rods on to the lower reaches.

I cast my Parsons' Glory, the third fly of the pattern I had used that day, into three more pools and one long, swift-flowing stretch, but the noonday strike—often a peculiar characteristic of Taupo waters—seemed to have passed. An occasional small fish gave a tug at the tail of the fly, and once, in the Schoolmaster Pool, I had a good fish on momentarily. He took the fly as it swung round under some overhanging manuka bushes, but my concentration must have relaxed, because I was late in tightening on him and at his first jump he threw the hook.

The "Houghton" has been more than satisfactory, and only last month in 12 days' fishing I landed seventy trout in the Tongariro river, averaging over 8 pounds and including two over 14 pounds.
Letter from New Zealand quoted in Hardy Brothers Catalogue, *1925.*

I trudged on round two more bends, happily conscious of the burden of fish I was carrying, and there before me was Delatour's Pool without a rod on it. Camp, food and beer were only a few hundred yards away, but the temptation was irresistible.

Delatour's can hardly be described as an attractive pool, compared with some of the perfect water upstream. There is a stretch of river flat and marshy ground on the left bank and a blunt peninsula of flat land on the other side where the Mangamutu Stream flows into the main river. It is an exposed, unsheltered pool right at the roadside, but its deep waters do hold fish in astonishing numbers, as I had seen for myself a few hours earlier. Indeed, during a major run the fish in Delatour's Pool lie so thick that it is impossible to count them.

The pool is best fished from the right bank, facing downstream, and in those days it was quite easy to cross the main river about 30 yards above the pool itself. At a spot on the right bank just above the confluence of the two streams and conveniently marked by a large, flat pumice rock, the knowledgeable angler stood and cast as long a line as he was able diagonally toward the left bank. Only thus was it possible to get a fly down to the fish, and even then the swirl where the two currents met often played tricks with your line, dragging it down in front of you so that you seemed to be fishing deep, yet buoying it up downstream so that the fly might be only a foot or so beneath the surface.

It was an interesting pool to fish, not only because you had to experiment with the current to sink your fly (weighted flies, casts or lines, by the way, are illegal in fly water at Taupo), but also because, if you did manage to hook a fish, there were so many things he could do to you. He could go headlong downstream and under the bridge, if you let him, and you had no hope of following him down; he could make a dash up the Mangamutu to the possible haven of weed and snags; he could charge upstream in the main river; or he could use the wide expanse and secret depths of the pool for his tantrums.

I waded across the river at the regular ford, hung my earlier catch up in the shade of a manuka bush (there is never any lack of this useful scrub which many New Zealanders call tea-tree), and started

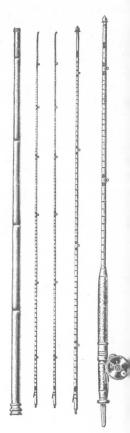

The Houghton dry fly rod. "Under scientific tests these rods show an amount of resiliency never before attain (1898).

in to fish the pool. It is a companionable place to fish if you are in the mood for company. Cars pull up at the roadside immediately in front of you and whole family parties engage you in friendly conversation, doing their innocent best to distract your attention from line and fly.

I had been fishing for about 10 minutes, had exchanged pleasantries with several parties, angling and otherwise, passing over the bridge, and had just been asked the inevitable question—"How's the fishing?"—by a substantial family group which had disgorged itself from a car, when a fish quietly and almost casually took my fly. Seldom in this pool does a trout strike fiercely. Generally the feeling is barely distinguishable from a drag on the line, as if the fly were passing over a stone. You strike quickly with the left hand and hope that the line is straight enough to transmit the strike firmly to the fish.

On this occasion, all went according to plan. I had only about half a dozen gathers of line in my left hand when I struck the fish, and as soon as he felt the hook he tore the line from me and yards more from the reel. Invisible but powerful, he bolted straight for the bridge. I was beginning to wonder when I should have to try the desperate business of stopping him when he came dramatically to the surface and leapt hugely into view.

The family party on the roadside shouted deliriously, and the three children among them went scrambling across the bridge and down to the left bank for a better view of the proceedings. I dismissed these distractions from my mind and got down to business with the fish, which was still leaping not more than 10 yards from one of the bridge piles. Another run and he would be under the bridge for certain. Slowly I moved backward on the bank, and the fish, no longer airborne, came quietly upstream. That was old Awhi Northcroft's counsel: "They come when you walk; they run when you reel." I even managed to recover some line in the process.

Abruptly the reel screamed again and the line described an arc to the right as the trout plunged for the shelter of the Mangamutu. He was actually a few yards up the side stream before I stopped him. Once again I tried walking backward, and the fish came with me. As soon as I had him clear of the mouth of the creek I started quickly to get line back on the reel; he still had far too much out for my liking. But where the gentle pull of walking had found him accommodating, the sharper pressure of the reel roused him to fury. Off he went downstream, running and leaping, and once again I thanked all the gods of fishermen when he stopped short of the bridge.

With a combination of walking and reeling I brought him back and recovered a satisfactory quantity of line. Then he started to move upstream of his own volition. For a moment the line went slack and I thought I had lost him, until I saw the line cutting back against the current. I reeled in furiously to tighten on him again. He was past me and swimming powerfully before the full pressure came back to the rod. He began to take line off me again, moving upstream, and I could not hope to follow him for any great distance. He was moving for a bend of deep water, malevolent with snags.

The time had come to shift the scene of the battle. I entered the water and started to wade diagonally upstream along the line of the ford where I had crossed earlier. I had the fish stopped now and was recovering line, reeling slowly as I waded. In a minute or so I was across, stepping up at a conveniently sloping stretch of river bank and congratulating myself on the fact that I had not given the fish a foot of slack line. Now I could get a pull on him which would bring him out of the current and round into shallow water, with a shelving sandbank nicely placed for the final beaching.

The trout turned and came downstream like a torpedo, and at the same time I found myself entirely surrounded by children. There were only three of them, I remembered afterwards, but at the time I seemed to be in the middle of a school picnic or a youth rally. Every way I turned, every step I took, in my swift reaction to limit slack, children encumbered me. I shouted to them to get to hell out of it, and noises of parental admonition came from the bridge— whether directed at me or at the offspring I could not be sure. But just as the trout moved past me I managed to find an unoccupied zone and moved quickly back to get a side strain on the fish.

If any children were trampled underfoot in the course of this operation I was mercifully unaware of it, but the manœuvre succeeded. The line tautened and strummed, and the fish was stopped a few yards away from the deep hole in the centre of the pool.

Mother and father had now joined the riverside convention and questions were hurled at me which I proceeded to answer in grunts and monosyllables while I endeavoured quietly to work the fish into the shallows. That last run, I thought, was probably his final effort, but I could not be sure. Foot by foot I eased him in toward the bank and placed myself exactly opposite the sandy strip on which I hoped

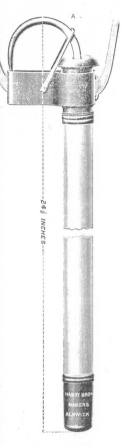

Hardy's New Zealand Gaff (1898).

to beach him. He was showing his broad rainbow side now, and there was little fight left in him. I steered him gently into the shallows and without too much strain on the cast had him out of the water and on to the sand.

The fish lay there gleaming in the sunlight, the rainbow markings beautiful beyond words. He gave a couple of despairing thrashes with his powerful tail, and then, from somewhere out of my range of vision, the pride and joy of the family party leapt forward to assist.

His hands were outstretched for the shiny filament of cast. He had only to break that and the fish could still slither back into the water. The most searing profanities rose to my lips, but before I could utter them young hopeful's feet had caught in a manuka stump and he pitched forward to lie on the river bank alongside a trout nearly as big as himself.

I moved forward with the line still tight, got my boot under the fish and hefted it a yard or two farther on to dry land beyond hope of escape. I turned round, half thinking it might be a good idea to repeat the operation a shade more forcefully on the recumbent child, but by this time he was on his knees, his eyes fixed on the still quivering fish.

"Ooh," he said, "what a beauty!"

And I forgave him everything.

The excitement over, I killed my fish, cut the hook out of the corner of its jaw where fortunately it was firmly lodged, and then submitted quite happily to the attentions of the family party. It had now converted itself into a quiz session. This was the first trout they had ever seen caught. Did trout always fight like that? Did I break many rods? Could they take a photograph of me holding the fish? I submitted and the family camera was duly brought into action. Could Richard be photographed holding the trout? Richard was thus photographed, although the bulk of the lovely 8-pounder was almost too much for him. And, after further expressions of mutual esteem, the family party returned to its car and drove off.

I had not offered them—could not possibly have offered them— the great trout that lay at my feet. It was only when they had driven away that I suddenly remembered the five others hanging in the manuka bush across the strem. To one of my earlier bag they would have been welcome.

I crossed the river again, brought back my fish and added the last victim to the bundle on the cord. I had weighed each fish individually on my pocket spring balance and I knew that I would have to walk down the road carrying 38 pounds of trout. Six fresh-run fish taken in a shade over 5 hours, the heaviest of them 8 pounds and the smallest 5.

O. S. Hintz,
Trout at Taupo, 1955.

FISHING IN NEW ZEALAND

Of the various epithets applied by its admirers to New Zealand, none appears to be more appropriate than that of the "Anglers' Paradise". Thanks to the exertions of the various acclimatization societies existing in the Colony, there is scarcely a brook, lagoon, or lake on which the lover of the rod may not spend a delightful and health recuperating holiday. Fish are plentiful, large and game, climatic conditions are bracing, accommodation is on the whole good and fairly inexpensive, and the traveller is well catered for in the matter of transport.

To angling may be added the delight and freedom of camp life. The tent should be light, of good quality, and ample size to accommodate the party with comfort. A serviceable size is 12 feet by 10 feet. It should be pitched in a sheltered spot on slightly rising ground, and round it must be cut a shallow ditch to carry off surface water. Capital camp "Liedowns" can be made of tussock or fern, covered with a waterproof sheet and such blankets as may be desired. A light bag in which to place all bedclothes during the day, to protect them from blow flies, is necessary. Individual tastes and requirements must determine the cooking utensils, quality and quantity of provisions, etc.

The fishing outfit should consist of three rods, a 14-foot fly rod, a $10\frac{1}{2}$-foot fly rod, and $11\frac{1}{2}$-foot spinning rod. For convenience when travelling three joint rods are the best. To the rods should be fitted good sound reels, to hold at least 60 to 80 yards of line. The stock of casts should comprise all sizes from extra fine to strong salmon. A gaff of telescopic form is more handy than a landing net and is not so liable to catch in undergrowth.

In flies, any of the killing British patterns are good. Every book, however, should include Alexandra, Coachman, Hofland's Fancy, Red and Yellow tipped Governor, Hardy's Favourite, March Brown, Coch-y-bondhu, Greenwell's Glory, and Capt. Hamilton's four special patterns. The trout sizes are 1 to 3 snecks, and for Rainbow trout, 5 and 6 limericks. Capt. Hamilton hooks are strongly recommended, and any flies can be had dressed on them.

Minnow fishing is the prime method for securing big fish, and when skilfully manipulated, never fails to award the user. Phantoms from 3 to $3\frac{1}{2}$ inches of various colours are all useful, spare mounts and hooks should, however, always be carried to replace broken or lost ones.

Waders are a necessity, and the brogues should be well made and strongly nailed.

Natural minnows, which can easily be procured along the weedy edges of the streams, make capital spinning baits.

Natural baits (grasshopper, etc.), are greatly used, and may easily be obtained for a trifling sum from most boys.

Trout fishing opens 1st October and extends to 30th April. The license fee for the whole season is £1, and it is issued by any Acclimatization Society. It is available for any part of the Colony if endorsed by the secretaries of the various local societies.

The month of October is usually squally, with frequent storms, and during this month trout are mostly killed with minnow, worm and blackfellow. November, December and January are the best months for fly-fishing, while for grasshopper, January and February are best. During March and April the weather is keener and the best lures are minnow, fly and worm.

The duty on fishing rods and tackle is 25 per cent, therefore it is better to take goods from England as personal luggage, which is free of duty.

Hardy Brothers Catalogue, 1920.

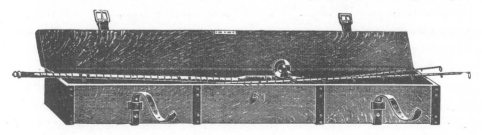

1912

ALBERT AND FRED

It took Albert only a season or two to graduate as a bachelor of angling, since when he has obtained his master's degree and even his doctorate. His own boundless curiosity taught him many things quickly which the average angler takes years to learn. He had right from the start an infallible eye for water; he knows almost intuitively where to place himself so that he can swim a fly naturally into a potential lie. He is never afraid to experiment. Yet things still happen to Albert, perhaps because he is one of those perennially happy fishermen who are happiest when things happen to them.

We were fishing at the mouth one night, not to any great advantage, as few fish were moving. But at any minute, we hoped, they might come on. Suddenly out of the darkness Albert roared.

"Fish ho!" A pause. "Blast it, I think it's a tiddler. No, by God, it's not!" The reel punctuated Albert's running commentary. "He's gone, I think. No, he hasn't. The sod's running in. I'll get a tight line on him before I bring him down. You blokes got your lines in? What the hell's the matter with this fish? He's still there shaking his head off, but I can't move him. Show a torch there, Fred. I may have a snarl in my line."

Fred Logan obliged. The beam of light from the torch showed Albert with rod upraised. At the very top of the rod, impaled, as it were, on the tip, was a furious yearling trout of about 8 inches. Albert had reeled line and cast right back through the end ring, and the fly projected from the tip like a miniature gaff, with the hook firmly through the jaws of the protesting trout.

"What do you think of that?" Albert expostulated. "The little so-and-so might have busted the tip."

Among all the Taupo fraternity Albert is unique. His zest for fishing is boundless, his exuberance natural and infectious. He is that best of all fishermen, one who does not grizzle or moan when the fishing is unconscionably hard, but goes off into out-of-the-way places, never caring whether he catches fish or not, content merely to be angling for them.

It will interest you to know that I recently took an 18-pound rainbow on one of your "Houghton" rods, 11-foot without steel centre. The rod had been in use for 15 years and is still in good order.
Letter from New Zealand quoted in Hardy Brothers Catalogue, *1925.*

At times Albert affects to be concerned when his wife, Twinks, leads him in the day's tally. She does so by dint of sticking to a beat of pools which she knows intimately and fishes with skill.

"Can't have this," says Albert. "Be expected to stay home and cook the flaming meals next."

And off he goes, up the river, or down to the mouth, or off to the Hatepe, or away to the Waikato River, to return roaring with laughter, often with a limit and always with a saga of improbable adventure arising from the day's sport.

If he is not fishing, Albert is generally helping some other fisherman to repair gear. Or lending a hand with odd jobs round the Lodge. Or cutting firewood. Or taking some tyro under his wing, telling the new chum where to fish, when to fish, how to fish, all in a flow of general conversation which encompasses the novice as if he were Albert's peer in knowledge and experience. There are others just as friendly and just as helpful as Albert, though none can match his exuberance or his gift for putting beginners at their ease.

"Damn it all," says Albert, "I was a beginner myself once. And that's not very long ago."

All of which goes to demonstrate the essential friendliness of Taupo fishing. Anglers from overseas who are used to a more exclusive sport often take a few days to accustom themselves to a gregarious pursuit of trout. But if they are real fishermen they soon adapt themselves to Taupo ways. I have seen a rather aloof Englishman arrive at Taupo with an impossibly light rod, an inadequate reel and line, a brave collection of miniature dry flies the like of which Taupo trout have never encountered, and a touching belief in his ability to catch rainbows by chalk stream methods. Within a few days someone has fitted him out with a pair of deep waders, someone else has rigged up a stouter rod for him, with reel and line, half a dozen or more have presented him with flies of legendary potency. And in another day or two everyone is calling him Charlie.

"You people are the most friendly fishermen I've struck anywhere," a visiting Scot once informed a few of us, yarning over supper in the Lodge. "Why, it's even dangerous here to ask a man what fly he's using. He can tell by your speech that you aren't a New Zealander and he promptly wants to empty his fly box into your pockets. He knocks off fishing himself to look after you. He'd wade out, if he could, catch a fish bare-handed and hook it on your fly. No thanks. Not another. It's time we used my bottle."

It is not always like that, of course. Out of every individual trout fishing brings either the best or the worst. All Taupo waters have their quota of impossible creatures—men who will sit on pools, taking selected limits from them, putting back fish after fish before they finally consent to kill the final one; men who will crowd you out of water you are fishing; men who will cast across you; men who will refuse to yield way when you are handling a fish. The presence of such mean-spirited folk is part of the price we pay for the inestimable privilege of open water.

But they are a minority, thank God, these ill-mannered anglers. The ignorant beginner soon learns the unwritten etiquette of the craft. The river-hog ultimately yields to the pressure of angling opinion about his antecedents, manners and probable place in the hereafter; he goes off and fishes in surly solitude.

There are always some who will not learn. Back before the war, a Very Important Person was staying at the Waitahanui Lodge with his wife and two daughters. The younger daughter was a novice but would not admit it. The VIP asked Fred Fletcher to take her out on the river and give her some casting lessons.

Fred took all this as part of the day's work and led the young miss to an easy stretch of water, waded in with her and proceeded to instruct her in the handling of rod and line. She was a poor pupil, impatient and supercilious. Finally Fred stood behind her, in the best attitude for teaching anyone how to cast, his right hand holding her right hand on the rod, his left hand holding her left hand on the line. And in this fashion he started to demonstrate the rhythm of casting.

After a minute or two the young female broke away angrily. "I don't know why we are going through all this nonsense," she said. "After all, I learned casting from one of the best professionals in England."

Fred grinned. "Well," he drawled, "he didn't make too good a job of it, did he? You carry on and wrap yourself up in your own line and then cable your ruddy professional to fly out here and untie you."

There were also the two American tourists living opulently somewhere in Taupo and visiting Waitahanui daily more to brag about their own skill and the extreme costliness of their gear than to fish. They were the Americans of pre-war English musical comedy, loud-voiced, harsh and arrogant—a type mercifully rare in real life. After a couple of days Fred loathed the sight of them.

We were standing on the Lodge verandah one morning when the Americans arrived in their glossy hired car and started assembling gear at the roadside. Fred muttered some most horrible oaths, seized his huge Hardy "Murdoch" from the rod rack on the verandah and strode across the road down through the lupins to the Boat Pool. It must have been on his very first cast that he hooked a fish. He probably knew exactly where the fish was lying. Fred knows a lot about fish.

At the first screech of the reel the Americans abandoned their preparations and went crashing down through the lupins to see what was happening. Fred leaned back on his massive rod, winched the astonished fish in without giving it an inch of line, beached it, tugged the fly out of its jaw, put his boot under its gleaming 8 pound bulk and propelled it back into the water.

"Jeez," protested one of the Americans "What in Pete's name did you do that for?"

"Oh," said Fred, looking up as if he had noticed them for the first time, "we always put those little b——s back here."

O. S. Hintz,
Trout at Taupo, 1955.

ANGLING IN TASMANIA

The "Southern Isle," with scores of splendid lakes—ranging in size from Great Lake with its 100 miles of shores to the mountain tarn, and drained by a veritable network of rivers and streams, each and all well stocked with trout, justly claims the title of "the premier angling state" of the Australian Commonwealth. The history of the acclimatisation of various members of the Salmonidae family to our waters is an epic of patient endeavour. The indigenous freshwater fish, with the exception of the beautiful cucumber mullet or herring, now almost extinct, afford but indifferent sport to the angler. Most of the rivers carry a plentiful stock of blackfish which, though of a sluggish and dead-hearted nature, are much prized for their edible qualities.

All the lakes and streams have been stocked with brown, Loch Leven or rainbow trout, while some of the lakes contain all three varieties. The estuary waters of the larger rivers contain migratory trout, and afford good fishing. The *fario* appears to have developed migratory tendencies, and we possess two distinct classes of it—the non-seagoing abounding in the fresh waters, and the migratory ranging the estuaries and lower river reaches. These fish are mostly caught on spinner or natural bait, and rarely take a fly. The lakes, however, afford the best sport for fly fishing. The migratory trout run from about 2 to 6 lbs., but many fish of 10 lbs. and over are annually taken. The record rod and line trout was caught in the Huon River many years ago by Governor Hamilton, and weighed $28\frac{1}{2}$ lbs.; the record Great Lake brown trout scaled $25\frac{1}{2}$ lbs., and the largest rainbow $15\frac{1}{2}$ lbs.

GREAT LAKE

This, the largest of our many lakes, some years ago afforded brown trout fishing that could not probably be rivalled anywhere, the average weight of the fish being about 10 lbs.; and specimens of 15 to 20 lbs. were frequently taken. They still exist in good numbers, but only occasional large fish are caught. The rainbow has, however, flourished amazingly, and large catches, under favourable conditions, may be made—with spinner or fly-fish of 8 to 10 lbs. being fairly common. There are two government accommodation houses erected at the north and south ends of the lake, each situated adjacent to the best fishing localities in the area, and are easy of access. The method of fishing mostly in vogue is trolling or spinning from motor or row boats, although there are many good grounds for wading or shore fishing. A most suitable outfit for spinning or trolling in the lake is: A "Hardy Bros." "Corbett" No. 2 or "Wee Murdoch" rod, a "Silex Major" $3\frac{1}{2}''$ to $4''$ reel, with 100 yds. of suitable line. Gold or brown and gold $2''$ Devons are favourite baits. Those who are prepared to give the fly a fair trial will not be disappointed. The writer, from his own experience at the lake, is confident that more fish, and, of course, infinitely superior sport, can be had with the fly. When fish are "on the take" with the spinner, they will also fall to a fly, while on the days when spinners do not interest them much they will still succumb to the fly. For fly-fishing a Hardy's "Houghton" or "Tournament" 10 ft. rod, a

Trouting (*The Mansell Collection*)

"St. George" (3¾ in.) or "Perfect Salmon" reel (3¼ in.), a "Filip" No. 1 trout line, with 50 yards of backing, is an ideal outfit for wet fly work in the lake; the fish run large, and are vigorous fighters.

DRY FLY

The Shannon River, affords what has been characterized by expert "dry fly" artists as "the finest dry fly fishing in the Southern Hemisphere." During December, January, and February the continuous and varied hatch of fly life is truly wonderful, and the rise of fish equally so. The water is very clear and fine tackle is necessary. Good catches are regularly made, and phenomenal bags are frequently recorded. They range in size from 2 or 3 lbs. to 8 lbs., and are mostly brown trout. The writer has used, and can confidently recommend, a Hardy's "Houghton" or "J. J. Hardy" (No. 1) rod, but, of course, any Hardy dry fly rod is suitable for the work. A heavy line is a *sine qua non*—strong down-stream winds being frequently experienced. A Hardy's "Filip No. 1 Trout" line is perfect. A "St. George" or "Perfect Salmon" reel, with 40 yds. or so of suitable backing for line, a "H. S. Hall," 2½ yds. tapered to 3 × cast, complete an ideal outfit. The most deadly flies (Sizes 1 to 3, Hardy hooks) are: Greenwell's Glory, Blue Dun, Olive Quill, Coachman, Black Gnat, Stream Jock Scott, Red Spinner and Dark Variant. I have found as a general rule Dr. Baigent's and J. J. Hardy flies most effective, and are taken much more readily than the ordinary standard patterns, while, on calm, bright days when fish are midging or smutting the "J. W. Dunne" smallest varieties often prove irresistible.

LAKE LEAKE

This popular resort is the happy hunting ground for the wet fly artist and the spinner expert. The fish—rainbow and brown trout—average nearly 4 lbs. There are two good accommodation houses, with boats and guides; and the lake can be reached in a few hours from Hobart or Launceston. The main line railway passes through Campbell Town (22 miles from the lake) where cars can be obtained. A mail motor service also connects with the lake. The most popular form of fishing is by wading; Hardy's rods are here, as elsewhere, deservedly popular. On one visit to the lake the writer found *nineteen rods at work, of which seventeen were Hardy's*. Years ago small salmon flies were mostly used, but nowadays trout flies are more in evidence. Greenwell's Glory, March Brown, Cock-o-bondhu, Orange Grouse, Teal and Red, and Soldier Palmer are good killers, and Jock Scott, English Thunder and Lightning, and Irish ditto are still old favourites among the small salmon flies.

OTHER LAKES

The Chudleigh Lakes comprise a series of beautiful lakes and tarns—all well stocked, and the fish run to a goodly size. They are reached by a good pack track from Deloraine, near Launceston. Huts, for the accommodation of visitors, have been erected. Lake St. Clair, our most beautiful lake, is more often visited for its wonderful scenery than for fishing, although large trout lurk in its crystal depths. Lake Echo contains the largest trout in the island. A $24\frac{1}{2}$ lb. fish was taken last season. The only lure that proves at all successful is a live bait—termed "a rover"—and this also applies to Lake Sorell which possesses a large stock of good fish. The Hartz Lakes, Wood's Lake, Tooms Lake, Arthur Lakes, and others, also afford good fishing but it is necessary to camp at these resorts.

STREAM FISHING

All our rivers, streams, and brooks contain trout, and the visitor can get good fishing. The Commissioners of Fisheries, the controlling body appointed by the Government, pursue an active course of propagation and liberation of trout fry from the hatcheries.

Hardy Brothers Catalogue, 1937.

TROUT FISHING IN NEW SOUTH WALES, AUSTRALIA

The Commonwealth of Australia has evinced considerable interest in the exploitation of the wealth locked up in its ocean waters, and the different States of the Union are not less active within their boundaries in fostering the freshwater fish of their inland waters.

New South Wales, by reason of its wide range of climate, and the fact that it contains the highest mountain ranges in the Continent, offers through the medium of its many swift-running streams, a wide field for the propagation and conservation of freshwater fishes. None have been acclimatized with such splendid results as the trout, and to-day in almost any of the mountain streams a splendid day's sport can be enjoyed by the angler.

The fishing season starts on the 1st November, and lasts until 30th April; no license fees are demanded, though stringent regulations compel the return to the water of fish below a certain standard. In most of the best known resorts, other attractions are linked with the sport. It is a matter of a few hours by rail from Sydney to the main Southern table-land, to the Monaro Plains, Kiandra, Kosciusko, and the Yarrangobilly Caves. These are all great show places, and are amongst the most renowned of the State's tourist resorts, and they stand in the centre of districts which have well stocked trout streams. Excellent facilities have been provided to indulge in the sport. The Government establishments at "The Creel", a shooting and fishing bungalow erected at the junction of the Thredbo with the Snowy River, two snow fed streams, and the palatial Hotel Kosciusko, 9 miles further up Mt. Kosciusko, amid glistening snow fields, bid fair to vie with their old world prototypes at Davos Platz, St. Moritz, and Aldenboden, and at the Yarrangobilly Caves house visitors will find every comfort and convenience. A round trip through the Kosciusko district can be made by rail to Cooma, thence motor or coach through to Tumut. Besides these well-known resorts, a break can be made into less frequented streams at Queanbeyan, Dalgety, and Jindabyne. The last-named is the country seat of Sir Joseph Carruthers, ex-Premier of the State, an ardent follower of the rod, who has always been an enthusiastic worker for the advancement of the sport, and in introducing the most improved fishing tackle. In a recent public utterance this gentleman indicated how favourably the angler in New South Wales was situated in comparison with his confrère in the British Islands, who has to pay large sums for his fishing rights. In New South Wales no charge whatever is made for licences, and indeed, the trout streams for miles and miles flow through the public estate.

All tourists who can use the trout rod and fly have a wide field for enjoyment in the western fishing centre environing the world-famed Jenolan Caves. The Fish River, which through countless ages has hollowed out the deep caverns decorated in such a lavish manner by nature, is a perfect miniature trout stream, and trout have been seen in the underground river of the Caves. Tarana and Oberon, two centres in the vicinity, are annually productive of very fine catches of trout.

On the Northern table-land of New South Wales also, there are many fine trout streams, and enthusiastic sportsmen of this part have

The Tasmanian lakes continue to offer every increasing inducement to the lovers of the "gentle art". Big hauls have been made from time to time, but that made by a party of four anglers during the Easter Holidays beats the record. Those who have visited the lakes cherish abiding recollections of its glorious scenery and bracing climate, and there are not a few of them who have equally abiding recollections of the old time stories that Brownie tells of the early Bushrangers, and entertaining them whilst they sojourn with him on the way to the scene of fishing operations. The access to the lakes is easy. A party of three gentlemen left Launceston by express train, and reaching Tunbridge the same afternoon were driven by Harris to Lake Sorell, where they passed a comfortable night at old Brownie's. On the following day they proceeded to the Great Lake, and there found a friend who had 10 days' sport prior to their arrival, during which time he landed 263 pounds weight of brown trout. Fishing was commenced the next morning, and continued for 6 days, the result being 496 pounds weight of trout. The record is a phenomenal one. The eighty-two fish caught turned the scales at 759 pounds, being an average weight of $9\frac{1}{2}$ pounds. The largest trout weighed 20 pounds, whilst, as will be seen from the appended list, the smallest was $2\frac{1}{2}$ pounds. The record is as follows:—

Party, four rods, 6 day's fishing, 1 day blank. Weight:—11, 16, $13\frac{1}{2}$, 11, 5, 4, $3\frac{1}{2}$, 3, 3, 3, 3, $2\frac{1}{2}$, 10, 18, $9\frac{1}{2}$, 8, $9\frac{1}{2}$, $7\frac{1}{2}$, 18, $10\frac{1}{2}$, 8, $13\frac{1}{2}$, 10, 5, $15\frac{1}{2}$, $11\frac{1}{2}$, $6\frac{1}{2}$, $9\frac{1}{2}$, $8\frac{1}{2}$, 12, 5, $4\frac{1}{2}$, $8\frac{1}{2}$, 14, 12, $11\frac{1}{2}$, $6\frac{1}{2}$, 14, $11\frac{1}{2}$, 10, $11\frac{1}{2}$, $8\frac{1}{2}$, $11\frac{1}{2}$, $18\frac{1}{2}$, 8, 7, 8, 13, $14\frac{1}{2}$, $5\frac{1}{2}$, 12.

One rod, 10 days (several blank days, rain):—6, $14\frac{1}{2}$, 6, $16\frac{1}{2}$, $11\frac{1}{2}$, 11, $9\frac{1}{2}$, 14, 12, 11, 6, $13\frac{1}{2}$, 11, $14\frac{1}{2}$, $4\frac{1}{2}$, 8, 20, 5, $9\frac{1}{2}$, 10, 4, $7\frac{1}{2}$, 3, 6, 9, 3, $3\frac{1}{2}$, 4, 4, 3.

The biggest haul for any one day was made on the 16th, when 14 fish weighing $159\frac{1}{2}$ pounds were landed, while the next best day realized twelve fish, weighing $124\frac{1}{2}$ pounds. Individual bags for 1 day's fishing aggregate 52 pounds and 53 pounds. Such magnificent sport cannot be surpassed, and the record just achieved will doubtless lead many sportsmen in the mainland to visit Tasmania and occupy the comfortable quarters and excellent accommodation provided for fishermen at the Great Lake.

Letter quoted in Hardy Brothers Catalogue, *1907.*

for a generation or more rigorously and steadily conserved the fish till the present day the angler can get a splendid day's sport quite close to any of the New England towns, preferably Walcha, Armidale, Glen Innes.

It is only during the last few years that trout fishing has become popular in New South Wales, and the residents have just commenced to realize the value of these fine trout streams, which have been placed amongst the finest in the world by trout fishers from the British Islands and Canada. The establishment of a Government Tourist Bureau has done a great deal towards the dissemination of information concerning the sport, and the fact that enthusiastic tourists have now made a regular practice to visit the State in the season for its fishing, has stimulated local interest.

Hardy Brothers Catalogue, 1912.

1886

THE MAKING OF A FISHERMAN

The road began to wind upwards; Trophim, the coachman, shook the reins, and called out cheerily, "Gee up, my beauties! Dyoma's close"; and our good horses set off at a fast trot. Already we could see the green valley through which the river flowed with its thick green border of wood. My father looked out of the window: "Look, Seryozha," he said; "do you see that strip of green running straight to the river, with sharp white points sticking up here and there? Those are the felt covers of the waggons in which the Bashkirs pass the summer—the Bashkir caravans. If it were not so far, I would take you to see them; well, we'll manage it some day." I looked eagerly and saw far off the summer quarters of the Bashkirs, with their flocks and droves of horses grazing round them. Though I had often heard of this from my father, it was the first time I had seen it myself. And now at last the river came in sight, and a number of islands, and the long bend of the channel in which the river formerly ran. The descent into the wide green valley was steep and winding: it was necessary to wedge the wheels and drive down carefully; the delay tantalized my impatience, and I ran from one window to the other, making as much bustle as if I could hasten the approach of the longed-for halt. I was told to sit down and be quiet, and had reluctantly to obey. But at last we reached the river bank, just by the ferry; the carriage turned and stopped under the shade of a gigantic poplar; the doors were opened, and I sprang out first, in such haste that I forgot the fishing-tackle in my box. My father smiled at my haste and reminded me of the tackle. I begged to go and fish at once; but he told me not to be in a hurry—to wait till he had given directions for my mother's comfort and for the feeding of the horses: "Meanwhile, you can walk about with Yephrem and take a look at the ferry; and get some bait, both of you!" I caught Yephrem's hand, and we walked to the ferry. The Dyoma lay before me—not a broad river, nor very rapid, but the sight of its smooth still water brimming to the level of its banks was of wonderful beauty. Fish, large and small, were constantly jumping. My heart beat hard, and I trembled at every splash, whenever a pike in pursuit of the small fry sprang above the surface of the water. On each bank there was a stout pole driven into the ground, to which a dripping rope, as thick as a finger, was fastened; along the rope ran a raft, made like the wooden floor of a room, and supported on two huge wooden beams. I soon noticed that one man could drive the raft with ease across from bank to bank. The two ferrymen were Bashkirs, and wore Bashkir caps, conical and made of felt; they talked broken Yephrem, otherwise Yevséitch (that was my name for him), holding my hand tight, walked with me on to the raft, and asked one of the Bashkirs to take us across. He very readily cast the raft loose from the landing-place, raised his brawny arms, turned to face the opposite bank, and then, standing firm on his feet, began to draw the rope towards him with both hands. The raft parted from the bank and began to float across the stream; in a few minutes we were on the far bank, and Yevséitch, still holding my hand, walked along the side in search of good places for fishing—he was a very keen fisherman—and then took me back across the river in just the same way. Next he began to talk to the ferrymen, who lived in a hut of wattles situated on the bank, and asked where we could get worms for fishing: he spoke in broken Russian, hoping they would understand him better, and mixed words of Tatar with it. One of the Bashkirs quickly guessed what was needed, and led us to a small shed, where two horses were standing out of the sun; here we found abundance of the worms we wanted. On coming near the carriage, I saw that all preparations had been made: my mother was lying down in the shade of a leafy poplar, the canteen was open, and the *samovar* was beginning to hiss. Provisions for our meal had been bought overnight in the Tartar village; even oats were not forgotten, and fresh new-mown hay for the horses was bought from the Bashkirs. We were in the middle of noble trees; and the great variety—there were fruit trees and other kinds—was strikingly picturesque and beautiful. Wild cherries, as large as forest trees, were covered already with their dark fruit; clusters of service-berries were turning red; bushes of ripe black-currants filled the air with their fragrance; the pliant clinging stems of the bramble, covered with large blackberries still green, wound round everything they touched; of raspberries, too, there was abundance. My father made me look at this profusion which he much admired; but I confess that my mind was so full of fishing that the richness and beauty of the scene around were but dimly felt by me. As soon as we had finished tea, I began to beg my father to show me how to fish. At last we started, accompanied by Yevséitch. He had already shaped some tree-branches into rods; we made floats out of the thick green reeds, tied on our lines, and began to fish from the raft, relying on the information of the Bashkirs. Yevséitch had prepared for me a very light rod with a thin line and small hook; he now put on a piece of soft bread, dropped the line, and put the rod in my right hand while my father held me fast by my left. The same instant the float turned and sank in the water, Yevséitch called out, "Pull, pull!" and with a great effort I pulled out a fair-sized perch! I trembled all over like a fever-patient, and was quite beside myself with joy. I caught my prey in both hands, and ran to show it to my mother, Yevséitch going with me. My mother was unwilling to believe that I could have caught the fish myself; but choking and stammering with excitement, I assured her that I had really pulled out that splendid fish with my own hands; and Yevséitch, to whom I appealed, confirmed my statement. My mother had no liking for fishing; she rather disliked it, and I was much hurt by her cool reception of my joyful tidings; but, worse still, when she saw me so excited, she said I would make myself ill, and must not leave her till I had calmed down. She made me sit down by her, and sent Yevséitch with a message to my father, that she would send me when I had rested and become calmer. To me this was an unexpected blow; the tears literally gushed from my eyes, but my mother had the firmness to keep me till I was quite quieted. After a little my father came himself to fetch me. My mother was not pleased: she said she had never supposed, when she let me go, that I would fish myself. But my father persuaded her to allow me, for this once, to catch a few more fish, and my mother, after some time, consented. How grateful I was to him! I believe that the disappointment would have made me ill, if I had not been allowed to go. My little sister begged to go with me, and, as our fishing was only 50 yards off, she was allowed to go with nurse to watch our sport. When we got there, my father showed me some big perch and trout which he had caught in my absence; the other fish were not taking then, because, as Yevséitch explained to me, it was too late in the day, and too hot. I caught a few more perch, and each gave me nearly as much delight as my first. As I had leave only for a short time, we soon returned. My father told Makéi, the cook, to boil and fry some large trout, and to give all the rest of the fish to the servants, for them to make fish stew of.

I went quite mad over fishing! I could think and speak of nothing else. My mother was vexed, and said she would forbid it, as such excitement might lead to illness. My father assured her that the second time would be different and that my excitement would pass off; I was convinced that it never would, and listened in terrible suspense to the decision of my fate. The baited hook, the quivering and diving float, the bending rod, the fish flapping on the line—the mere recollection of these things drove me wild with excitement. For the rest of our halt I was unhappy, not daring to speak about fish even to my father or sister; and indeed all seemed put out by something, and in this frame of mind we resumed our journey. On the way my mother tried to explain to me why it was wrong to abandon oneself so passionately to any amusement, how risky it was and even dangerous on the score of health; she said that even a clever boy might turn stupid, if he forgot everything else for the sake of a mere sport; I, for instance, instead of looking contentedly out of the window, or reading my book, or talking to my parents, was sitting as silent as if I had been drowned.

*   *   *

There it was at last, my noble lake, which I had so long desired to see; and noble it really was. The lake of Kiishki was three *versts* in length and full of bays and capes; in breadth it was very uneven, varying from 150 yards to half a *verst*. The far side was formed by a wooded height, which sloped gently down to the water. On the left, the lake ended suddenly in a narrow channel, by means of which the Byélaya poured into it during the spring floods. The other end of the lake hidden by a bend of the shore, was close to the large village already mentioned, called Kiishki after the lake. The Russians naturally called both, and also the new Russian village Sergéyevka, by the name of *Kishki*; and the name suited the lake very well, because it was long and crooked. The pure transparent water, the sandy bottom, the leafy woods mirrored on the surface, the green grass on the banks—all made such a delightful picture that my father and Yevséitch were charmed as well as I. Our side was especially picturesque, covered with young grass and field-flowers; there being no houses there, it was free from all pollution. A score of oak trees, of uncommon height and breadth, grew on the bank. When we got to the waterside, we saw a wooden jetty projecting over the water, and a boat moored to it; these were fresh delights for me. Both were new: my father had arranged about them beforehand, because the water was so shallow, that it would have been impossible to fish without the jetty; it turned out very handy also for washing clothes. The boat was intended for fishing with a net. Behind the jetty stood an enormous oak, whose trunk would have required several men to surround it with their arms; and near it was the tallish stump of another oak, far thicker than the surviving tree. For curiosity, we all three climbed on to this mighty stump, and took up only a little corner of it. My father said that twenty men could have sat on it. He made me look at the axe-marks on the stump and on the tree, and told me that the Bashkirs, the real owners of the land, made marks of this kind on great oaks every 100 years. Many of their old men had assured him of this custom. On this stump there were only two marks, but five on the living tree; as the stump was much thicker and therefore much older, it was evident that the remaining marks were on the severed part of the trunk. My father added that he had seen an oak very much thicker, which had twelve marks and was therefore 1,200 years old. I don't know how far the tales of the Bashkirs were true; but my father believed them, and to me they seemed gospel truth.

The lake swarmed with large fish of every kind. In flood-time the fish came in from the river; and, when the water began to fall, the native inhabitants blocked the channel of communication which was neither broad nor deep, so that all the fish were imprisoned in the lake till next spring. Large pike were constantly jumping out of the water in pursuit of the small fry which rushed wildly before them. In places near the grass banks, there was a ripple caused by shoals of fish crowding towards the shallows and even jumping out on the bank; I was told that these were dropping their spawn. The commonest fish in the lake were perch and especially bream. We shook our lines free and began to fish. My father took the largest rod with a strong line, baited it with an uncommonly fat worm, and cast as

far as he could; he wanted to catch something big. Yevséitch and I had smaller tackle and small brandlings for bait. Our sport began instantly: fair-sized perch and pollen, a fish I had not seen before, took constantly. I got so excited—mad, Yevséitch called it—that I trembled in every limb and was hardly conscious of what I did. Every moment, a fish was landed and the line thrown in again; and my shouts, and Yevséitch's attempts to instruct me and restrain my transports, caused such a din that my father said, "It's impossible to get anything worth taking here beside you." He got into the boat with his big rod, and rowed to some distance, where he anchored himself with a stone and a rope, and he began to fish. The fish were so numerous and so easily caught, that my excitement began to cool down; and so did my attendant's, who, to tell the truth, had been quite as excited himself. He began to consider how we could catch bigger fish. "We must go deeper, my little falcon," said he; "I'll put more worms on the hooks, and throw in a third line baited with bread." Of course I agreed at once. We raised our floats, so that they no longer stood but lay on the water; we put on larger worms, and Yevséitch fixed nearly a dozen on his own hook; then he baited the third line with a piece of bread-crumb the size of a hazel-nut. At once the fish stopped taking, and complete stillness began to reign around us. Then, as if on purpose to confirm what my father had said, a big fish of some kind took his bait; he played it a long time, while Yevséitch and I, standing on the jetty, took a lively interest in his proceedings. Suddenly he called out, "Broken away!" and pulled up his loose line; the hook, however, was all right. "I didn't give it time to swallow the bait," he complained; again he baited his hook and again threw in his line. Yevséitch was much distressed. "Dear, dear," he said, "no other fish will take now; the first getting away is a sure sign of bad luck." I had not seen the fish, because my father had not raised it to the surface; nor had I felt its weight, as I was not holding the rod; and I did not understand that it was possible to judge the size of a fish by the bending of the rod. Hence I did not take the loss so much to heart, and said that perhaps the fish was a small one. For some time we sat in perfect silence, without getting a single bite. I got tired of it, and asked Yevséitch to alter my tackle to what it was at first. He did so, and at once my float turned up and the fish began to take. But Yevséitch made no change in his own tackle, and his floats lay quietly on the surface. I had now caught more than twenty fish, two of which I could not pull out

1898

without Yevséitch's help. To tell the truth, he had quite enough to do, in taking each fish off my hook, throwing it into a bucket of water, and baiting the hook again. This left him no time to attend to his own lines; and so he did not notice at once that one of the rods had vanished from the jetty, a fish having carried it 50 yards away. Suddenly Yevséitch gave such a yell, that I was frightened and Soorka who was with us began to bark. Yevséitch began to beg and beseech my father to catch the floating rod; and my father hastened to fulfill the request: he pulled up the stone by which he was anchored, and, using the oar as a paddle, quickly caught up the rod and pulled out a very large perch, which, without unhooking it, he placed in the boat and brought over to us on the jetty. In this incident I took a much more lively interest; the anxiety of Yevséitch and his cries for help had excited me; I jumped for joy, when we carried the perch to the bank, unhooked it, and placed it in the bucket. Apparently the fish were frightened by the noise and motion of the boat as it came near; for they stopped biting, and we sat a long time, waiting in vain for more victims. Only towards evening, when the sun was near setting, my father caught a large bream, but kept it in the boat, for fear of frightening the fish near him: he held up his prize with both arms, that we might see it from where we were. The pollen were beginning to take with me again, when my father suddenly noticed that a mist was beginning to rise off the lake, and told Yevséitch to take me home. I was very unwilling to go; but I had had such a delightful day's fishing already that I did not venture to ask leave to stay. With both hands helping Yevséitch to carry the bucket full of water and fish, though he did not need my help at all and was rather hindered by it, I went gaily back to my expectant mother. While I was fishing—either pulling out a fish, or watching the motion of the float, or momentarily expecting a bite —I felt only the excitement of fear and hope and the avidity of the sportsman; real satisfaction and complete happiness only came now, when I recalled all the details with delight and told them over to Yevséitch, who as a partaker of the sport, knew them as well as I did, and yet, like a true sportsman, found equal pleasure in the repetition and recollection of every incident. As we went, we both spoke at the top of our voices and interrupted one another; sometimes we even stopped and set our bucket down, in order to complete some exciting reminiscence—how the float bobbed and was dragged under, how some fish resisted or broke away; then we caught up the bucket again and hastened on. My mother was sitting on the stone steps or, to speak more accurately, on the two stones which took the place of steps as an approach to our unfinished abode; she heard us coming some way off, and was surprised that we were so long in appearing. "What were you and Yevséitch arguing about so loudly?" she asked, when we got close. Again I began to describe our doings, and Yevséitch joined in. Though I had noticed more than once before that my mother did not care to listen to my eager descriptions of fishing, at that moment I entirely forgot it. To confirm our story, Yevséitch and I kept pulling out of the bucket first one fish and then another; then, as this proved troublesome, we shook out all our catch on the ground; but alas! our fish produced no impression whatever upon my mother. When my story came to an end, I noticed that a small fire was burning in front of my mother with the smoke of its few sticks blowing straight in front of her. When I asked the reason, she replied that she did not know what to do, for the midges; and at the same instant she looked at my face and cried out, "Just look what they've done to you! Your face is all swollen and bleeding." In fact, I was so bitten by the midges that my face and neck and hands were all swollen; and yet, in my passion for the sport, I had never noticed it. Never in my whole life and in no place have I found such multitudes of midges; and they were reinforced by another kind of gnat which I find even more intolerable, because it makes its way into the mouth and nose and eyes. The abundance of trees and of stagnant water accounted for the number of insects. At last the midges actually routed us, and my mother and I retreated to our own room. Having no door or windows, it offered no protection; but we sat down on the bed under an open-work canopy; and though it was stuffy sitting under it, yet we had peace. A canopy is the only specific against the attacks of midges and mosquitoes. It was dark before my father returned; he had caught two more large bream, and said that the fish had gone on taking, and, but for his fear of alarming us, he would have stayed all night in the boat. "Oh, when shall I be grown up," thought I, "and spend whole nights with Soorka fishing on the bank of river or lake?" The boat, I confess, rather alarmed me. . . .

The passion for fishing steadily grew stronger; merely from fear that my mother would forbid me to sit by the lake with my rod, I forced myself to work at reading, writing, and the first two rules of arithmetic, under my father's teaching. I became rather artful at concealing my thoughts, and often started long discussions with my mother, while all the time my one thought was how soonest to escape with my line to the jetty, and when every moment of delay was a sore trial. The fish were taking wonderfully: there were no bad days, or only to this extent that sometimes we got few large fish. My little sister sometimes went with her Parasha to fish, but found no pleasure in it and was soon driven home by the midges.

At last we began to have visitors. Once there was a fishing party; General Mansuroff, the kindest of men and devoted to all forms of sport, was there with his wife; so was Ivan Bulgakoff, with his wife too. A great expedition to drag the lake was planned; the net was got, I think, from the Bashkirs, and also some boats. Two of the largest boats were lashed together and covered with planks laid across and nailed down so as to form a little raft, with a place for the ladies to sit on. In the stillness of a wonderful moonlight night, we all except my mother set out for the water. I sat with the ladies on the raft. Quickly and cautiously the net was brought up and let down into the water, so as to surround a long reach of the lake where the bank was shaped like a prolonged semi-circle. Countless shoals of bream came to the shallow water there at night. As soon as the sides of the net had been drawn close to the bank, the multitude of imprisoned fish began to be evident; from the raft we watched the centre of the net, where such a commotion was soon visible that our ladies, and I with them, uttered cries of excitement; many large fish, chiefly pike, leaped over the top of the net or dashed into the narrow space between the sides and the bank. The fishermen, who had been silent till now while dragging the net or drifting in boats beside it, now began to shout and slap the water with the net-ropes, in order to force the fish back into the centre of the net. We got the raft ashore quickly, to watch the process of drawing out the catch. For a wonder, I did not share the general excitement and so was able to watch attentively the whole lively and animated scene. Mansuroff and my father were more excited than anyone else. My father, who acted only as manager, was constantly calling out: "Keep the edges even! Get the bottom ropes closer together! See that the centre does not get out of place!" Mansuroff went beyond mere words. He waded knee-deep in the water, caught hold of the bottom ropes of the net, and dragged them along, pressing them at the same time against the shallow bottom; for this purpose he had to bend double and walk backwards. His wife (a sister of Bulgakoff) and Bulgakoff's wife, in spite of their excitement over the fishing, laughed heartily at the ridiculous figure he thus presented. At last, whole heaps of dripping meshes, forming the sides or wings of the net, were brought out and thrown down, and the centre appeared, not long and narrow as when empty, but broad and round, owing to the multitude of fish it contained. It soon became difficult to draw the net along the shallows; and the risk of breaking the centre made it necessary to stop. Then the upper ropes were held up high, to prevent the fish from leaping over; and men with buckets and pails dashed into the water and caught hold of the fish which were forcing their way into the sack-like centre and filling it to bursting. The men filled whatever they carried with fish, rushed to the bank, shook out their victims on the ground, and dashed back for more. When the weight of the draught was thus lightened, the whole party caught hold of the top and bottom ropes with a will, and with a loud shout drew the centre out on to the bank. We caught so much more than we expected, that we had to send for a cart. Most of the fish were gold and silver bream, which sparkled bright in the moonlight; but there were also pretty large tench and dace and perch; the pike had all managed to scramble out, thanks to their cunning, said the fishermen. What a scene it was of bustle and excitement and noise! The ladies too were keenly interested. Many a time I heard Yevséitch call out, "That's something like a bream! As big as a shutter!" But it seems that I was born an angler; for even then I kept saying to Yevséitch, "If only we could land a bream like that with the rod!" I even felt depressed by the netting of so many big fish, which might have taken our bait; I felt sad to see the lake emptied in such a way, and said to Yevséitch that we should never have such good sport again; but he comforted me by declaring that we should do just as well as ever—the lake was large and the stock of fish enormous; and our jetty was a long way from the place where the net had been drawn. "You shall see for yourself to-morrow, my little falcon," said he: and I was quite reassured and able to take a more lively interest in what was going on. By degrees order was restored: the cart was filled with large fish, and the rest were carried in buckets and pails. All the company walked merrily home behind the loaded cart; and merriest of all was General Mansuroff, though he was covered with mud and wet nearly to the waist.

Sergei Aksakov,
Years of Childhood.

TROUT FISHING IN SOUTH AFRICA

Fifty years ago, there were no trout in South African rivers. Ova had to be imported, and sorry results were recorded when it arrived. It seemed as if all the elements of cussedness were at work to prevent success, but, because of determination on the pioneers' part, failure proved only victory deferred.

To-day trout fishing is to be had in Cape Province (including East Griqualand), Natal, and the Transvaal. There is one other Province, the Orange Free State, where a start has been made, with trout acclimatization, especially in the Bethlehem district. At present the Fisheries, both coastal and inland, come under the Provincial Administrations, and Natal is the only Province in South Africa which has taken the question with due seriousness.

The law in South Africa is that only the artificial fly be used for trout. The rainbow predominates. He has behaved very well indeed on the whole in South Africa; his roving habits have not been unduly exercised here. He has plenty of rations, his main requirement (apart from purity of water); and he puts on weight. It seems likely that South Africa will develop as New Zealand has done, into a rainbow-trout country. Not but what the brown is in South Africa; and in some rivers—especially the Mooi of Natal—he gives sport of the first rank; but the tendency is for the distributions to consist of rainbows rather than of browns. The plan of not mixing the two breeds in a river has been wisely adopted.

FLIES: AND WHERE TO GO

The wet fly is used more than the dry. Nevertheless, if a man likes the dry fly, let him not be without hope that he can employ it on occasion. In the early part of the season—(close time is for three months only, from 1st June to the end of August)—if rain has not fallen, then small flies and fine casts are the order; though fly fishermen do not here fish with the very small flies as in England. To strike an average, one would say that No. 12 old scale is the size of fly generally used, taken over the season.

The intending visitor should equip himself with a booklet (distributed free upon application), issued by the General Manager of South African Railways and Harbours, and obtainable in London at the office of the High Commissioner for the Union of South Africa, Trafalgar Square, or in Johannesburg through the Publicity Department of the South African Railways and Harbours. One risk must be frankly disclosed and accepted. In South Africa there is a rainy season, and if you hit it your fishing will be upset. In the second half of August, and in the first half of May, it can generally be relied upon that there will be no heavy rainfall in the Transvaal or Natal, but neither of these periods is in the trout fishing season, and it is possible that it will be considered whether one or both should not in future be included. Weather risks have always to be taken by any fisherman, and it is not very likely that the heavy weather we get from time to time will deter visitors from coming.

Any or all of the following flies are likely to be effective: March Brown (preferably with silver body), Red Spinner, Greenwell's Glory, Woodcock, and Yellow, Hardy's Favourite, Mooi Moth (for Natal), Butcher, Zulu, Hare's Ear, Coachman (for evenings), Wickham's Fancy, Soldier Palmer, Coch-y-bondhu, small Black Gnat, Teal and Claret, Red Tag, Red Ant, and Blue Jay. For the big rainbows a larger fly is generally used—such as a 7 or 8 Jock Scott—and fly fishermen on these occasions prefer a 2x cast to 3x, though generally speaking 3x is the popular cast. Few of the trout rivers are wider than the average trout stream and therefore the ordinary fly rod is applicable; a 9-foot to 10½-foot "Hardy" is the usual thing. The Umzimkulu river in Natal is, however, something like a salmon river, but the long rod is not in demand as a rule. No licence is required in the Transvaal, and all information as to trout fishing in that Province can be had from the Hon. Secretary, South African Fly Fishers' Club, P.O. Box 2927, Johannesburg, who also will welcome inquiries about the very fine trout fishing to be had from the Trout Bungalow, Nottingham Road, Natal. A long stretch of the Mooi river in that district is rented by the Club, and the Bungalow is excellently run. In Natal a trout-fishing licence has to be bought, and this can be done at the nearest magistrate's office.

The Cape Province has the biggest field to offer for trout, and it

1907

is divided into the Western Division and the Eastern Division (the Eastern includes East Griqualand, very good for rainbows). In the Western Division of the Province, trout fishing is to be had at Somerset West, 30 miles from Capetown, also near Stellenbosch, so that visitors from overseas can soon be satisfied if they arrive at the right time, but it must be emphasized that permission to fish must first be obtained, and this proviso applies practically throughout South Africa. Where angling clubs exist, procedure is naturally rendered easier for visitors, who at small cost can be elected to membership, and thus enjoy the right to fish on rented waters. Other trout centres in the Western Division of the Cape Province are Caledon, Paarl, Simondium, Ceres, and Worcester. In the Eastern Division, Cape Province, trout fishing is to be had in the King-williamstown District at the Pirie (where there is a notable reservoir with a river running through it), at Somerset East, and at Queenstown (two reservoirs); and East Griqualand is particularly attractive, especially the Maclear district. Natal has for years been famed for its Mooi river, and in addition, there are the Bushman's river, the Umgeui, the Loteni, the Umzimkulu, and the Umkomaas. Nottingham Road is the best-known centre for trout fishing in Natal, this being the station for the Trout Bungalow. Himeville (Pietermaritzburg-Donnybrook railway line) is another capital trout-fishing centre; it has an hotel, and four or five trout rivers are available by motor car runs. Estcourt is the station for the Bushman's river, and Dargle Road for the Umgeui. Then in the Transvaal Province a delightful holiday is to be had at Machadodorp, in the Eastern district, three or four streams are full of trout, which though not big are very game. Another good trout-fishing area is that of Lydenburg. Half a dozen streams hereabouts yield baskets. Then the Northern Transvaal has the Haenertsburg district with its Helpmakaar river; and the Broederstroom river is only a few miles off.

Both hold trout, and the scenery on the way thither from Pietersburg is very fine, reminding one of the Scottish Highlands. An effort is being made by the Rand Piscatorial Association to promote trout acclimatization near Johannesburg.

It should, in conclusion, be mentioned that the indigenous yellow fish takes the fly and comes a very good second to the trout.

Hardy Brothers Catalogue, 1923.

THE TROUT ROD
IN SOUTH AFRICA

As I hear that quite a number of those brave young fellows who whipped the Huns back to the other side of the Rhine are thinking of coming to some climate which is better suited for gas-induced chest weaknesses than Great Britain, it occurred to me that a short note about trout fishing in South Africa might be found useful at the present moment.

Incidentally it may be mentioned that those who think of farming out here, unless really exceptional men, do very little without substantial capital, and I would further add that the conditions here are so different to those in Great Britain that a man before he buys land should certainly spend at least a year working as pupil or assistant on a farm in the district in which he intends to settle. If he can devote a second year to a course of education at one of the agricultural colleges so much the better. There are, however, certain areas of irrigated lands where small holdings are likely to be available for settlers and where a certain amount of co-operation (as to machinery, etc.) will reduce capital expenditure. The Sunday River Settlement is one of the best of these. There are others as to which disinterested advice is essential.

The Government have very little good land to offer, but they are arranging for settlements for the benefit of returned South African soldiers, and they also make money advances on very moderate terms. All the details as to Government assistance can be obtained in London at the Imperial Institute or from the official representative of South Africa, or from the South African Settlers' Advisory Committee, which has a London office at 58, St. Mary Axe, E.C. The headquarters of the committee is at 60, St. George Street, Cape Town, in which a public-spirited South African, Mr. J. W. Jagger, M.L.A., takes a keen and practical interest.

Trout were introduced in South Africa a good many years ago

and have as a rule flourished exceedingly. There is a Government trout hatchery at Jonkers Hoek, near the old Dutch town of Stellenbosch, which lies amongst mountains, vineyards, and orchards, about 40 miles from Cape Town. From this hatchery trout fry and eyed ova have been distributed far and wide. Needless to say some of the best stocked streams are those in the neighbourhood of the hatchery, notably the Eerste River and Laurens River. In a similar district, but in another watershed some 20 miles from Stellenbosch, are the sources of the Great Berg River, and these are fairly well stocked with both rainbow and brown trout. The former run from about $\frac{3}{4}$ to $1\frac{1}{2}$ pounds and are fairly numerous. Brown trout are rather scarce, but here and there one comes on big fish of 4 or 5 pounds. One sees an occasional blue dun at the river side, but generally speaking water flies are scarce. I was told that there was a may-fly rise of about 3 days' duration, but I doubt if it is the same fly as ours of the same name.

You may be interested to hear that the Houghton rod which I purchased from you in June–July 1933 proved ideal for rainbow trout in Rhodesia and Nyasaland where considerable accuracy is required in the more overgrown streams.

Although I had intended using it solely for dry-fly work, it has been pressed into service for tiger fish when my spinning rod was broken. A month ago it landed an accidental turtle.

Letter from the Sudan quoted in Hardy Brothers Catalogue, *1937*

Other notable rivers in the Cape Colony are the Breede, fished from Ceres and other places, and the Hex and Witte Rivers, for which Worcester is the centre. In the Eastern district there are the Buffalo River (King William's Town) and the Keiskama, while some of the best fishing of all is to be had in the Transkei territories in the Wilderbeeste River and many other streams where the trout breed very freely. That district is rather remote. In Natal I came across a most charming trout stream, one long series of falls and perfect pools. It is called the Mooi River, and is stocked with Loch Leven trout. It has several sister streams rising in the same mountain range.

A Government regulation applies to all or nearly all rivers prohibiting all methods of trout fishing except with the artificial fly. A Government trout licence costing 10 shillings must be taken out. I need hardly say that landowners are beginning to appreciate the value of their trout fisheries, but permission is still freely given, and in many instances the landowners have pooled all their interests in a club or association which practically anyone can join.

In regard to tackle, 50 yards of not too light a line, a trout rod which is strong enough to play a 4-pound or 6-pound fish, and casts varying between those one would use on the Itchen and those suitable for large sea trout would meet every necessity. A second rod about 7 feet long would be useful for waters canopied by trees, of which there are many in the South.

Rainbow trout like flies with plenty of glitter and colour. They are not good surface risers, and the big brown trout will hardly ever take a small fly. At the same time I think one should have a few flies dressed for floating. As a general rule the most killing flies are such as we use at home for lake and sea trout, including sundry well tried favourites—Claret and Mallard, March Brown, Alder, Red Palmer, Black and Teal. Very small salmon flies are a good deal used. I have tried the dry-fly again and again, but caught few fish with it. Indeed, one sees few rising fish as a general rule, except just at sundown, and then the fish are often smutting.

Waders are constantly worn, but it is weary work trudging along in them under the rays of an African sun. They give considerable protection from snakes, which one does not often see, are useful for wading up tree-covered streams, and for crossing rivers. I rarely use them, preferring to miss water here and there than have to bear the weight of them. On the open portions of rivers the man who can cast a good line does not need them.

As for dress, the climate is a little warmer during the summer than in England, while the nights are often colder. There is no winter to speak of. The sun works round by the north. Winter begins about April, summer in October. Over nearly the whole of South Africa the principal rainfall is in summer, but in the grain and fruit district of the South West coastal belt there is a winter rainfall which does not work in with trout fishing arrangements. On the high velt, which includes practically all the inland portions, the nights are often very cold. Coming back from the Mooi River, water left in the railway carriage wash basin froze hard one night. This was 4,500 feet above sea level, and the railway people had run short of blankets!

It will be seen that nothing very special in the way of clothes or tackle is necessary. Quite a good lot of flies and tackle can be bought in Cape Town, where there are departmental stores almost rivalling Whiteleys or Harrods. On arrival in Cape Town, the fly fisher should get in touch with the Secretary of the Publicity Association, and purchase Mr. Manning's book on *Trout Fishing in Cape Colony*, which is published at the *Argus* Office. It contains a most useful map.

I must not forget to say that many men catch small sea fish here on the fly rod, using a piece of mackerel skin on a small hook, and as a rule casting into rocky pools. Quite a variety of fish are caught. Mackerel are fished for in the same way from boats round which they may often be seen swimming, and fight even better than trout. A silvery fish resembling shad and called elf will occasionally take bright salmon flies, and that fishing is as good as for sea trout in the sea.

John Bickerdyke,
Journal of the Flyfishers' Club, 1919.

REAL AND FANCIED ANGLERS

Almost everyone is now-a-days a "*piscator*". The *Fanatico*, about Easter, goes off as busy as the cockney on his hunter, when bound to Epping. He generally takes a great many things, and kills a few fish. The old angler takes a few things, and kills a great many fish. Some dark, warm, windy, drizzly days, early or late in the season, and particularly when a fine breeze blows from off the banks of a river, where no one has begun fishing, the trout are so easily taken, that a basket full is but little proof of skill. One might then almost train a monkey to catch a trout. But, at other times, and particularly when fish are well fed, is the time to see who is, and who is not, an angler. About ninety in a hundred fancy themselves anglers. About one in a hundred *is* an angler. About ten in a hundred throw the hatchet better than a fly.

Peter Hawker,
Instructions to Young Sportsmen, 1814.

THE DUFFER

Some men are born duffers; others, unlike persons of genius, become so by an infinite capacity for not taking pains. Others, again, among whom I would rank myself, combine both these elements of incompetence. Nature, that made me enthusiastically fond of fishing, gave me thumbs for fingers, short-sighted eyes, indolence, carelessness, and a temper which (usually sweet and angelic) is goaded to madness by the laws of matter and of gravitation. For example: when another man is caught up in a branch he disengages his fly; I jerk at it till something breaks. As for carelessness, in boyhood I fished, by preference, with doubtful gut and knots ill-tied; it made the risk greater, and increased the excitement if one did hook a trout. I can't keep a fly-book. I stuff the flies into my pockets at random, or stick them into the leaves of a novel, or bestow them in the lining of my hat or the case of my rods. Never, till 1890, in all my days did I possess a landing-net. If I can drag a fish up a bank, or over the gravel, well; if not, he goes on his way rejoicing. On the Test I thought it seemly to carry a landing-net. It had a hinge, and doubled up. I put the handle through a buttonhole of my coat: I saw a big fish rising, I put a dry fly over him; the idiot took it. Up-stream he ran, then down-stream, then he yielded to the rod and came near me. I tried to unship my landing-net from my button-hole. Vain labour! I twisted and turned the handle, it would not budge. Finally, I stooped; and attempted to ladle the trout out with the short net; but he broke the gut, and went off. A landing-net is a tedious thing to carry, so is a creel, and a creel is, to me, a superfluity. There is never anything to put in it. If I do catch a trout, I lay him under a big stone, cover him with leaves, and never find him again. I often break my top joint; so, as I never carry string, I splice it with a bit of the line, which I bite off, for I really cannot be troubled with scissors and I always lose my knife. When a phantom minnow sticks in my clothes, I snap the gut off, and put on another, so that when I reach home I look as if a shoal of fierce minnows had attacked me and hung on like leeches. When a boy, I was—once or twice—a bait-fisher, but I never carried worms in box or bag. I found them under big stones, or in the fields, wherever I had the luck. I never tie nor otherwise fasten the joints of my rod; they often slip out of the sockets and splash into the water. Mr. Hardy, however, has invented a joint-fastening which never slips. On the other hand, by letting the joints rust, you may find it difficult to take down your rod. When I see a trout rising, I always cast so as to get hung up, and I frighten him as I disengage my hook. I invariably fall in and get half-drowned when I wade, there being an insufficiency of nails in the soles of my brogues. My waders let in water, too, and when I go out to fish I usually leave either my reel, or my flies, or my rod, at home. Perhaps no other man's average of lost flies in proportion to taken trout was ever so great as mine. I lose plenty, by striking furiously, after a series of short rises, and breaking the gut, with which the fish swims away. As to dressing a fly, one would sooner think of dressing a dinner. The result of the fly-dressing would resemble a small blacking-brush, perhaps, but nothing entomological.

Then why, a persevering reader may ask, do I fish? Well, it is stronger than myself, the love of fishing; perhaps it is an inherited instinct, without the inherited power. I may have had a fishing ancestor who bequeathed to me the passion without the art. My vocation is fixed, and I have fished to little purpose all my days. Not for salmon, an almost fabulous and yet a stupid fish, which must be moved with a rod like a weaver's beam. The trout is more delicate and dainty—not the sea trout, which any man, woman, or child can capture, but the yellow trout in clear water. . . . My ambition is as great as my skill is feeble; to capture big trout with the dry fly in the Test, that would content me, and nothing under that. But I can't see the natural fly on the water; I cannot see my own fly,

Let it sink or let it swim.

I often don't see the trout rise to me, if he is such a fool as to rise; and I can't strike in time when I do see him. Besides, I am unteachable to tie any of the orthodox knots in the gut; it takes me half an hour to get the gut through one of these newfangled iron eyes, and, when it is through, I knot it any way. The "jam" knot is a name to me, and no more. That, perhaps, is why the hooks crack off so merrily. Then, if I do spot a rising trout, and if he does not spot me as I crawl like a serpent towards him, my fly always fixes in a nettle, a haycock, a rose-bush, or what not, behind me. I undo it, or break it, and put up another, make a cast, and, "plop", all the line falls

in with a splash that would frighten a crocodile. The fish's big black fin goes cutting the stream above, and there is a *sauve qui peut* of trout in all directions.

Andrew Lang,
Angling Sketches, 1891.

IS FISHING A DISEASE?

Is fishing a disease? As an answer to this in the affirmative has been given by a great medical authority, we may look upon it that the question has been definitely settled, and that the fact is proven. It happened in this wise. As there was a doubt in his mind, and in that of his own particular doctor, as to the existence or not in a portion of his anatomy of a certain rare and interesting ailment, a friend of the writer was despatched to a great consulting physician to be thoroughly overhauled. After a somewhat lengthy inquisition, involving the use of a stethoscope, much tapping, and the wearisome iteration of the words "ninety-nine" came the complimentary and comforting sentence of "All Clear".

During the process of replacing his clothes, the patient was addressed in a contemplative manner by the great man. "I don't suppose," he observed, "that you suffer much from nerves?" "No," was the reply, "I have looked down the barrels of my rifle at what Jorrocks would call 'the biggest stag wot ever was seen' without a tremor—it is like shooting at a mark—but," he added, "a 2-pound trout lying under a stump at the opposite side of a river has led to such beatings of the heart and such shakings of the hand that I have been unable to change my fly!" Then came the dictum of the great man. Shaking his long and delicate finger in the patient's face, he said, warningly, "It's a disease, and *I've got it myself*!" There you have it in a few trenchant words.

Now what is the nature of this disease? Is it endemic, epidemic, communicable, contagious, infectious? Is it curable? Has it readily recognized symptoms? And has it, as in the case of such other well known types as scarlet and Malta fevers, sequelæ which are, for the most part, the reverse of benign? Let us try to answer these queries.

It may, though widely spread, be rightly classed as endemic, since it is found to exist permanently in the vicinity of chalk streams and of certain other rivers in the British Isles. It has even extended its ravages to the Antipodes, and has, of late, broken out on several of our Fronts. Though rife, as we have said, in the immediate neighbourhood of rivers, it gives way, curiously enough, when these rivers become polluted by sewage, tarred roads, or by the presence in their waters of acids and other chemicals.

Inmate of lunatic asylum to angler: "Come inside!"
(From a Punch *cartoon, 1897)*

Sufferers wander far from infected localities, but their blood always gives a prompt reaction when tested. It may, at times, and notably in the spring of the year, be detected in their speech. In extreme cases a lethargy which has been noticeable during the autumn is thrown off, and the patient may be heard to babble of green fields and limpid streams. Epidemic, it may seem to be, from the above, since it is proved to occur at stated seasons and with seemingly unabated virulence. It has been known to be communicable, though instances of this are rare, and the disease may be described in these cases as imitative and not true to type. Treatment for this form is unnecessary, and the disease soon wears itself out. It is certainly not contagious, and is only infectious in a minor degree. In fact, the manners and speech of those afflicted have been known to be abhorrent to those who are not receptive, and are therefore immune from the attacks of the bacillus, a streptococcus of the comma series. It yields to no known treatment, and may be said to be incurable, though sufferers have been known to live to great ages. Diagnosis is easy, since the symptoms are well marked. Some of these, together with their appearance at stated seasons, have already been described. At the annual recrudescence of the disease the patient begins to exhibit a dislike to the ordinary business routine, and, if watched at this time, he will be found to be taking a morbid interest in insects of all sorts, his eagerness in their study and in attempts to imitate them by fashioning flies, for instance, of feathers of birds and of hair from the smaller mammals, would be amusing were it not pathetic. His efforts in this direction almost amount to mania, some of his productions being ludicrous in their wide divergence from the shape or colour of any insect known to entomologists. To some of these freak productions he loves to give the name of "lure".

My, but it was a sight, one of the four, 11¾ pounds, in a ripping torrent. But all held and he came to gaff like a pearl of priceless beauty.

Letter quoted in Hardy Brothers Catalogue, *1907.*

The calls on his purse at this season will be very heavy, and sufferers have been known to imperil their financial position by prodigal outlays on the implements of what they may be heard to call their "craft"; for these the disease gives them a morbid craving.

Perhaps the most serious and distressing symptom of the malady is the brain degeneration which it engenders: this may be correctly classed as one of the sequelæ. "Fishermen", as those who suffer from it are known, have an inherent difficulty in restricting themselves to anything approximating the exact truth when recounting their experiences. The tendency to embroider would appear to be irresistible. This is so well known that efforts have been made to segregate them in clubs where this tendency is recognized and allowed for. Thus herded together, wonder inspiring anecdotes told by sufferers who may be otherwise men of high moral rectitude, fall harmless on accustomed ears.

The disease is interesting, and one that will repay careful study, but the interest of such study cannot, it should be stated, fail to be damped to a certain extent by the fact that all treatment has failed, and that it must therefore be pronounced incurable.

Journal of the Flyfishers' Club, 1918.

You can hardly believe what that Wye rod did; I had just killed two Salmon 11½ and 12½, using light leaders and short-dressed Hardy's make Mar Lodge, when I was fast to a 24½ pound Salmon fresh from the sea. That fish fought and eventually ran under the boat before we had time to get to the shore with the canoe.

The line must have got caught under the canoe; we could not get it cleared, and this Wye rod before I knew it went clear under water from the tip to the centre of the middle joint shaped like a half circle. I looked at the rod after the salmon had been gaffed; the tip was a little twisted, but within an hour it was right back to its normal shape. I killed three or four nice fish with it.

Letter from New Brunswick quoted in Hardy Brothers Catalogue, *1937.*

FISHING IN KASHMIR

Trout were first introduced into Kashmir in 1900 and having weathered many vicissitudes now flourish there exceedingly. Every year sees a few fish of upwards of 7 lbs. brought to the net. Among noteworthy specimens one of 14½ lbs. was taken from the Upper Bringhi river on the 24th July, 1924, by Lt. Col. Sir S. Hissam-ud-Din, Khan, Kt., C.I.E., O.B.E., of which a faithful model was produced by Hardy's and now hangs, with many other trophies, in that veteran sportsman's house in Peshawar, N.-W.F.P. This fish was taken with a small Peacock and Jungle lure on a Hardy 9 ft., steel centre rod.

The Kashmir Valley is drained by the Jhelum River into which most of the trout streams eventually find their way.

Space does not permit of a detailed description of the many rivers but the following notes may be of use to a prospective visitor.

The season opens on the 1st April and closes on the 30th September. Limit, 12 inches. Fly only on most waters, but spinning is permitted on certain beats particulars of which are supplied by The Director, The Game Preservation Dept., Srinagar, Kashmir State, to whom applications for licences and permits must be made. If a visitor desires to follow any definite tour programme it is advisable to apply for permits on 1st January when booking opens. Any information required is afforded readily by the above State official who generally is an European. It is practically all wet fly-fishing, although the dry fly can be used on parts of some of the streams, e.g. the Burdwan and Kokernag. There is good black bear and barasingh shooting in some of the nalas in the vicinity of trout streams. The cost of trout fishing licences is Rs. 5 per day, Rs. 25 per week or Rs. 150 for the season. The exchange value of the rupee is approximately 1s. 6d.

It is as well to take with one all tackle, etc., likely to be required. The best rod for general purposes is from 9 to 10 ft. and it is advisable to take along at least two in case of accidents. A 9 ft. "Gold Medal" or "Perfection" and 10 ft. "Houghton" "Crown Houghton" or "Tournament" are useful types. An 8 ft. 6 in. "Victor" is eminently suitable for use where spinning is permitted.

The most popular flies and lures are: Peacock and Jungle, Fig. 7, Demon and Dandy lures and Watson's Fancy, Teal and Green, Silver and Gold March Browns, Peter Ross, Butcher, Woodcock and Yellow, Wickhams Fancy, Mallard and Claret and Coachman flies on Hardy hooks Nos. 5, 7 and 9. There is another fly, a proved killer, invented by the writer of these notes, of which Hardy's have the dressing. He also favours Capt. Hamilton hooks Nos. 4, 5a and 8.

Casts tapered to 0x, 1x or 2x. Finer not advisable.

The best spinning baits are Gold and Silver Devons and Phantoms of from 1 to 2 inches. The "Sylph" also proves attractive. A supply of "Crocodiles" No. $3\frac{1}{2}$ both leaded and unleaded should be taken. One of these mounted with a species of minnow locally called "gurran" is a deadly bait especially when used in deep pools with a sink and draw motion. This bait is so effective that its use is only to be recommended when other baits fail to attract.

SIND RIVER

Divided into five beats and permits granted to two rods on each. Spinning permitted in all but the two upper beats. Best months, April, May and from mid-August to the end of September. Snow water coming down is likely to make the river practically unfishable in other months. Total length of good trout water is about 18 miles. Permits are issued for 7 days on each beat. There is a tributary stream, the Wangat, which enters the main river at the junction of the upper and middle beats and for which a permit for two days only is granted.

BRINGHI RIVER

Divided into five beats and permits granted to two rods on each of 7 days. This is a well-stocked river affording delightful fishing. It fishes well throughout the season except when logging is in progress, but the best months probably are May and August. The above illustration is of trout taken from the upper beat of this river, fly only permitted, in September, 1929. The largest fish weighed 3 lbs. 10 ozs. In 1931 fish of over 6 lbs. in weight were taken on every beat of this excellent river.

A tributary, the Nowboorg, divided into two beats, enters the upper beat of the Bringhi. The Nowboorg is one of the best stocked rivers in Kashmir, in fact, in the opinion of many, it is over-stocked. The scenery in the Nowboorg valley is indescribably beautiful. Permits are granted for 7 days on the Upper Nowboorg and 2 days only on the Lower.

About one mile across country the left bank of the Lower Bringhi brings one to the Kokernag. This is a placid, shallow stream, fringed with willows. It holds many extensive weed beds and in this respect is unique among Kashmir streams. Vast numbers of fresh-water shrimps live among the weeds. Kokernag trout, owing to their good feeding, are generally in perfect condition with deep pink flesh. Permits granted for two days only.

The Achhabal is another excellent river holding many rainbow trout as well as brown, but in 1931 H. H. The Maharajah included this stream among his own private reserves but whether this is to be a permanent arrangement or not is not known. The Kooljam is similarly preserved, as also the Thricker, possibly the best water in Kashmir and holding many fish of upwards of 5 lbs.

The above are the principal waters but very good sport is to be obtained in small streams such as the Burdwan, Madmatti and Erin, all of which involve interesting journeys from Srinagar through wonderful scenery.

LAKES

Two lakes, Vishensar and Khrishensar, in the Haramukh range at an altitude of 12,000 feet, have been opened for fishing this year, 1932. They contain a very large number of medium sized fish but doubtless there are some big fellows awaiting the fortunate angler. The route to these lakes lies through magnificent scenery and the wild flowers are wonderful. Here may be found the lovely blue poppy.

It is understood that Satpora lake, in Baltistan, a few miles from Skardu, is shortly to be stocked. This will enable the big game sportsman *en route* to Baltistan and Ladakh to secure Ammon, Markhor, Ibex, Tibetan Gazelle, Red and Black Bear, etc., to introduce into his journey a pleasant interlude with the rod. Complete and comfortable camp outfits can be obtained from numerous firms in Srinagar at very low cost, and the rates for transport, too, are low. Living is comparatively cheap and it is possible to the experienced or to well-advised strangers for a party of two to live "all-in" upon about Rs. 500 per month. This amount includes hire of camp, transportation charges, wages of all servants, food, drinks (moderate), and a proportion of the cost of a season license. It is questionable if so cheap a trout fishing holiday could be obtained anywhere else in the world.

A native shikari (gillie) who knows the river well can be engaged for about Rs. 30 month or Rs. 1 per day.

A visitor from afar would be well advised to take with him a mahseer rod and tackle, and to fish for some of these game fighters in the Jhelum River near to Srinagar at Shadipur, Sopore, Baramulla and other places. Fish of from 15 to 30 lbs. are not uncommon and almost every year one or two in the neighbourhood of 50 lbs. are taken. Any salmon spinning rod of about 12 ft. will serve for this purpose. The best season for mahseer in Kashmir is from 15th July to 15th September.

Hardy Brothers Catalogue, 1937

FISHING IN NORTH AMERICA

Trout fishing in the Northern United States and Canada begins in April and continues until August or September. Most states and provinces exact a licence fee and in certain Canadian territories additional fees are required for fishing particular waters. The average cost of a non-resident licence is 5 dollars for all fish except salmon.

As a rule salmon licences cost more. Eastern streams provide excellent speckled, brown, and rainbow trout fishing and there is an abundance of bass, pike, and muskellunge. New Brunswick has by far the best eastern salmon fishing although other provinces should not be overlooked. The salmon of the east is the lordly Atlantic salmon, perhaps the most prized game fish in the world. It is identical with the salmon of Britain and northern Europe and a weight of 15 or 25 pounds is a good average for the Canadian rivers, although larger fish are frequently taken.

In northern Quebec and within a very limited range the Ouananiche (*Salmo salar ouananiche*), or so-called "land-locked salmon", is eagerly sought and the fish is a fine scrapper. It is a blood brother of the Atlantic salmon in everything but weight and should not be confused with the lake trout (*Cristivomer namaycush*).

On the Pacific coast the best of the five species of salmon, from the angler's point of view, is the King salmon, known locally as the tyee or chinook. It averages around 20 pounds but very much larger fish are taken at times. It enters the coastal rivers in the spring and will take the fly but trolling is the favourite method of fishing for it. On Vancouver Island an effort is being made now to encourage the use of light tackle for taking tyee salmon up to 75 pounds in weight.

The steelhead, so closely related to the rainbow trout that it is frequently said to be the same fish with the addition of sea-going tendencies, is perhaps the closest American relative to the common trout of England. It is a great game fish and abundant on the Pacific coast, the Klamath and Rogue rivers being among the most noted of the steelhead waters. The run starts in the Klamath in July but the best fishing comes in September when the fish run larger and are more plentiful.

Bass fishing is a typically American sport and the fish is a great fighter. Small-mouthed bass, usually given credit for being better fighters than large-mouth, although not running nearly so large, are fairly well distributed in Quebec, Ontario and Minnesota. Large-mouth bass attain their greatest size in the warm waters of the Southern states. The universal method of fishing for both species is plug casting with a short single-handed rod, but fly-fishing with fairly heavy trout tackle is becoming exceedingly popular in sections where this method of angling can be successfully used. Less sporting is still fishing with live or dead bait. The summer months are best in northern districts.

From Fishing in American waters, *1875.*

The range of the great muskellunge (*Esox masquinongy*) is limited to eastern and central Canada and to the northern edges of a few of the border states. His weight and deep-bred arrogance is something to be considered. Forty pounders are not uncommon.

Closely related but seldom given much credit as a game fish (and nowhere officially) is the great northern pike. He is widely distributed, covering the entire northern range of states and provinces and it is said to be plentiful throughout Alaska, Siberia, and Europe. Both pike and musky can be taken on bait-casting tackle of the lightest kind and in the cold and invigorating waters of Canada either fish will put up a terrific battle. These fish are taken throughout the summer and early autumn. Trolling is another very successful method of fishing for them.

SUITABLE TACKLE

Trout:—For the heaviest fishing a bamboo rod of good action, from 8½ to 9 feet long and weighing approximately 5¾ ounces is generally preferred. Such a rod will take the great trout of the fabled Nipigon or the 10-pound steelheads on the Rogue and is capable of casting the heavier lures used in bass fly-fishing. For smaller waters rods weighing from 4 to 5 ounces are perhaps more popular. Reels should have narrow spools and capacity sufficient for a fairly long running line. Leaders on the larger streams need seldom run finer than 1x but there are many waters where 4x leaders in 9-feet lengths will be needed during periods of low and clear water. Flies cover a wide range from the size 1/0 popular on the Nipigon, size 6 for steelhead and so on down to the smallest hooks for fine work. As a rule Canadian trout and mountain trout rise best to flies of gaudy colour. Favourite patterns in both wet and dry flies are the Parmachenee Belle, Coachman, Royal Coachman, Grizzly King, Professor, Silver Doctor and Queen of Waters. A few of the more sombre hued flies such as the Black Gnat, Flight's Fancy, Grey Drake, Brown Palmer, and Cahill should be on hand for use in the very early season and for more southern waters. For such streams as the Saranac and many of the streams of Canada where wading is possible a wading staff is an essential to safety. Many of the larger streams are fished from boats or canoes.

Largemouth bass (from T[...] American Angler's Boo[...] 1865)

I beg to express my appreciation of the performance of the "Hardy" rods which I have used. I have landed perhaps several hundred Black Bass weighing from 3 to 5 pounds each with the "Fairy" cane built fly rod, which I have used since 1912, without apparent injury to it.
     Letter from America quoted in Hardy Brothers Catalogue, *1922.*

Salmon:—Dry-fly fishing for eastern salmon is becoming an increasingly popular sport. It is a sport that brings the fisherman the keenest delight and which, with light tackle, takes his measure as an angler. The rod most generally used is from 9½ to 10 feet long and weighs about 8 ounces like the "De Luxe" salmon rod and the "Houghton". It is also quite practical to use these rods for fishing the smaller wet flies. They must have a good action in order to drive a fly into the wind, and a detachable handle extension is a necessity when playing a heavy fish. Nine-feet leaders are the rule, of tapered single gut in medium and heavy weight. For wet-fly fishing the most generally used rod is from 14 to 15 feet in length the "Special" and the "Paradox". This applies to all the larger rivers of Canada but on Newfoundland and Nova Scotia rivers many anglers prefer rods

Smallmouth bass (from Gam[...] Fish of the Northern Sta[...] and British Provinces, 18[...]

12 feet in length *viz.* the "Hebridean"; the "Wye"; the "Gold Medal". For most of the New Brunswick and Nova Scotia water the popular sizes are 2, 4, and 6 double hooks and 1/0 single hooks are standard. The Dusty Miller, Thunder and Lightning, Durham Ranger, the Butcher, and the Black Dose are among the best. Incidentally, in 1932 the New Brunswick government added a considerable amount of free fishing to that already established. Eastern salmon is exceptionally good during July.

Bass:—Here the characteristically American sport of plug casting comes into wide use. The rods used weigh between 4 and 6 ounces, depending upon the weight of the plugs, and are between 5 and 6 feet long. The reel, in use, is on the top of the rod and above the hand. Many anglers believe that the short butt type of the rod gives better action and if the rod is too light and whippy it makes the casting of a $\frac{5}{8}$ ounce lure, the average weight of baits for bass, pike, and musky, unnecessarily difficult. Silk casting lines, hard or soft braided and testing from 8 to 24 pounds are very popular. A 12-inch cable wire trace is always used between the lure and the line. Bass and musky fishing begins in most districts 1st July and continues until October or November.

Black flies and mosquitoes are bothersome during the spring fishing in many sections and the angler should always be prepared for them with headnets or some repellent lotion for applying to the skin. Warm clothing and sufficient items of extra tackle to make replacements should always be carried.

The smallest rod you made me this year is perfect for small streams and bushwhacking. I have used it every day for the last 5 weeks, fishing dry most of the time, and landing on an average of forty fish a day.

Letter from Wisconsin quoted in Hardy Brothers Catalogue, *1907.*

Nowhere in the world is there such a variety of inland fishing to be obtained as that to be found in north America.

Hardy Brothers Catalogue, 1934.

Frontispiece from Fishing in American Waters, *1875.*

SPRING IN
BRITISH COLUMBIA

One day, in British Columbia, you will wake up and find that the snow-flaked mountain opposite you has lost its flat, metallic colours of white, blue, and rock-grey. And the lake itself, instead of looking black as ink against the white snow marge, is a bowl of quivering blue haze. The sun feels unusually hot on your face. You can *smell* the forest behind you. Spring has come.

This was the real fishing! Spring, with the fly. I used practically the same flies I would use in Scotland, with the addition of the Cowichan Coachman, which was a plum and white wing, invented and tied by an English lady down on the coast. The seductive Alexander I found a dud in British Columbia, though I heard of other people having spectacular luck with it. Butcher, Zulu, the old reliable March Brown, Silver Doctor, Jock Scott, Grouse and Claret, Teal and Green, Teal and Red, with the exception of the Peter Ross (which I did not have there), these were the same flies you would use in Scotland, the Shetlands, or the Outer Isles. I nearly always used the Butcher for a tail fly, the Zulu for a dropper, and rang the changes with the intermediate fly. I used the same set-up in the Balkans, in the swift mountain streams of the Dinaric Alps with equal (if not better) success—plus the Peter Ross and particularly the hackle Blue Upright. I took the side-gangs off my spinning baits, finding I caught more fish by trusting solely to the tail gang. They didn't foul-hook so much, or near-hook. And I found a 2-inch gold and silver, flat "Reflex" Devon—with one scarlet bead at its tail above the treble hook—outstandingly the best artificial lure. Again I emphasize the deadly attraction of that red or scarlet.

I had secured my house-boat then, this unpainted board shack built on a long raft of cedar logs; and in the lonely neck below Bald Mountain, where I moored it the next spring, I could always see the trout swimming about us in the calm of the early morning. I'll confess that in the very early spring I caught them with night-lines, baited with the illegal salmon eggs; but that was before they would take the fly. One had to live! I have caught them from our raft; but usually I left them alone in my vicinity. There was one big buck trout who *lived* under our raft. We used to watch him coming out— he used it for shade on the very hot days—and we would see him investigating the various bits of food we threw over to tempt him. We often debated whether he knew he was safe or not.

The partner of the Englishman who lived across the lake had come from tea-planting in Ceylon, found that the "ranch" in British Columbia was not the paradise he had expected when he sank his money in it, and he was soured. About the only thing that interested him now was fishing. He rowed across to me one dawn with the remark that he heard the Rainbow had started to take the fly "like anything!" in the river down below. What about it?

I don't know which is the most exciting; the thud when a fish takes the wet fly under the water, the "sup" as some big fish will turn and take a dry fly down—just before you hit him—or the last moments when you are, anxiously, about to land him. All of them of course surpass anything that a spinning bait can give you. There is nothing like the fly, or the pleasure of casting it.

On this swift river a line of logs had been laid along the other bank, linked by short sections of chain, to shunt off down-coming drift wood, brush, logs or whatever came down from the lake, so as to keep the river open. These early trout seemed to be lying always along these logs. It was not an easy cast owing to the high brush behind you, but when it fell and you saw your line sweeping down you knew that at any second the strike might come. A 2-pounder would be a good fish in that swift water—too much if he took to the white water right away. Our bags were never very large, perhaps ten each in a day. A 2½-pound fish was the biggest I remember getting there. But with a fresh spring wind blowing around you and that joy of being just alive, which comes after the long winter, every day was exhilarating.

I did not get hold of a 70-pound salmon, but I did get one of 56 pounds, and one of 40 pounds, besides lots of little ones under 20 pounds. My wife got three which weighed 120 pounds, viz.:—43, 40, and 37 pounds, besides about a dozen between 20 and 7 pounds. These fish were all caught on your "Murdoch" rods; and, in fact in the week these rods killed over 300 pounds of fish—not counting several very large fish that got away. I never saw such fish in my life. The 56-pound fish I had on 47 minutes, and he took me down the coast 2 miles before we could get him killed.

Letter from British Columbia quoted in Hardy Brothers Catalogue, *1907.*

There was a pool below where the house-boaters, and those who lived near the store, had a miraculous rise on some evenings. I have fished it with three or four boats on it, with fish rising all around us.

The back-drop of all this was the heavy fir forest, with the mountains above the timber line shining in the sun high above. The Cutthroat ran larger, but did not seem to have the same drive that animated the fine fighting Rainbow. Nor were they so good to eat. And by far the most memorable fish to me from those 2 years were two 2½-pound Rainbow, alike to the ounce, that I caught within ½ hour of each other in my own bay. Both of them put up such a battle that I thought they must be 4 pounds at least. We were so sure of a fish when we wanted one that one night we had invited the old Irish doctor over to dinner I didn't go out until the very last minute. The consequence was that I did not get a rise. Darkness had come down. I saw the long oblong of light from the open door of our houseboat, even heard the doctor's voice, sarcastically inquiring had I gone down to *buy* a fish from the hatchery—when a big brute, about 3 pounds, took my fly while it was sinking to the bottom.

Several times in the darkness he got under my boat without my knowing it, until I heard his fins and tail fluttering as he jumped behind me on the other side. My wife and the doctor, too, could hear the splashes; and he called—"Is that our dinner?" I called back that I thought it was. Then, with the fish in the boat, I yelled back triumphantly: "All right, Eve—put on the frying-pan."

Negley Farson,
Going Fishing, 1942.

FISHING IN CANADA

Canada offers some of the finest fishing in the world, but it is a mistake to imagine that every river and lake is an aquarium. Fine waters are now practically depleted near the centres of population. Such a state of affairs, however, does not affect the visitor, as by spending a comparatively short time in travelling he can, if he wishes, cast his line upon actually virgin waters. The following lines will point out merely a few places where the best sport can be obtained, the chief difficulty being to keep the list within reasonable bounds. Mention is made of reliable "guides" at each point, for upon the capacity or otherwise of one's guide depends nine-tenths of the success of an outing.

ATLANTIC SALMON

The impression appears to exist that all good salmon fishing in Eastern Canada is in the hands of clubs or private individuals. It is true that many of the rivers are held in this way, chiefly by Americans, but the visitor will find little difficulty in having the courtesy of any river extended to him upon application. Free fishing is to be obtained on the Tobique River and the south-west branch of the Miramichi River, and fishing quarters can be reached within 24 hours of leaving Montreal. In both rivers fly is the principal lure, and the fish are free risers. Fishing opens 1st February, though as a matter of fact it is of little use fishing before the beginning of July; the first 3 weeks of this month are the best, though good fishing is obtained, if the water keeps up, until the close of the season on 15th August. . . .

Salmon fishing is also to be obtained in Newfoundland. One of the best rivers is the Gander. . . . The Codroy is also a fine stream, and comfortable quarters can be had at South Branch, at the Bungalow kept by Tankins Bros. Fishing in rivers of Quebec for salmon is practically all controlled, that is to say, on such rivers as are accessible, but here again, permission is generally accorded to visitors by the owners of the fishing rights.

PACIFIC SALMON

Trolling is the principal method employed on the Pacific, but it is quite wrong to imagine that the Pacific salmon is never taken on a fly. Fish are caught by this means every year, though few have the patience to persist in this method, when they see others catch quantities by means of trolling with a spoon. There are several kinds of salmon, the principal being the Tyee (or Chief) and the Cohoe. The former runs up to 70 pounds; 40, 50, and 60 pounders are common. The Cohoe are smaller, an average weight probably about 12 pounds, but they are very sporting fish. The best fishing is at the mouth of the Campbell River on Vancouver Island. One can stay at the

Willows Inn and here get boats and guides at reasonable prices. Enormous quantities of fish are caught every year; the best time is the month of August, the salmon not coming from the north until the beginning of that month. The best spot is along the bar at the mouth of the river, where the tide runs at such a pace that fishing is practically restricted to high and low water, and the commencement and end of the ebb and flood tides. It is safe to assert that a visitor to Vancouver Island will catch as many salmon as his strength will admit his playing, if he spends a fortnight in August at the mouth of the Campbell River. No licence is required to catch salmon in British Columbia.

TROUT

We will omit mention of the Lake Trout, which though they run to great size are not game, the speckled trout (*Salmo fontinalis*) gives all the sport desired. In New Brunswick the Miramichi River before-mentioned gives trout which will average between 1 and 2 pounds. Another excellent spot, especially during the month of June, is Bonney River, N.B. The proprietor of the hotel there has sporting camps at selected points where his visitors get comfortable quarters and the best fishing at reasonable rates. Quebec and Ontario have waters too numerous to mention, so we will confine ourselves to a notice of three places on the north shore of Lake Superior, where undoubtedly the cream of trout fishing in Canada is found. First must be mentioned the Nipigon River whose fame extends to many parts of the world. . . . The only complaint the writer has ever heard of the Nipigon is that it is too easy, for in spite of the fishing it gets year after year the stock keeps up. From its source in Lake Nipigon to its mouth, the river is only 40 miles in extent, and the whole of this 40 miles contains scenery which alone is well worth the trip. Fish are caught up to 7 and 8 pounds, principally in the heavy water at the foot of the rapids with the fly, and provide grand sport and need grand tackle. There is a special licence required to fish the Nipigon, the fee being $15.00 for 2 weeks, $20.00 for 3 weeks, and $25.00 for 4 weeks. The Nipigon has the name, but it is doubtful if it is superior to the Upper Steel River for fishing. This river is more difficult to get at, but the best part can be reached in 1 day after leaving the railroad by canoe. . . . The first nine taken there by the writer in August weighed 27 pounds. Two fish during a week's fishing weighing 6¾ pounds and 6 pounds 10 ounces respectively were taken. Flies and mosquitoes are rather troublesome in June, and probably the best months for the visitor would be July or August. The Slate Islands in Lake Superior, little known, but which have grand trout lakes and streams, are also reached from Jack Fish by a 14-mile trip on a tug. These islands are uninhabited but have the great advantage of being free from mosquitoes and flies. . . .

Apart from the Nipigon the licence for fishing for trout in Ontario

The improved "Halcyon" Spinner (1907).

It may be of interest to you to hear that I am extremely pleased with a 10½-foot steel centred split-cane rod which I had from you a few years ago. This season I have given it some outrageously severe work in Canada and can see no harm done to it. I have used it for trolling for big trout from a canoe, in which a big rod is too cumbersome. Whipping a salmon reel to the butt and dragging a large spoon or natural bait at the end of 40 yards of salmon line. On getting into a fish, I have several times had the butt in the bottom of the canoe and the tip in the water directly beneath. In Newfoundland I had some extraordinary grilse fishing, for which the rod served me admirably and excited the admiration of my Newfoundland friends. I took out of one pool, which had previously been fished by three other rods, eight grilse, averaging 4½ pounds and lost almost as many more, within a couple of hours.

Letter quoted in Hardy Brothers Catalogue, 1907.

is only $2.00 per rod. It may be mentioned here that the guide furnishes every requisite with the exception of fishing tackle, and moreover life under canvas is to be preferred to the average hotel accommodation. In Alberta there is the Old Man River, whose waters teem with trout; they do not run to the same size as the Lake Superior trout but are exceptionally sporting. The North and South forks of this river are best reached from Lundbreck Station, and Messrs. Mason and Green of this place will supply guides, horses, and necessary outfit. . . .

The "Halcyon" Spinners I found excellent for Small Mouth Black Bass, Pike, Pickerel, Perch, Rock Bass, and other sorts of fish in the St. Lawrence River.

Letter from Canada quoted in Hardy Brothers Catalogue, 1925.

OUANANICHE

There is really only one locality where this fish is obtained, and that is around the Upper end of Lake St. John in Northern Quebec. Headquarters should be made at Roberval reached by train from Quebec, and the best time for fly-fishing is the month of June. Later in season the fish are taken with minnow. The Ouananiche, that lives in the waters of the Grand Discharge, is probably the hardest fighting, liveliest and most sporting member of the trout species, and a visit to Roberval is sure to be repeated.

This year I did much better, as in the 6 weeks I was on the river, I killed 122 salmon. The first cast I used killed sixty-five salmon, but I then had to lay it aside as it had become too short. I never use points, but the fly to the cast line, which, of course, becomes shorter and shorter from constantly changing the fly. The next cast killed forty-seven fish, when it also was too short. I thought it a pity to waste such superlatively good gut, so I knotted the two casts together, making one good long one, and with this I fished until I left the river, killing ten more fish with it, so the upper half of this cast has now killed seventy-five salmon, and the lower half fifty-seven. It is still quite sound and not at all frayed, and I intend to commence operations with it next season, and, barring accidents, expect to kill at least thirty more salmon with it.

Letter quoted in Hardy Brothers Catalogue, 1902.

BASS

Bass are found practically all over Quebec and Ontario, both in lakes and streams, and as fighters no fish can beat them. A fight with a bass of 4 or 5 pounds on a fly must be experienced to be properly appreciated. Bass have far more endurance than trout and fight to the very last gasp. The only trouble is that they will not rise at all times. The American art of casting with a floating bait is extremely sporting, and probably the best all round method for taking bass. They will also take any ordinary troll and live-bait. Places especially recommended are several points on the waters of the Rideau, reached from Ottawa, Chaffey's Locks, Jones Falls, and Newburgh being specially good. There is hotel accommodation at each place, and guides and boats can be obtained there.

MASKINONGE

This fish is well named the "fresh water tiger". Though similar in appearance to a pike it is very different in its fighting qualities. On reasonably fine tackle he will put up a fight that will test any one's endurance. This fish has been caught up to 75 pounds in weight, but nowadays a 40 pound fish is considered good. Probably the two best places where the big fish are to be obtained are the waters of Lake St. Louis in Quebec, near Montreal and also near the Thousand Islands. The former waters every year provide 30 and 40 pounders during the month of August. Accommodation can be obtained at the Clarendon Hotel at St. Anne de Bellevue, where guides and boats are also obtained. St. Anne de Bellevue is only 24 miles from Montreal, and a visitor to Canada with a couple of days to spare should certainly try a fall with the big fish.

A WORD AS TO TACKLE

For all kinds of fishing one's rods and reels must be of the best workmanship: the lines strong, gut heavy, and flies large. For salmon fly-fishing the 16-foot "Hi Regan" is just the thing. For trolling the Pacific salmon a "Murdoch" or "*Salmo Esox*" spinning rod fills the bill. For trout, Hardy's rods are the only ones in the writer's opinion that are really fit to stand the big strain rods are subjected to—the steel centre is advisable. The question of reels we will leave to the individual himself, and with regard to lines it is merely necessary to state that in addition to being suitable to the rod, they must be of the very finest material. For trout Second Marana gut is quite fine enough, and for salmon twisted gut casts are desirable. Flies for trout fishing are much larger than those used in Great Britain, but when fishing for big trout it is well to take along some of the flies recommended for bass, this being specially the case with the rivers to the north of Lake Superior, where Silver Doctor, Jock Scott, and the Parmacheene Belle are the favourite and most killing flies for the big fish.

Hardy Brothers Catalogue, 1912.

FISHING IN NEWFOUNDLAND

Newfoundland affords undoubted attraction to the angler. Here salmon, sea trout, and lake trout abound. The salmon and sea trout are to be found in all the large rivers, although the streams on the West Coast are the best, as they have not been well fished over, being less accessible than the other parts. Lake trout fishing is obtainable in nearly every watercourse in the island, and its possibilities have been increased by the fact that a local club has for many years past been engaged in stocking the inland waters with California rainbow trout, hatched out in a hatchery of their own work. Loch Leven trout were also introduced some years ago and extensively distributed, and the native trout, so-called, but really a species of char, are amazingly abundant.

Rod fishing in Newfoundland is by no means expensive. It can be obtained within easy reach of St. John's, and there is no need of a camp, as there are inns near many of the best spots. A guide, however, though not absolutely necessary, is very desirable.

The best salmon fishing is to be had directly the salmon start going up the rivers, generally about the second week in July. After they are once well up the streams they are much harder to catch. In the middle of July good sport, however, can be depended upon, given favourable weather and no east winds. Next to the salmon come sea trout, which afford excellent sport. Like the salmon, they must be followed up-stream, where the pools become filled with them. An ordinary catch is five to ten dozen, scaling from 1 pound up to 5 pounds.

The fresh-water trout, though smaller, often afford a very good day's diversion. They can be found in nearly every pond, and even close to St. John's, although most assiduously fished, yield very good results.

If the visitor, however, desires to see the country as well as secure sport, he cannot do better than to take a trip across country by rail to the Western shore, where he will find the Codroy and George's rivers afford excellent sport and splendid scenery. The three large rivers on the East coast—the Cambo, the Gander, and the Exploits—are also frequently visited by anglers; and there are also attractive salmon rivers on the south coast and above the Northern Peninsula.

Fishing for Atlantic Salmon in Canada, c. 1900 (Mary Evans Picture Library)

All the trout and salmon rivers in Newfoundland are open to sportsmen of every nationality on the same footing. A licence fee of $10 is exacted from every visiting angler, and the money thus obtained is used in paying game wardens. These wardens live on the rivers the whole fishing season and see the laws enforced. The trout pools and salmon streams everywhere over the Island are provided by nature with a practically countless supply of these fish, moderate in size, but gamey and good fighters, with flesh that forms excellent eating.

1888

The season, for trout and salmon in Newfoundland, extends from June until September, and every section of the seaboard has its own watercourse wherein the sport can be pursued.

All articles of equipment—canoes, tents, etc.—are now supplied by the best of the guides, and the services of reliable men who can both cook and otherwise help can be had for about $2 per day. Provisions and other necessaries can be purchased in St. John's.

The summer weather is delightful, the climate being similar to that of Scotland, and the fishing conditions generally resembling those in that country. The weather at that season is such that it is possible for visitors to remain in camp for many weeks, and as all the best sporting grounds are reached either by railroad or steamer certainly every week, and, in most cases, oftener, the visitor is in constant touch with civilization.

Hardy Brothers Catalogue, 1923.

RAINBOWS IN CHILE

This river was the Laja, racing down from the extinct volcano of Antuco in the far Andes. In the long flat sweeps it was a deep bottle-green . . . but swirling. Then it crashed through the rocks it had rounded through the ages, poured white over ledges, and emitted the continuous low roar of broken water. I remembered what the ambassador had told me in Santiago—"plenty of backing on your line"—and my heart sank.

At any rate, I told myself, put on the biggest cast you've got (it was a 2x), soak it well . . . and trust to heaven. It was well I did.

I had picked the side of a broad stretch of white falls where the main river swept past in frothing white water and where there was a lee of green water lying along the main current. I felt that if there were any big trout, waiting for something to come down, this was where they would be. It was easy casting, for there was no high brush behind me, and I kept as long a line as I could in the air, hoping to reach the edge of the white water. I think I must have been even more shocked than the fish when, on my very first cast, just as my fly was sweeping down about opposite me, I got that driving pull of a heavy strike. It was the first cast I made in Chile— and it was the best fish.

Without waiting for any more argument he went straight on down the river, sweeping through the white water, where he seemed to rest, or sulk, for a moment in the green water on the other side. It was lucky for me that he did; practically every foot of my line had been taken out. So there we were. I could not get across to him. Neither could I get him across to me. So I gave him the bend of the rod while I stood there and thought about it.

In these parts of Chile there is a very poor brand of peasant, which exists heaven knows how; they come about as close to living without any visible means of support as you would think man could get. There was the brush-board-and-thatched hovel of one of these ramshackle humans behind me now. Its inhabitants had evidently been watching me for some time. Now, seeing me standing there, apparently doing nothing, a small urchin impelled by curiosity came cautiously up to see what I was doing. We spoke no language in which we could communicate with each other; and when I unhooked my landing-net and snapped it open he almost fainted from fright. But he was a quick-witted little fellow, and, somehow, he comprehended what a net was. I made him take it from me.

So there were two of us standing there now. The fish had remained exactly where he was. I gave him a slow pull. The next instant the fish was going down along his side of the river and the boy and I were stumbling down along the boulders on ours. As I said, these strange, volcanic rocks had been rounded by time, and a more tricky, stumbling, infuriating river journey I have seldom made. For I was deep in the river by now, getting as close to the fish as I could get in order to win back some more line. In this fashion I took several yards back from him. Then I reached a high stretch of bank where the water was too deep, and so came back to land. It was now, I said gloomily to myself, that I would lose this fish. I remembered the big sea trout I had had on for 2 hours and 40 minutes, in the Shetlands. Here was to be another broken heart; for, some 50 yards below me, shone a long sloping shelf of white water in the mid-day sun.

Then the fish took it into his head to command operations. To my confused delight and dismay he came directly at me across the white water, so fast that I could barely strip in the line. I had no chance to reel in. Then he went on up the river, taking the line with him as fast as I could pay it out without fouling it. Then, boring against the line, as if he meant to jump the low falls, he again remained stationary over one spot.

This was exactly what the doctor ordered. I could not have asked him to do anything nicer. Reeling in as swiftly as I could, I worked my way up to him. So there, plus one Chilean boy, we were exactly where we had started over 20 minutes before. I knew it was 20 minutes, because twice during our tussle, I had seen Chillan erupt. That 2,000-foot sulphurous jet!

Now began one of the most beautiful battles I have ever experienced. For I had plenty of line in hand now; when he came past I gave him the bend of the rod for all I thought it could stand—determined he should never cross to the other side of that white water again. And every time I checked him. The green water was so glass-clear that when he swung in the swirls sluicing past me the sun caught and reflected the pinkish stripe along his strong sides. I could watch him fighting the hook. And then he spun in the sun, jumping. He was the very essence of fight. Furious, I think—still not frightened.

There is no doubt that in the ingredients of a fisherman's delight there is nothing comparable to being able to watch a fish fight like this. For I could see him, or his shape, nearly all the time. Chillan erupted once more.

But by now my gallant rainbow was a slow-moving, sullen thing. His tail working heavily, he lay in the green water about 20 yards out from me. And I looked around for the lee of some rocks and slowly worked him in a pool. It was almost still water. He was almost resting against the hook. And then, as the bank was high, and I was an idiot, I signalled the little Chilean boy to wade out and slip the net under him. . . .

The boy did. He was an eager boy . . . so eager that he stabbed the net at the fish . . . pushed him with it! Then he tried to scoop him in from the tail . . . I jumped. As I did, the boy actually got the fish into the net. I seized boy, net, fish, all at the same time, and threw them all up on the bank. There I dived on the fish.

It all goes to prove the hysterical condition into which some fishermen will get themselves. For this rainbow was not much over 6 pounds. But he was such a beautiful one! That was the point; that small nose, and those deep shoulders, and those firm fighting flanks. This fish had been living in clean water on crayfish galore. I sat on the bank and looked at him for nearly 20 minutes. I had him.

Then I sighed, got up, and went to fishing again.

Negley Farson,
Going Fishing, 1942.

THE LAST PLACE OF ALL

Mr. Theodore Castwell, having devoted a long, strenuous, and not unenjoyable life to hunting to their doom innumerable salmon, trout and grayling in many quarters of the globe, and having gained much credit among his fellows for his many ingenious improvements in rods, flies, and tackle employed for that end, in the fullness of time died and was taken to his own place.

*   *   *

St. Peter looked up from a draft balance sheet at the entry of the attendant angel.

"A gentleman giving the name of Castwell—Says he is a fisherman, Your Holiness, and has 'Flyfishers' Club, London,' on his card."

"Hm-hm," said St. Peter. "Fetch me the ledger with his account."

St. Peter perused it.

"Hm-hm," said St. Peter. "Shew him in."

I had a most excellent spring fishing on one of my old haunts. I go on the water early in February, and owing to a very early and warm spring, and slight snowfall in the hills, there was much less snow water than usual, and the large fish were showing in great numbers. My total catch for 39 days or part of days, was eighty-four fish, weighing 1,545 pounds. My thirty-two largest averaged exactly 30 pounds. My four largest 44, 41, 40, 40 pounds; best day six fish, 131 pounds.

Letter from Kashmir quoted in Hardy Brothers Catalogue, *1907.*

Mr. Castwell entered cheerfully and offered a cordial right hand to St. Peter.

"As a brother of the angle—" he began.

"Hm-hm," said St. Peter.

"I am sure I shall not appeal to you in vain for special consideration in connection with the quarters to be assigned to me here."

"Hm-hm," said St. Peter. "I have been looking at your account from below."

"Nothing wrong with it, I hope," said Mr. Castwell.

"Hm-hm," said St. Peter. "I have seen worse. What sort of quarters would you like?"

"Well," said Mr. Castwell, "do you think you could manage something in the way of a country cottage of the Test Valley type, with modern conveniences and say $\frac{3}{4}$ of a mile of one of those pleasant chalk streams, clear as crystal, which proceed from out the throne attached?"

"Why, yes," said St. Peter, "I think we can manage that for you. Then what about your gear? You must have left your fly rods and tackle down below. I see you prefer a light split-cane of 9-foot or so with appropriate fittings. I will indent upon the Works Department for what you require, including a supply of flies. I think you will approve of our dressers' productions. Then you will want a Keeper to attend you."

"Thanks awfully, Your Holiness," said Mr. Castwell. "That will be first rate. To tell you the truth, from the Revelations I read I was inclined to fear that I might be just a teeny-weeny bit bored in Heaven."

"In H—. Hm-hm," said St. Peter, checking himself.

*   *   *

It was not long before Mr. Castwell found himself alongside an enchantingly beautiful clear chalk-stream, some 15 yards wide, swarming with fine trout feeding greedily; and presently the attendant angel assigned to him and handed him the daintiest, most exquisite, light split-cane rod conceivable—perfectly balanced with reel and line—with a beautifully damped tapered cast of incredible fineness and strength—and a box of flies of such marvellous tying as to be almost mistakable for the natural insects they were to simulate.

Mr. Castwell scooped up a natural fly from the water, matched it perfectly from the fly box, and knelt down to cast to a riser putting up just under a tussock 10 yards or so above him. The fly lit like gossamer 6 inches above the last ring, floated a moment and went under in the next ring; and next moment the rod was making the curve of beauty. Presently, after an exciting battle, the Keeper netted out a bouncer of about $2\frac{1}{2}$ pounds.

"Heavens!" cried Mr. Castwell. "This is something like."

"I am sure His Holiness will be pleased to hear it," said the Keeper.

Mr. Castwell prepared to move up-stream to the next riser when he became aware that another trout had taken up the position of that which he had just landed, and was rising. "Just look at that!" he said, dropping instantaneously to his knee and drawing off some line. A moment later an accurate fly fell just above the neb of the fish, and instantly Mr. Castwell engaged in battle with another lusty fish. All went well, and presently the landing net received its $2\frac{1}{2}$ pounds.

"A very pretty brace," said Mr. Castwell, preparing to move on to the next of the string of busy nebs which he had observed putting up round the bend. As he approached the tussock, however, he became aware that the place from which he had just extracted so satisfactory a brace was already occupied by another busy feeder.

"Well I'm damned!" cried Mr. Castwell. "Do you see that?"

"Yes, Sir," said the Keeper.

The chance of extracting three successive trout from the same spot was too attractive to be foregone, and once more Mr. Castwell knelt down and delivered a perfect cast to the spot. Instantly it was accepted and battle was joined. All held, and presently a third gleaming trout joined his brethren in the creel.

Mr. Castwell turned joyfully to approach the next riser round the bend. Judge, however, his surprise to find that once more the post beneath the tussock was occupied by a rising trout, apparently of much the same size as the others.

"Heavens!" exclaimed Mr. Castwell. "Was there ever anything like it?"

"No, Sir," said the Keeper.

"Look here," said he to the Keeper, "I think I really must give this chap a miss and pass on to the next."

"Sorry! It can't be done, Sir. His Holiness would not like it."

"Well, if that's really so," said Mr. Castwell, and knelt reluctantly to his task.

*　　*　　*

Several hours later he was still casting to the same tussock.

"How long is this confounded rise going to last?" enquired Mr. Castwell. "I suppose it will stop soon?"

"No, Sir," said the Keeper.

"What, isn't there a slack hour in the afternoon?"

"No afternoon, Sir."

"What? Then what about the evening rise?"

"No evening, Sir," said the Keeper.

"Well, I shall knock off now. I must have had about 30 brace from that corner."

"Beg pardon, Sir, but His Holiness would not like that."

"What?" said Mr. Castwell. "Mayn't I even stop at night?"

"No night here, Sir," said the Keeper.

"Then do you mean that I have got to go on catching these damned $2\frac{1}{2}$ pounders at this corner for ever and ever?"

The Keeper nodded.

"Hell!" said Mr. Castwell.

"Yes," said his Keeper.

Journal of the Flyfishers' Club, 1930.

From The Angler's
Companion, *1847*.

Index of Sources

The publication dates given for books are the dates of first English-language editions.

AKSAKOV, SERGEI, *Years of Childhood*, translated by J. D. Duff (Edward Arnold 1916) 256

BARRINGTON, C. G., *Seventy Years' Fishing* (Smith Elder 1902), 218

'B. B.', *Fisherman's Bedside Book* (Eyre & Spottiswoode 1945), 123

BICKERDYKE, JOHN, [C. H. Cook], *The Book of the All-Round Angler* (Upcott Gill 1899), 181; in *Journal of the Flyfishers' Club*, 158, 269

BLACKER, WILLIAM, *Art of Fly Making* (London 1844), 10

BOWKLER, CHARLES, *The Art of Angling* (London 1746), 171

BROWNE, G. F., *Off the Mill* (Smith, Elder 1895), 90

BUCHAN, JOHN, *John MacNab* (Hodder & Stoughton 1925 Houghton Mifflin 1925), 220

CHAYTOR, A. H., *Letters to a Salmon Fisher's Sons* (John Murray 1910), 45, 53

COTTON, CHARLES, *The Compleat Angler*, Part II, (London 1676), 9

DENNYS, JOHN, *The Secrets of Angling* (London 1613), 28

FARSON, NEGLEY, *Going Fishing* (Country Life 1942 Harcourt Brace & World 1943), 216, 286, 295

GREY, SIR EDWARD [LATER EARL GREY OF FALLODON], *Fly Fishing* (Dent 1899), 12

HALFORD, F. M., *Dry Fly Fishing in Theory and Practice* (London 1889), 112

Hardy Brothers' Catalogue, (1886) 35; (1888) 101, 152, 153; (1894) 51, 64, 141, 165, 179, 198, 203, 226, 229; (1898) 20; (1902) 27, 163, 185; (1906) 12; (1907) 24, 25, 109, 136, 138; (1911) 26, 37, 132; (1912) 253, 288; (1920) 244; (1923) 266, 293; (1924) 61; (1925) 30; (1927) 68; (1931) 41; (1934) 66; 281; (1937) 209, 249; (1952) 17, 19, 71, 75; (1960) 143

HAWKER, COLONEL PETER, *Instructions to Young Sportsmen* (London 1814), 29, 272

HINTZ, O. S., *Trout at Taupo* (Max Reinhardt 1955), 235, 246